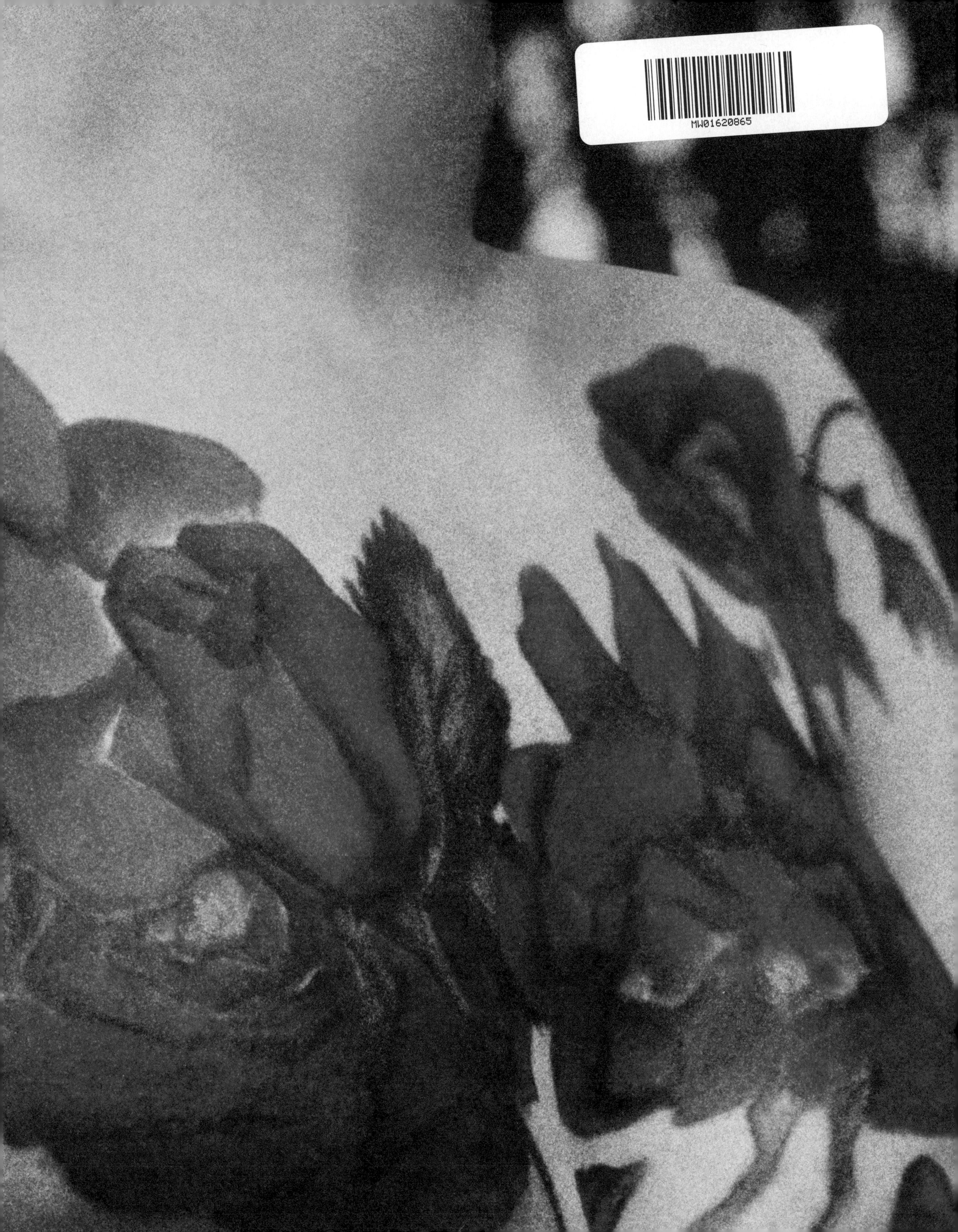

BODY PAINTING

MASTERPIECES BY JOANNE GAIR

BODY PAINTING

MASTERPIECES BY JOANNE GAIR

FOREWORD BY HEIDI KLUM

UNIVERSE

Foreword

Joanne Gair is one-of-a-kind. I first met Joanne when she was working as a makeup artist on various jobs—from commercials to editorial shoots—and from the very beginning, it was so clear that Joanne had more on her mind and more in her creative vision than simply makeup, though she was and is so talented at it!

We bonded when she body-painted me for the *Sports Illustrated* Swimsuit Issue on Necker Island, which I guess is not surprising when you consider the hour upon hour of extremely close-quarters contact that's necessary for one of these body-painting masterpieces to emerge. That was the first time I really got to experience the amazing process that happens with Joanne's work. This was at a point with *SI* when I had gotten the cover the year before, and it had really helped further my modeling career, so I was looking to mix things up—to go the next step and put a twist on the traditional swimsuit photos—and I was really lucky that I had a friend and artist like Joanne to experiment with me.

During the Necker Island shoot, I realized this was some hard-core business—no slacking. Joanne started painting on me right after dinner the first day we arrived and she literally painted the entire night through so we could start shooting at sunrise. I was already familiar with some of Joanne's work, of course, including the exquisite *Vanity Fair* cover she did of Demi Moore. For my first time undergoing the body painting, I was excited, anxious (in the best, most positive way), and really curious as to what the final result would be. I knew, though, that it would be an unusual shoot to say the least. And poor Joanne: I at least got to take some catnaps throughout the night (a girl needs her beauty sleep to look fresh for those early morning calls!). And it was a trip: every time I'd open my eyes after one of those brief rests, she'd be so much further along—it was as if a swimsuit were miraculously growing on my skin. I knew Joanne had to have such patience and that she could work so meticulously only because she has a true passion for her work and she totally gives herself up to it. It is inspiring to see, or rather be part of Joanne's method, and it makes you feel really lucky to be involved in the whole process.

Joanne's work is so detailed and duplicates the actual swimsuits to such a tee, that it's the ultimate *trompe l'oeil*—you really can't tell what's "real" and what's "paint"! For one of the suits—a tie-dyed one—we came up with the idea that I'd smear some of the paint onto my hand and hold my palm up, so people viewing the photo could see that the suit was indeed a Joanne Gair body-painted original. It was a quirky idea, but people responded like crazy and absolutely loved it—in fact, that particular photo ended up being the cover of German *Sports Illustrated* Swimsuit Issue.

Joanne is so colorful—not just literally, with her paints and the amazingly subtle shades of her work—but also in terms of *her:* her personality, character, way of looking at the world, the way she just is. She talks and laughs A LOT, with gusto, and that's how she approaches her work and her life. Like I said, when you have to sit there painting someone for that many hours, you really have to love what you do, and Joanne certainly does. And Joanne's like the perfectionist Energizer Bunny: she keeps going and going. Sometimes, I think the only reason any of her body-paint works get finished is because the photographer and editorial team are there waiting to shoot; if not, I bet she'd just keep painting and painting for a week straight!

Joanne is dazzlingly inventive and creative—a true original. To conceptualize the way she does and to work these creations out in her head, and also to have the skill to actually execute them into this incredible art form and to relay what's in her mind's eye for the whole world to see is really the definition of true artistry. To come up with the idea is impressive enough; to make it actually work is a whole other ballgame.

And also, it's not like she's styling with clothes. There are some models who are more comfortable with their bodies than others, but Joanne has this way of getting everyone into a groove—of making the models feel completely comfortable so that when they go in front of the camera, they don't feel "naked." It's funny that people often think "ooohhh, body painting, that's so erotic," and I guess that's one way to look at it, but I think if you really appreciate the final product, it's so clear that the body paint is an art form in and of itself.

I was a fan of Joanne's work from the moment she first showed me her books and portfolios. I love the Demi Moore picture that Joanne stylized as a Botticelli muse—she not only painted her so that it looks three-dimensional, but also stuck on actual fabric objects to make it even more multidimensional. It was really so elaborate, with the sleeves that look like they're blowing in the wind, and the amazing background, which is very striking and cool. And for myself, I loved when Joanne painted me as "Mother Nature" with the butterflies. It was actually a whole range of natural elements, including butterflies, vines, and vibrant-colored flowers, all done up with beautiful, flowing hair and an angelic expression; it was all really lovely. I ended up using this image as a double-page spread in my own book. Because there was a significant amount of skin exposed for this image, some people might think it wouldn't take as much effort as some of Joanne's other body-painting works that cover the entire body, but actually the opposite was true. Every single butterfly had so much detail—the dots, the stripes, the threadlike veins. If you look closely, it just boggles the mind that Joanne could recreate all that! Again, it's that patience, attention to detail, eye for beauty in imperfection as well as perfection, and a true artist's perspective that make Joanne stand out.

I'm so excited to work with Joanne again for 2006 *Sports Illustrated* Swimsuit Issue, not just as a body painter but also as a photographer. This shoot is different because

Joanne can really carry through her vision from beginning to end rather than handing it off at a certain point. No matter how much you consult with the photographer beforehand, different artists see things differently. This way, I like to think Joanne can have her cake and eat it too instead of spending all this time lovingly baking the cake and then watching someone else eat it!

I'm looking forward to seeing how Joanne's work evolves. Body painting is so ephemeral, just by its nature. It's not like a piece of artwork on canvas that hangs on a wall or in a museum somewhere. Of course, the photo becomes a recording and captures the image, but it's still different. There's something natural and organic about the temporary state of the body painting as artwork. It's a one-off in the best way. There is a certain sadness to it being there and then gone as soon as the subject washes the paint off, but there's also something gorgeous and poetic about it. It's like the passage of time doesn't ever touch this one original moment of existence.

Working with Joanne is a true pleasure; and it's always evolving as we experiment, play, and develop. Joanne has a childlike sense of wonder that I hope never goes away. And it's not just in her work. Her house is like a miraculous fairyland (Alice in Wonderland's got nothing on Joanne Gair!) with these incredible themed rooms where the four walls are not just four walls, but bursts of color, fabrics, unique furniture, and shards of stained glass that are reassembled in amazing ways. An object is not just an object in Joanne's world, and everything has an anecdote—how it was discovered on some adventurous trip, or it's a found object, or it has some incredible back story. Everything in her home is unexpected and surprising and inspiring—just like Joanne.

Heidi Klum
New York, January 2006

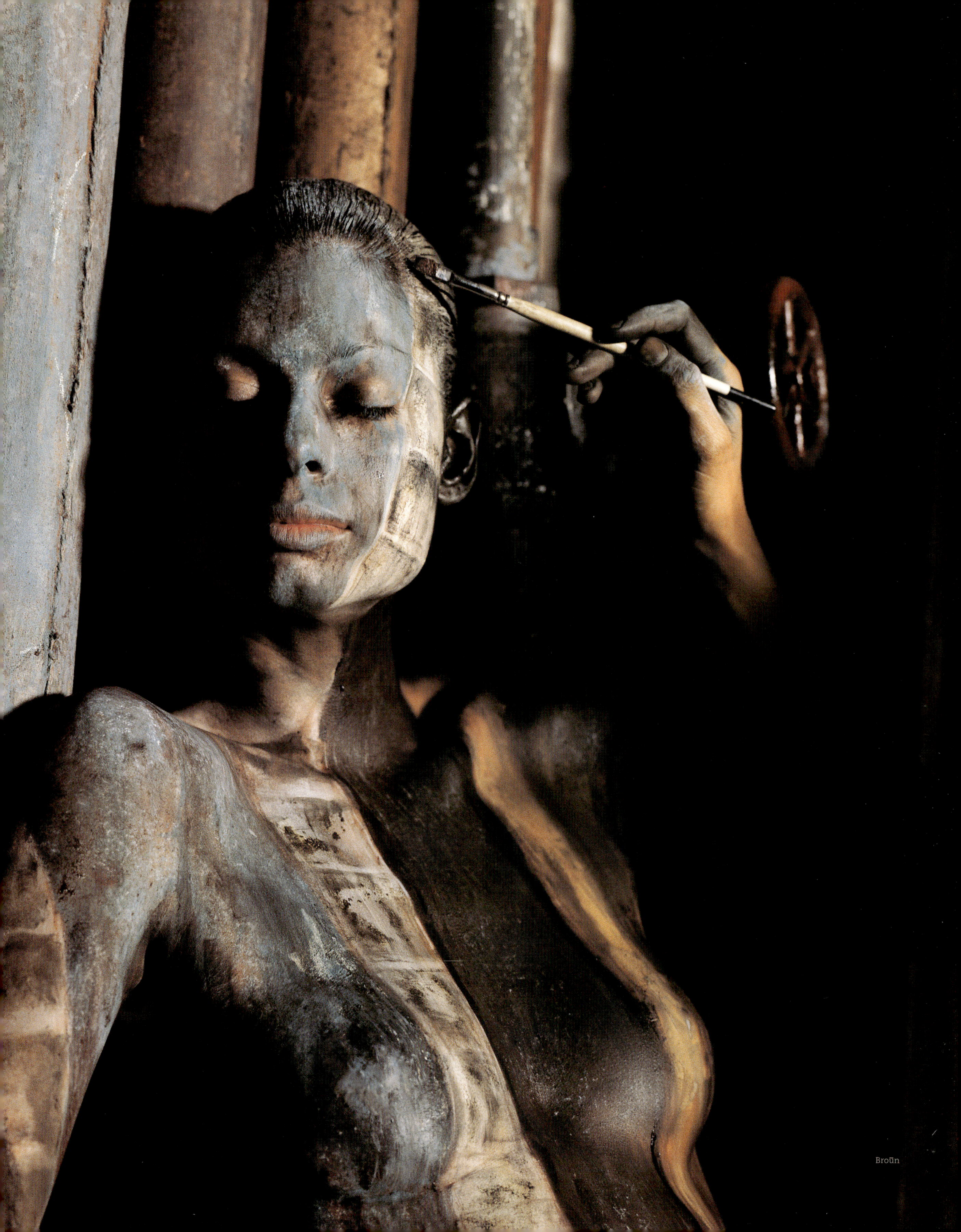

Broūn

The Journey—Part One

As I write this, *Body Painting* nears completion. Looking over the pages and images that represent the past twenty-plus years of my career in body painting and makeup, I do not feel nostalgic, but proud, with a sense of fulfillment. Proud of the work, which reflects a collaboration with the many photographers, art directors, editors, and models that I have had the honor of working with; and fulfilled by the quality of the images that were captured. With this book, a chapter of my journey is complete and available to view in all its colorful glory.

I am a New Zealander—a Kiwi. As a young girl, I was fascinated by the history of our native Maori culture and the way the Maori identified their tribal heritage through the facial skin adornment known as the moko. This fascination would later grow to embrace world cultural body and skin art.

I believe that life is made up of many defining moments that are only made possible by happenstance. In my journey, a big moment occurred in 1984. Having already spent five years away from New Zealand, mostly in Amsterdam and Australia, I touched down on American soil—Los Angeles, California to be exact, during the 1984 Summer Olympics—for what was meant to be a stopover of a few weeks on my way to London. In my possession was my first makeup and body-painting portfolio. It consisted of images primarily created in Australia—many shot with friends as models in my photographer friend Christian Lemech's studio, and often in the dead of night. Those were my early learning days of the craft. While I had completed a course in face makeup in Australia, I was self-taught in body painting. One example from this period is the Bob Watson image of Geeling Ng.

Armed with my portfolio and running out of money in Los Angeles, I was introduced to a top makeup agency through a young model. The Cloutier Agency, headed by Chantal Cloutier, recognized that I had something unique in my portfolio that was different from other makeup artists—it was, of course, the body painting. Based on this, I secured a working permit in about a week and a half. My trip to London was put on hold.

What I found interesting about my early days in Los Angeles was that I went from being an outside observer, viewing models and celebrities in the media, to suddenly working with them and helping them achieve their look or style. From advertising to print, to music videos and on to motion pictures, I was introduced to and then quickly entrenched in the industry.

In body painting your canvas is washable. The makeup goes on, the model brings the canvas to life, and the photographer captures it—then, as quickly as it has been applied, it is washed away, captured in time by the image. Body adornment can be something as small as framing an eye with my custom-made lashes. It can be tattooing a mouth. Or it can be the full-scale transformation of a body-as-canvas with my brush and imagination.

My early body-painting and makeup work during the 1980s was first embraced in the music industry on album covers and in music videos for artists such as David Lee Roth, Tina Turner, Grace Jones, Annie Lennox, and Mick Jagger.

In the late 1980s I was introduced to Madonna and first worked with her on the music videos "Express Yourself" and "Vogue." This was the beginning of a long working relationship. Many memorable and diverse looks and images came from this period, not to mention music videos and concert tours including 1990's Blonde Ambition Tour, which was captured in the documentary *Truth or Dare*. It was a highly creative and exhilarating time for me—traveling the world and working with a top entertainer who could push you to a whole new artistic level. I deeply value and treasure that collaboration. It was during this period that photographer Herb Ritts photographed Madonna for her concert-tour promotional material—one of the pictures became a signature Madonna image and appears in the following pages.

In 1992, I worked on a week-long editorial piece with Annie Leibovitz and Demi Moore. It was for a follow-up to the previous year's picture of a pregnant Demi on the cover of *Vanity Fair,* which I was also involved in. We shot in Hawaii and Los Angeles, and the black and white images that appear in this book featuring Demi with wings on her back were executed with ballpoint pen in Hawaii. On one of the days in Los Angeles we created a body-painting image that went on to become the now-famous cover. I remember that while painting Demi, as she watched the suit evolve through the day, she remarked to me, "Jo, this is going to change your life"—and it did.

Thanks to the collaboration with Annie and Demi on the *Vanity Fair* cover, my body painting became widely recognized. I was sought after more than ever by top companies worldwide for commercial and advertising work that would now feature body-painted models.

Demi and I continued our collaboration and friendship over the years. I had the privilege of working with her on several film projects in the mid- to late 1990s, and during that time we worked on additional body-painting images on the side. These images were photographed by Matthew Rolston and Peggy Sirota who, along with Demi, have graciously allowed for their publication here for the first time.

In 1998, *Sports Illustrated* approached me, interested in doing a few body-painted images for their 1999 Swimsuit Issue. I was a bit naive at the time, not realizing the exposure that a pictorial such as this would create. The plan was to shoot approximately five body-painted swimsuits on Richard Branson's Necker Island in the British Virgin Islands. This was to be the start of a long and lasting collaboration and friendship with *Sports Illustrated* Swimsuit Editor Diane Smith. In October 1998, while shooting the first set of swimsuits with photographer Antoine Verglas, I was asked to come back and shoot more images the following month. We ultimately shot thirteen body-painted swimsuits that made the 1999 issue and subsequent 2001 *Sports Illustrated* body-painting calendar. My body painting has since been featured in five additional swimsuit editions over the years, and a good collection of the work appears in this book.

The 1998 *Sports Illustrated* shoot was also the first time that I body-painted model Heidi Klum. Heidi and I had been working together during the past year on other advertising and editorial projects, including Victoria's Secret. She had graced the cover of the 1998 *Sports Illustrated* Swimsuit Issue and was excited and looking forward to being body-painted for the 1999 issue. Heidi's energy and enthusiasm were welcomed during the long process involved in creating the suits. She was a very interactive canvas, both

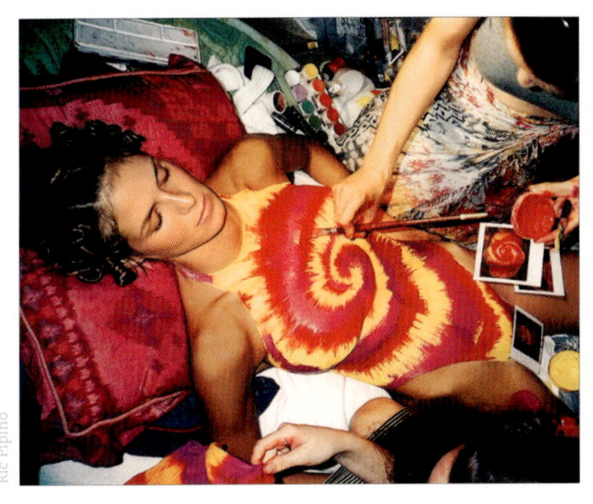
Ric Pipino

behind and in front of the camera. Her bubbly personality and playfulness brought the painted bathing suits to life. Since Necker Island, Heidi and I have gone on to do numerous body paintings and projects together. Heidi is always professional—a pleasure to work with, but more importantly a good friend.

In 2000, I worked on a beauty spread for *Black Book* magazine titled “Skinscapes.” New York-based photographer Eva Mueller and I were teamed together for the first time. Eva was known for shooting stark images with a humorous twist. She and I instantly clicked creatively. The images that appeared in the “Skinscapes” pictorial were organic landscapes on select parts of the female form. I am happy that many of the photographs from this project are now a part of the collection of imagery featured in this book.

There have been many personal and professional highlights during my career—having my work feature in the Auckland Museum as part of the 2001–2002 Vodafone Body Art exhibition was definitely one of them. Many of the images that appear in this book were featured in the exhibition—some printed life-size on canvas, six feet in length. I was very proud to be able to share the experience with my parents and family in my home country of New Zealand. This event was to be followed with an equally wonderful experience the following year with the start of my photography career.

In 2003, I picked up a camera. Not unlike earlier in my journey, I built my portfolio from scratch, photographing in and around locations in my Hollywood Hills home. In 2004 I was approached by a publishing firm in Auckland, New Zealand, to see if I was interested in body-painting and photographing a fun, body-painting themed book titled *Paint A'Licious*. I returned once more to Aotearoa, “the land of the long white cloud,” and spent ten wonderful months creating, body-painting, and photographing a lighthearted look at life. It was a tremendously gratifying experience, and for this I owe a great deal of thanks to publisher Geoff Blackwell.

After all these years, I find I still have a great passion and excitement for my craft. I treasure the friendships I have made and collaborations that have gone into my work over the past three decades. I want to thank everyone who has been involved and especially those who have consented to be a part of this book. One of the most gratifying things for me with body painting is that it is timeless. Now, relax, sit back, turn the pages, and enjoy the past twenty-plus years of my journey (part one).

Joanne Gair
New York, January 2006

Demi Moore Annie Leibovitz

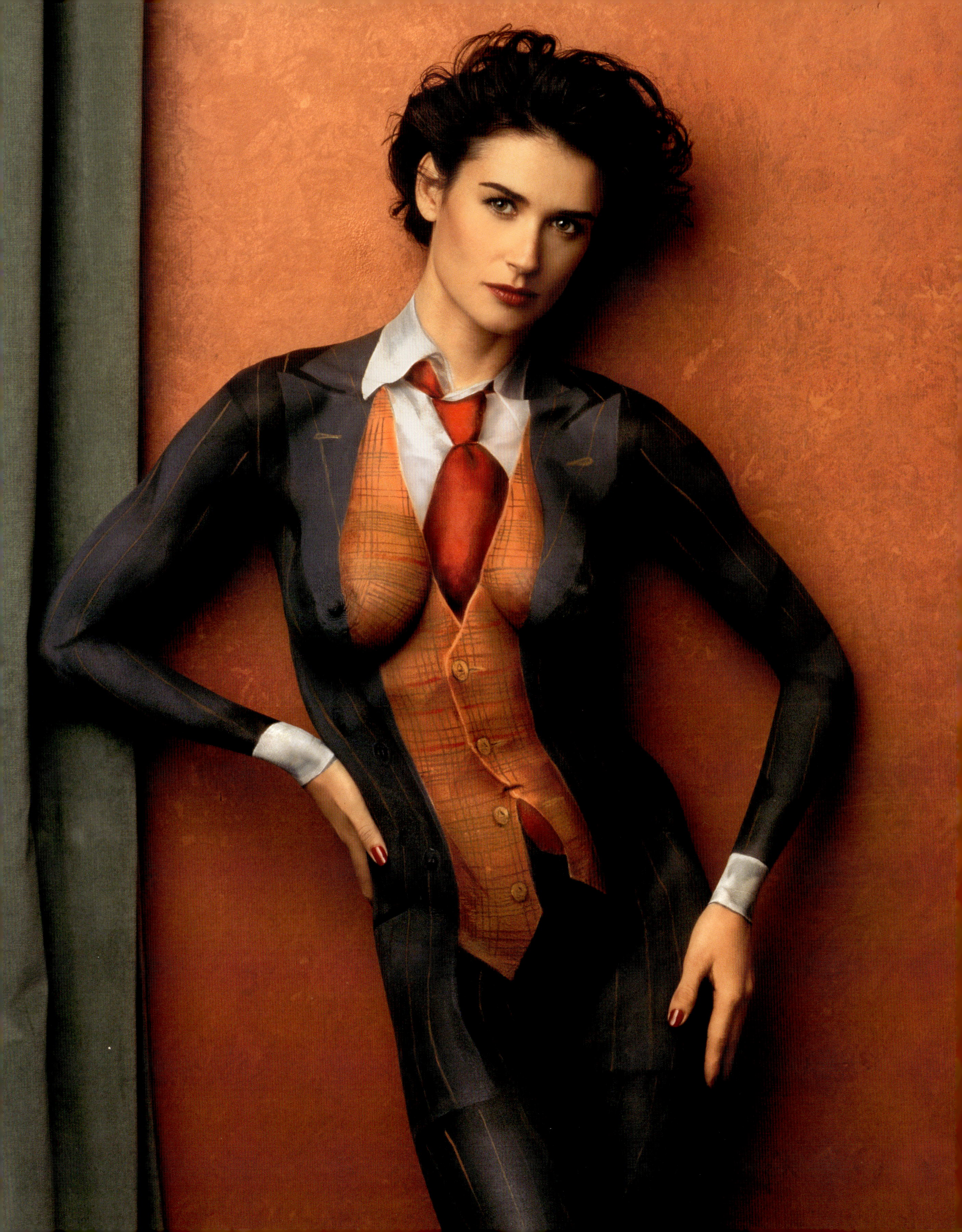

Goldie Hawn Matthew Rolston

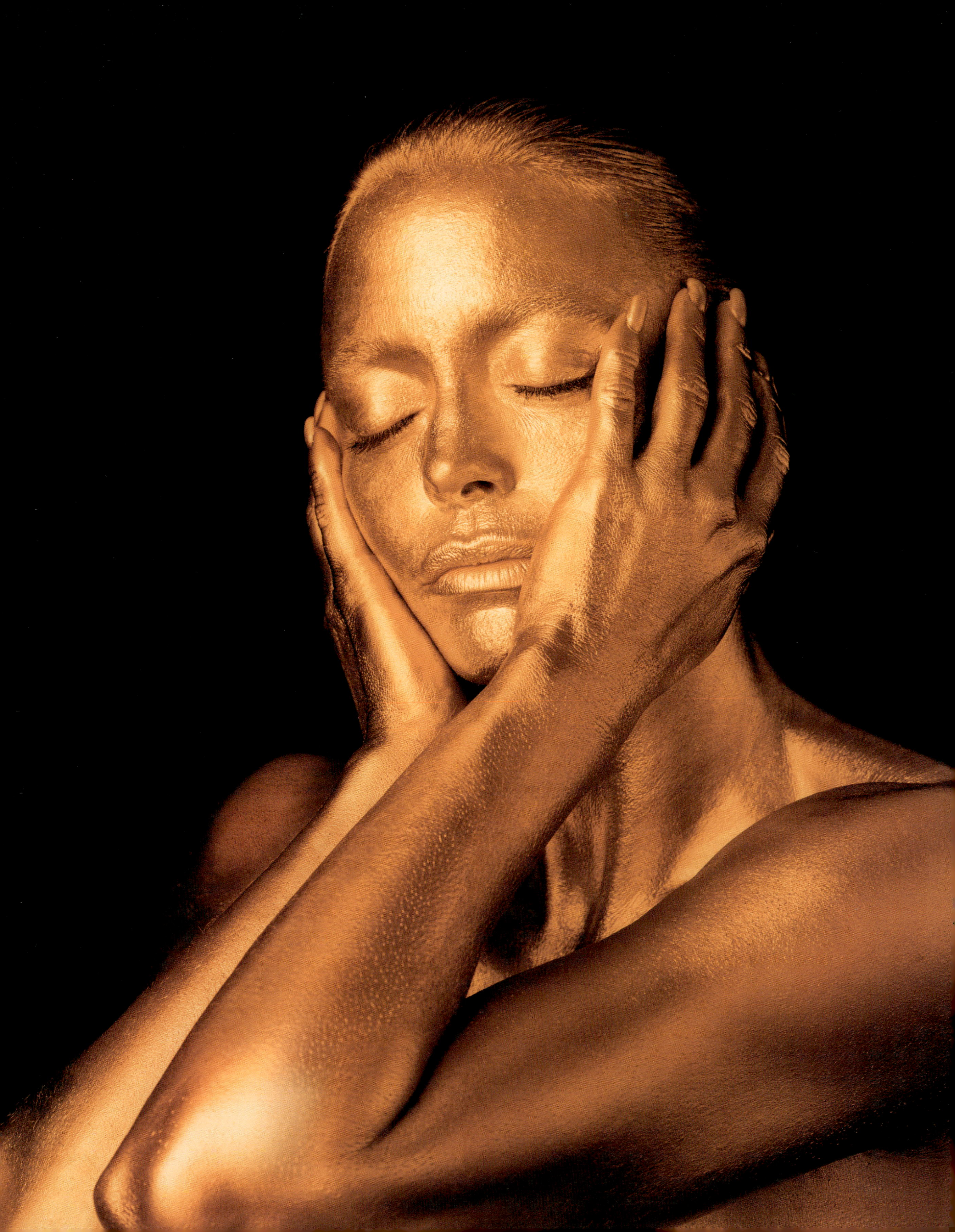

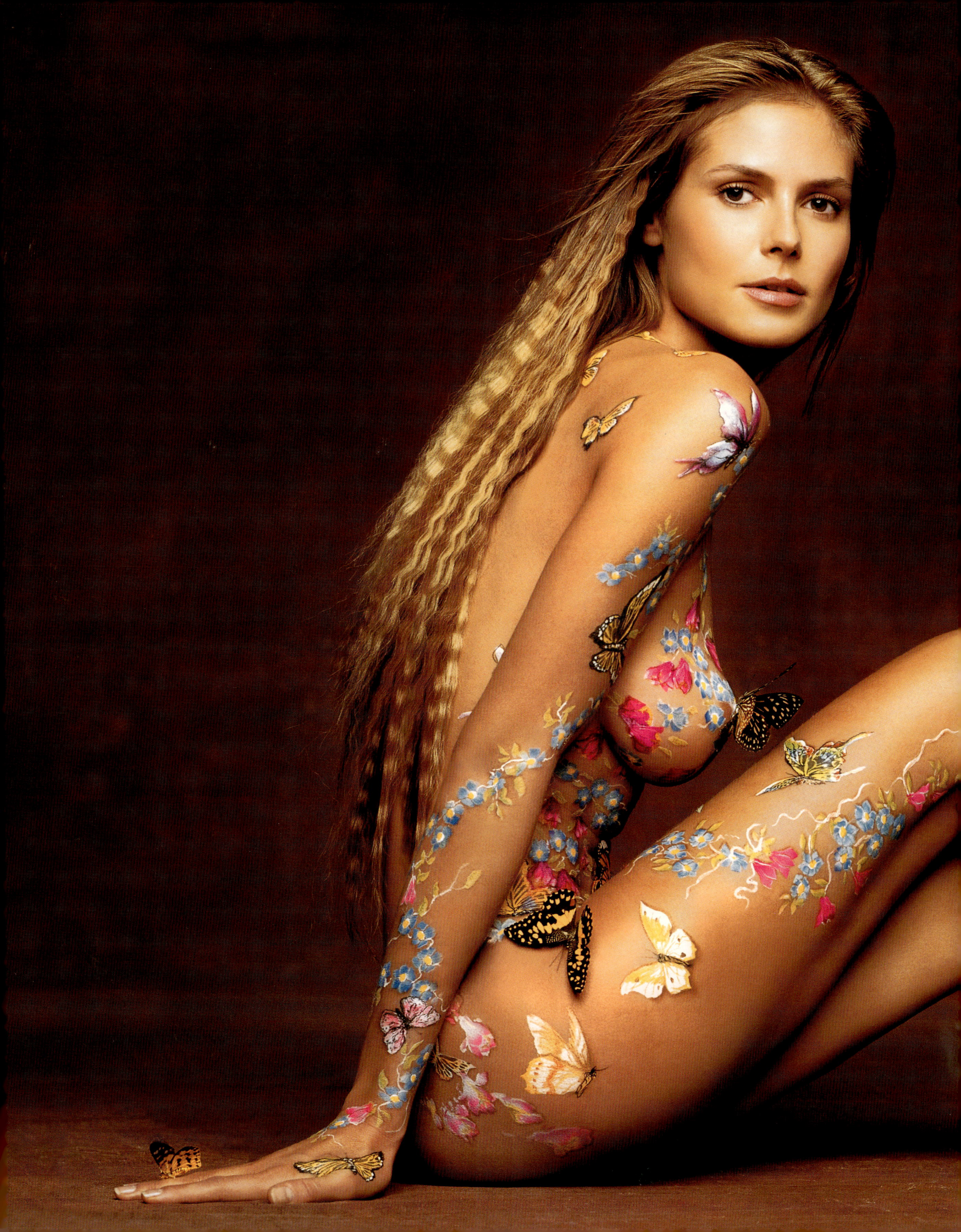

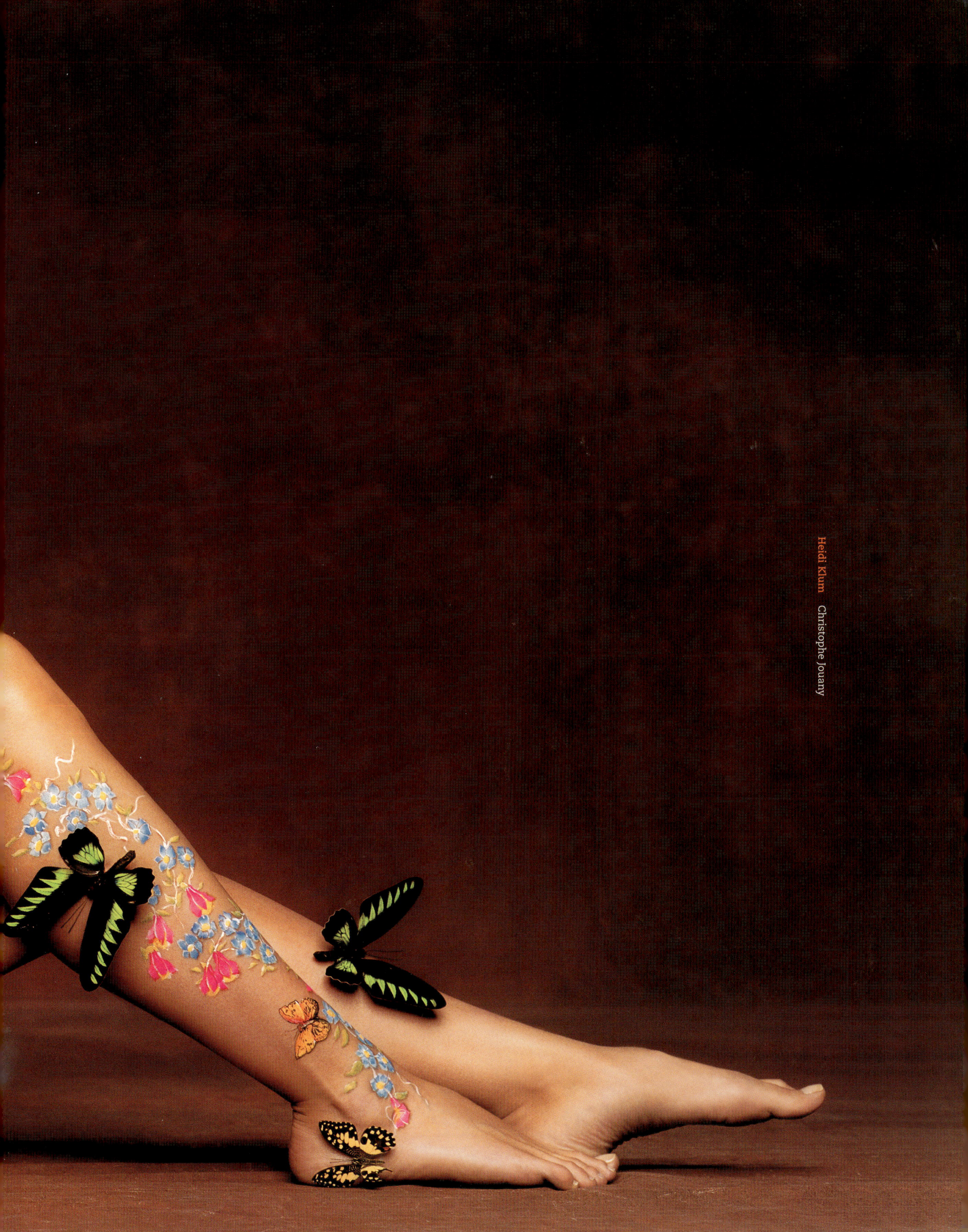

Heidi Klum Christophe Jouany

Heidi Klum Antoine Verglas

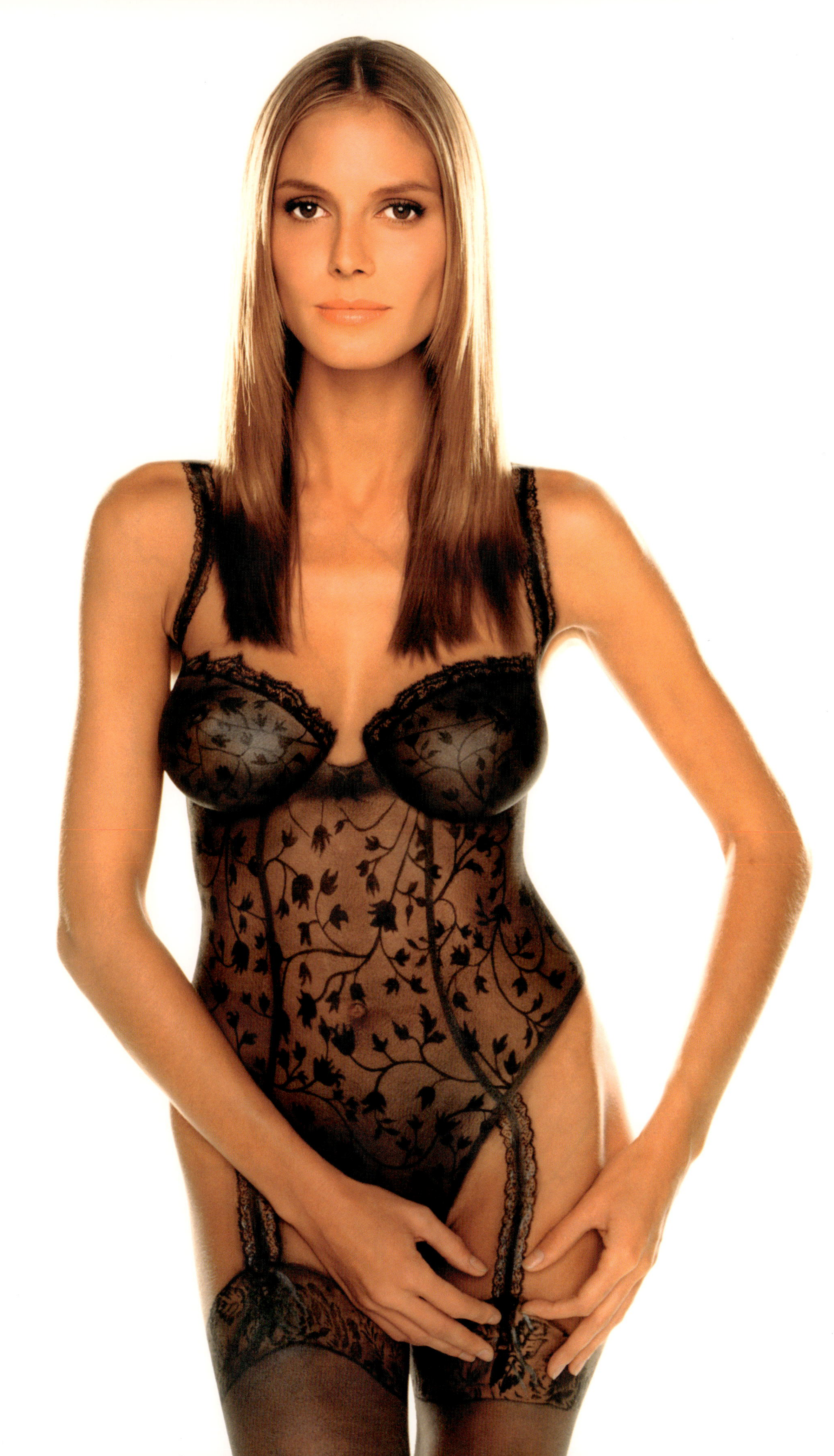

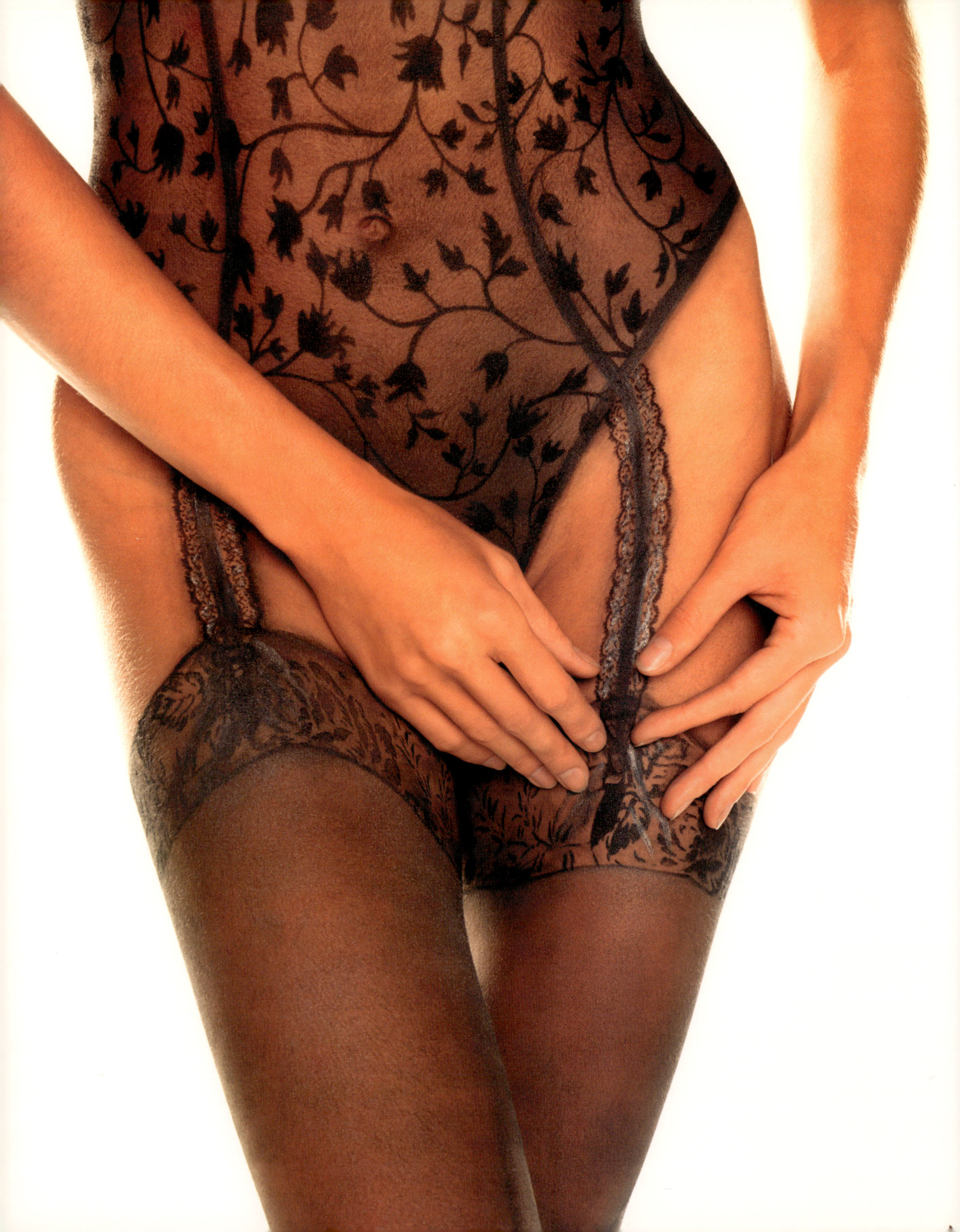

Heidi Klum Antoine Verglas

Elle Macpherson Tony Duran

[overleaf] Ken Browar

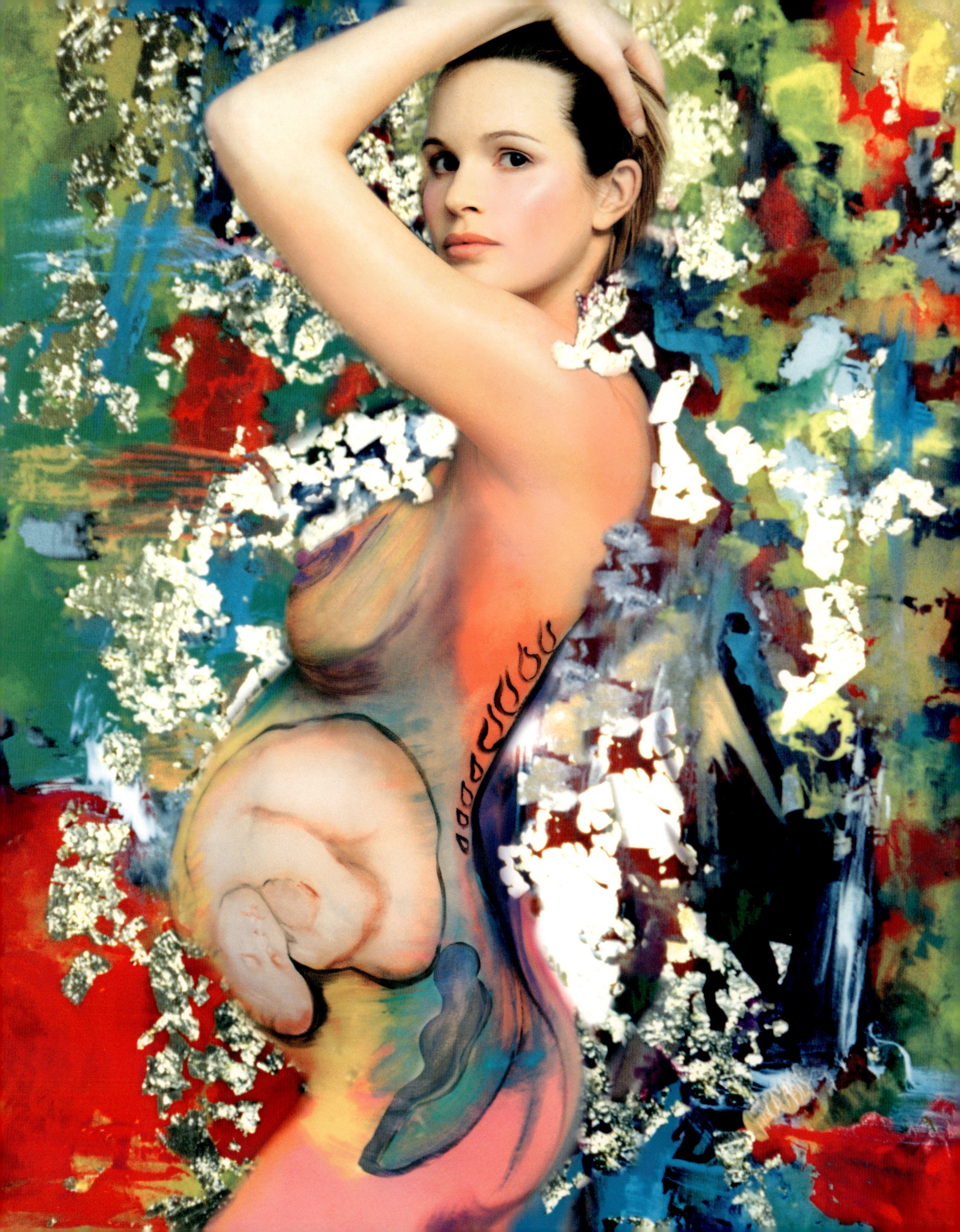

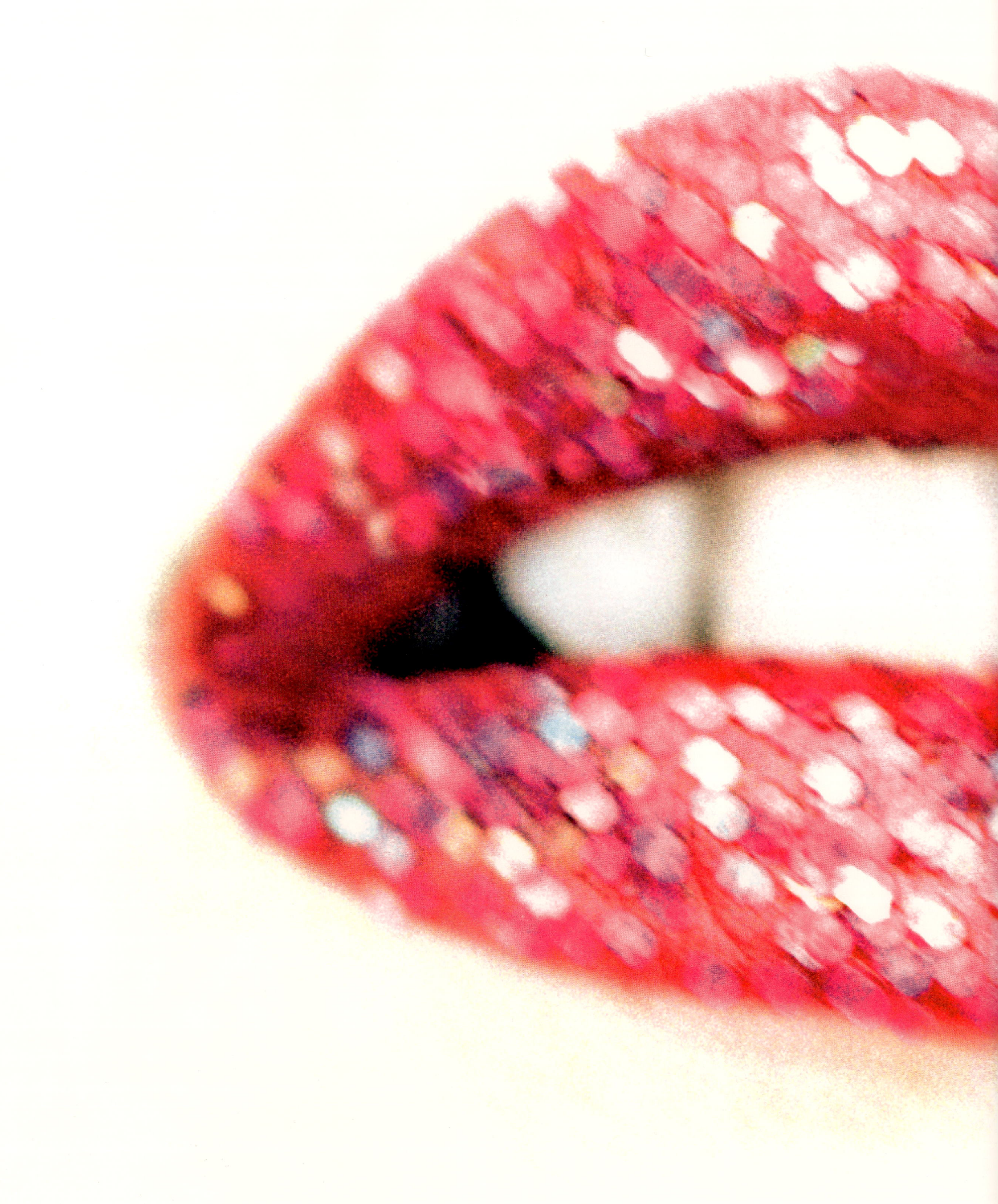

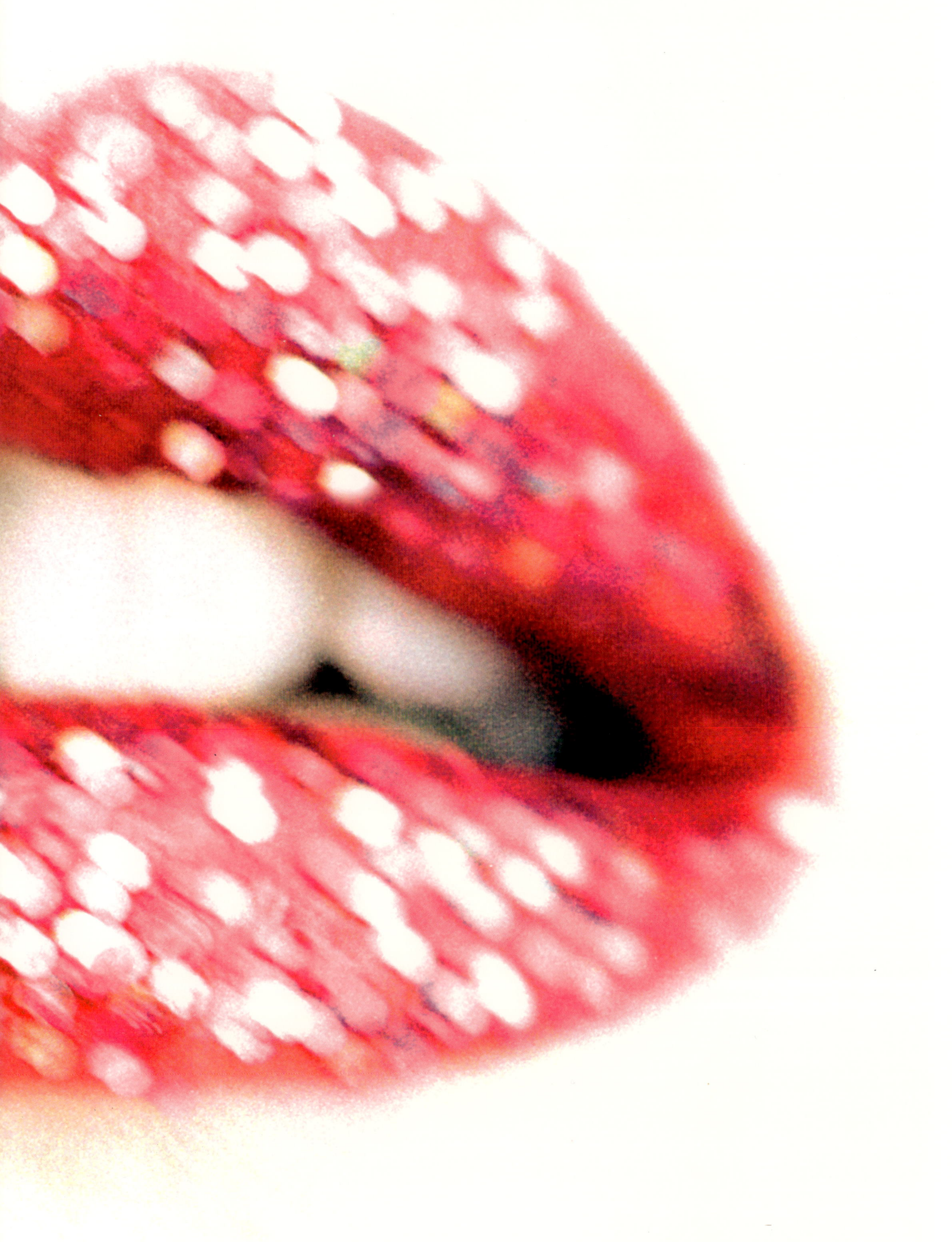

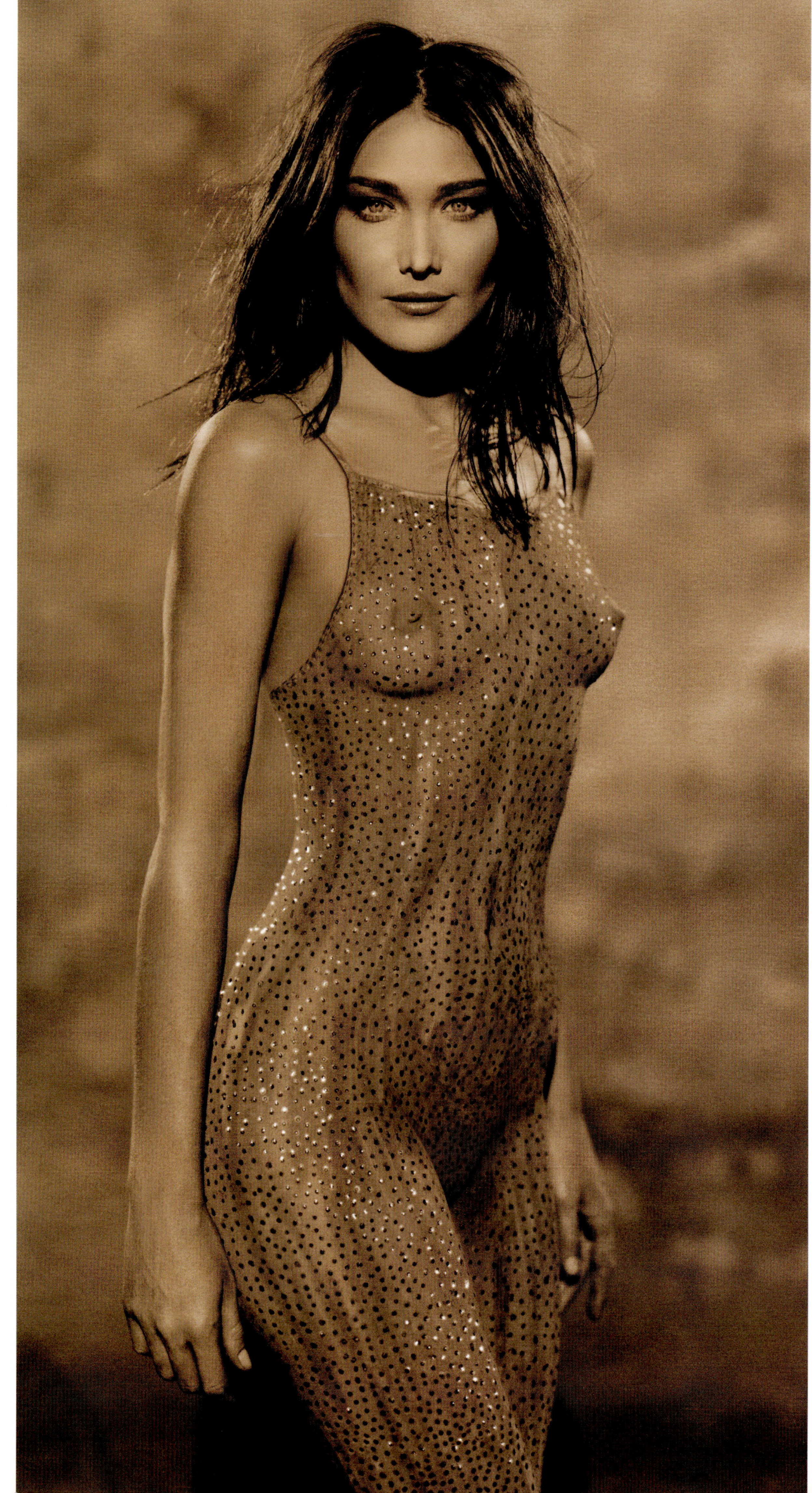

Carla Bruni Holger Eckstein

[overleaf] Sasha Tracy Bayne

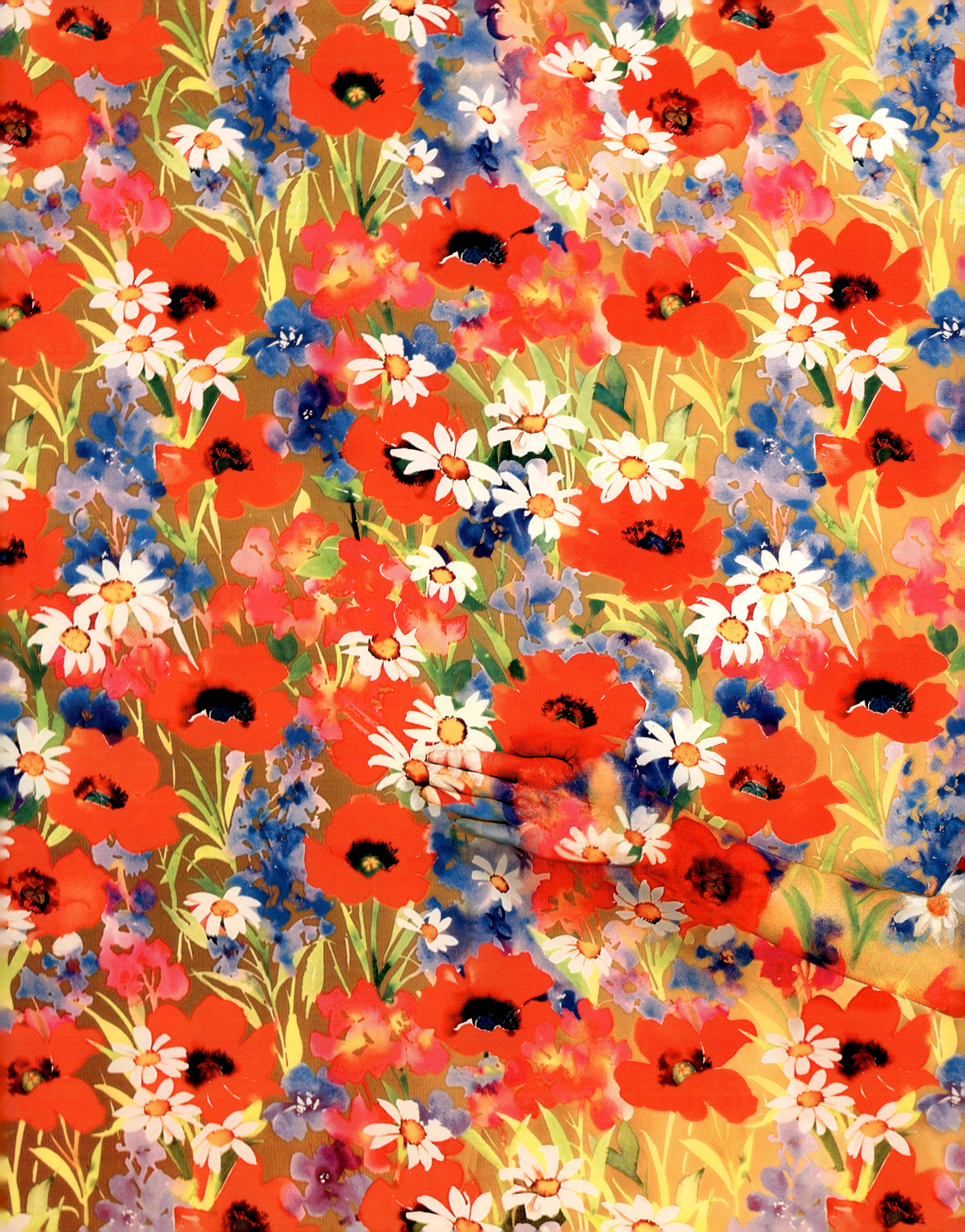

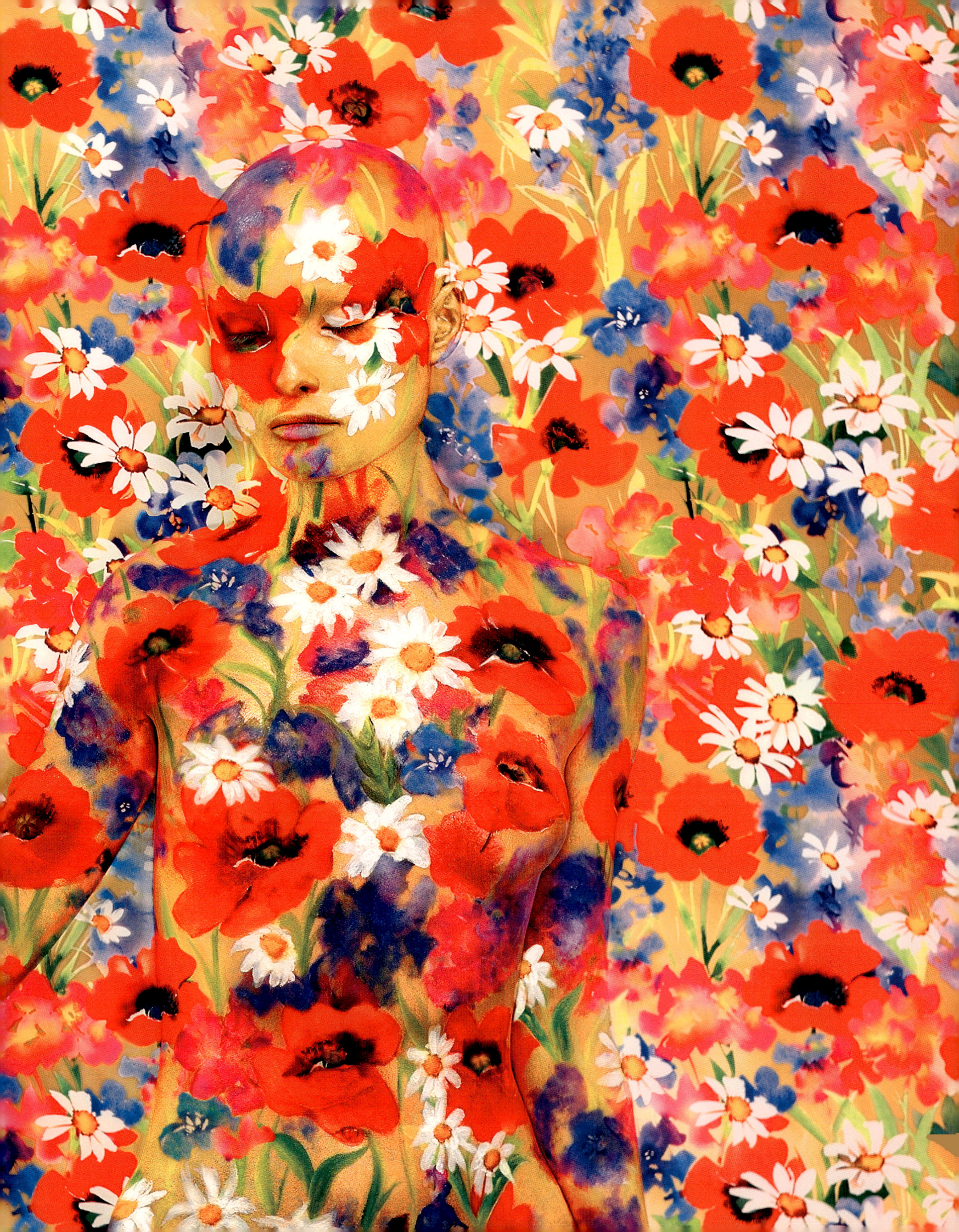

Demi Moore   Annie Leibovitz

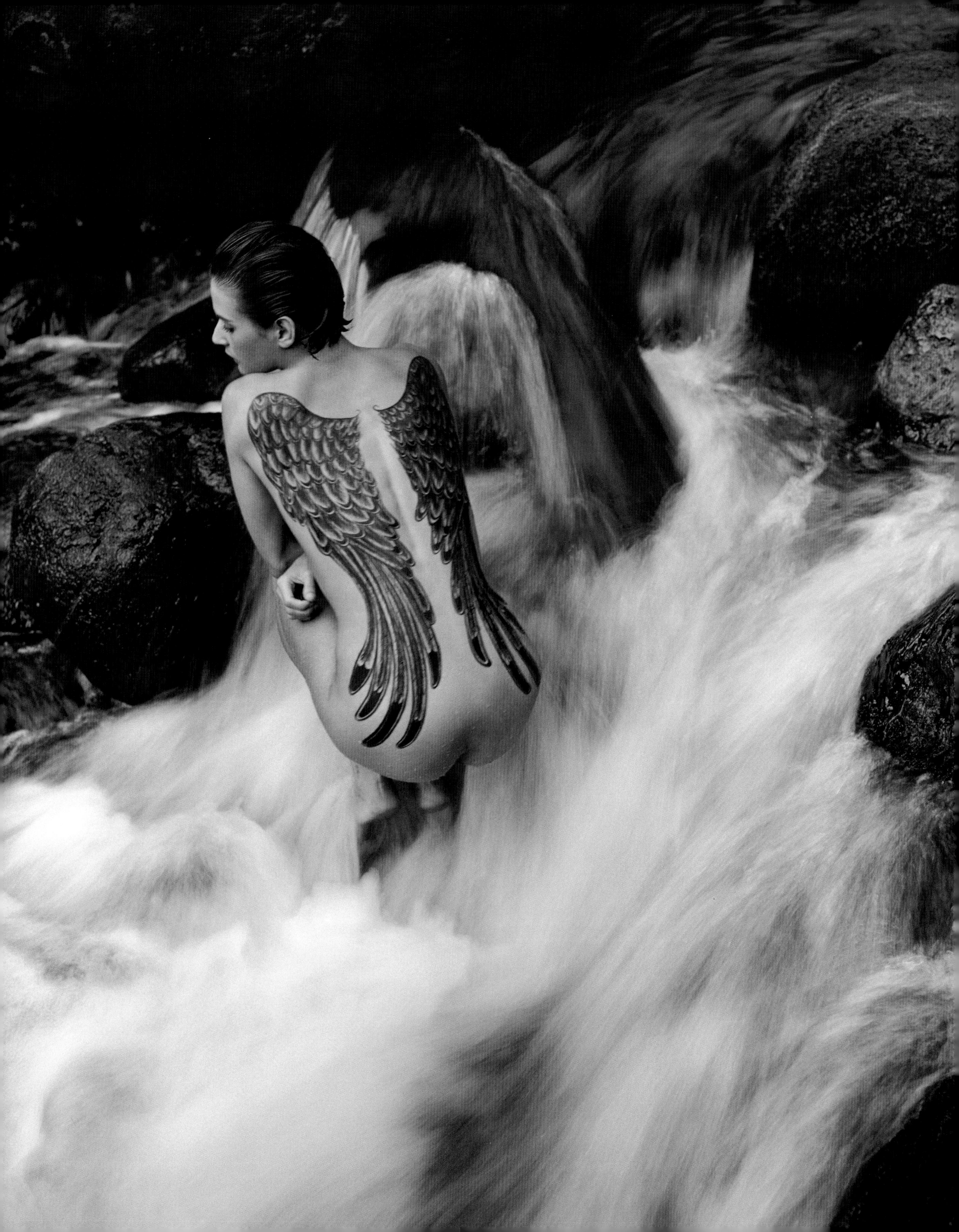

Demi Moore   Annie Leibovitz

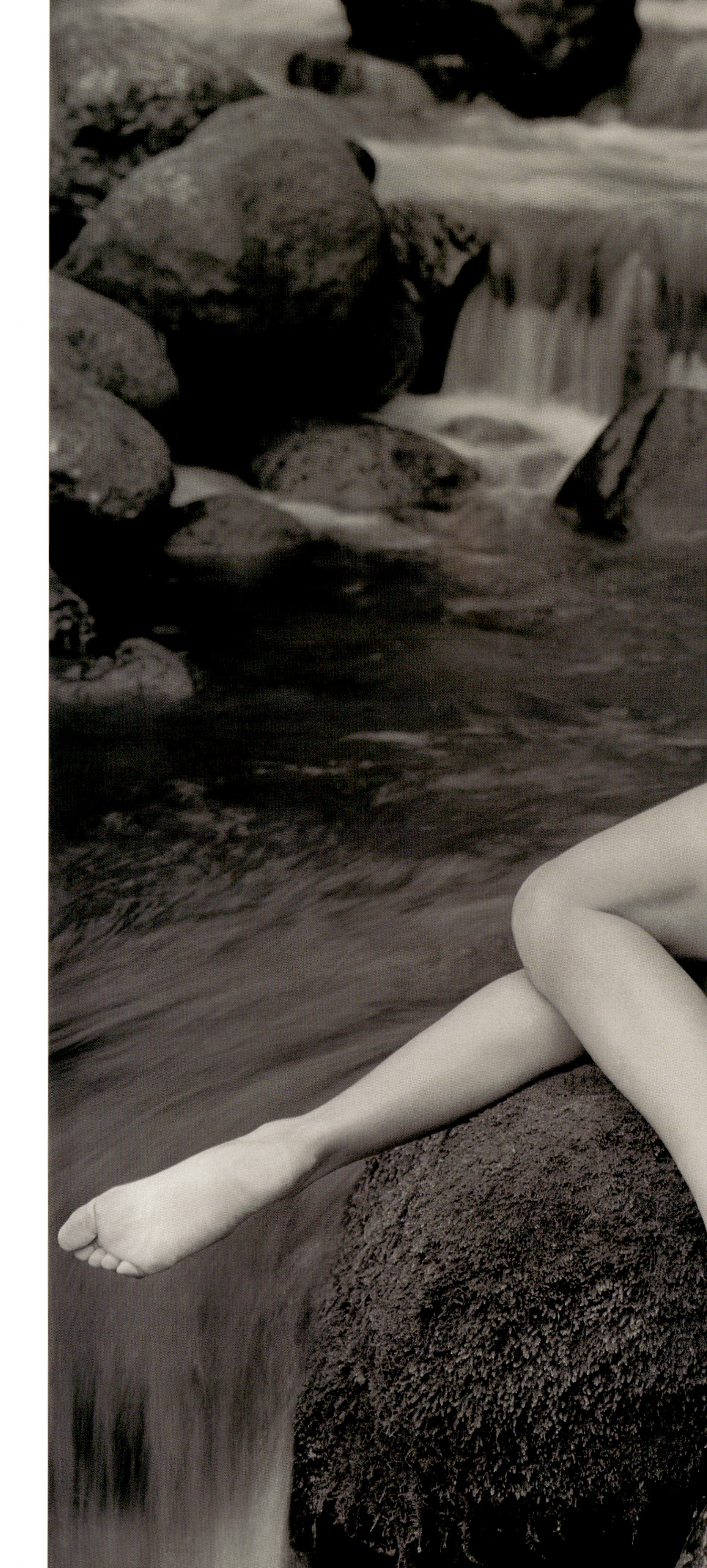

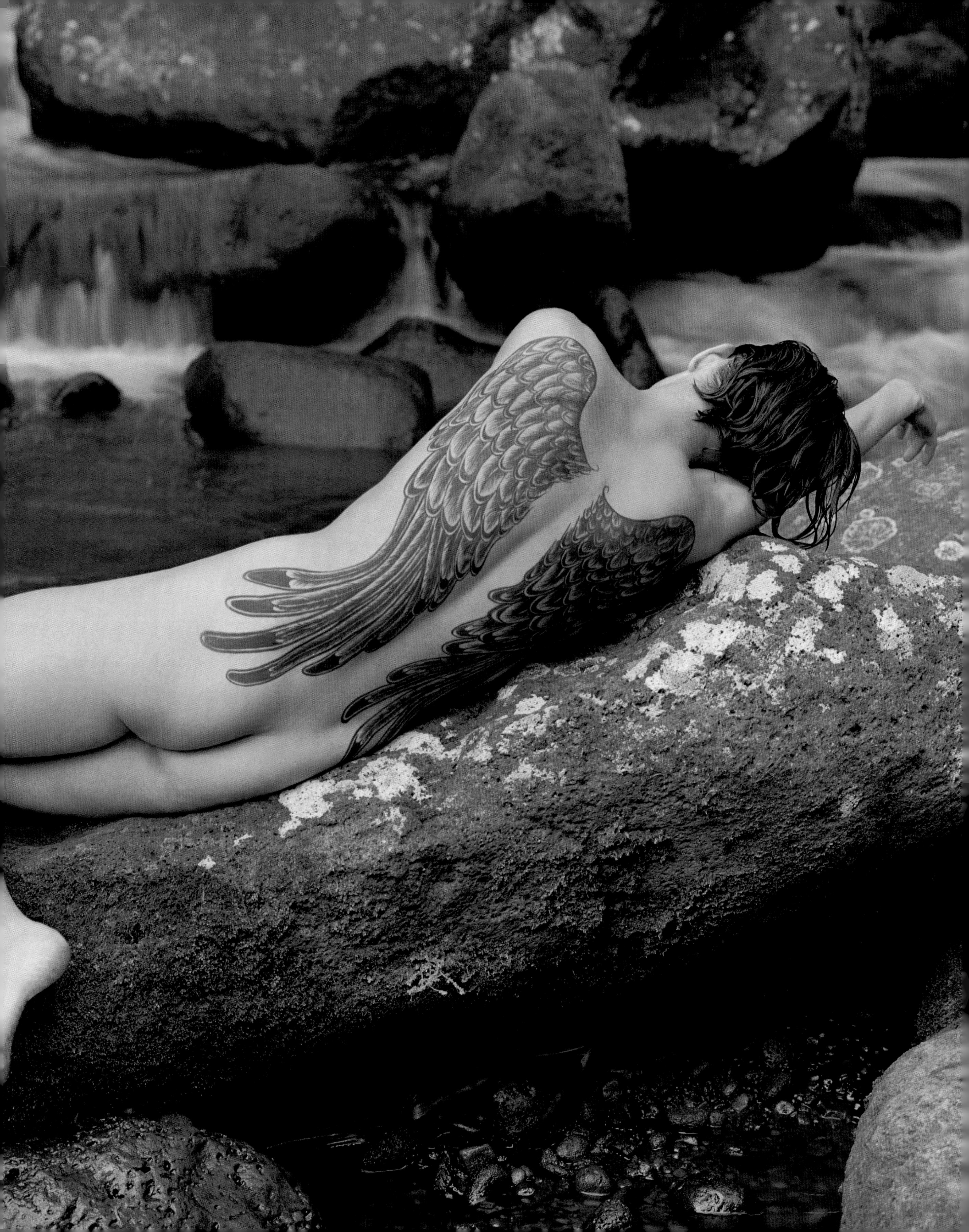

Madonna Herb Ritts

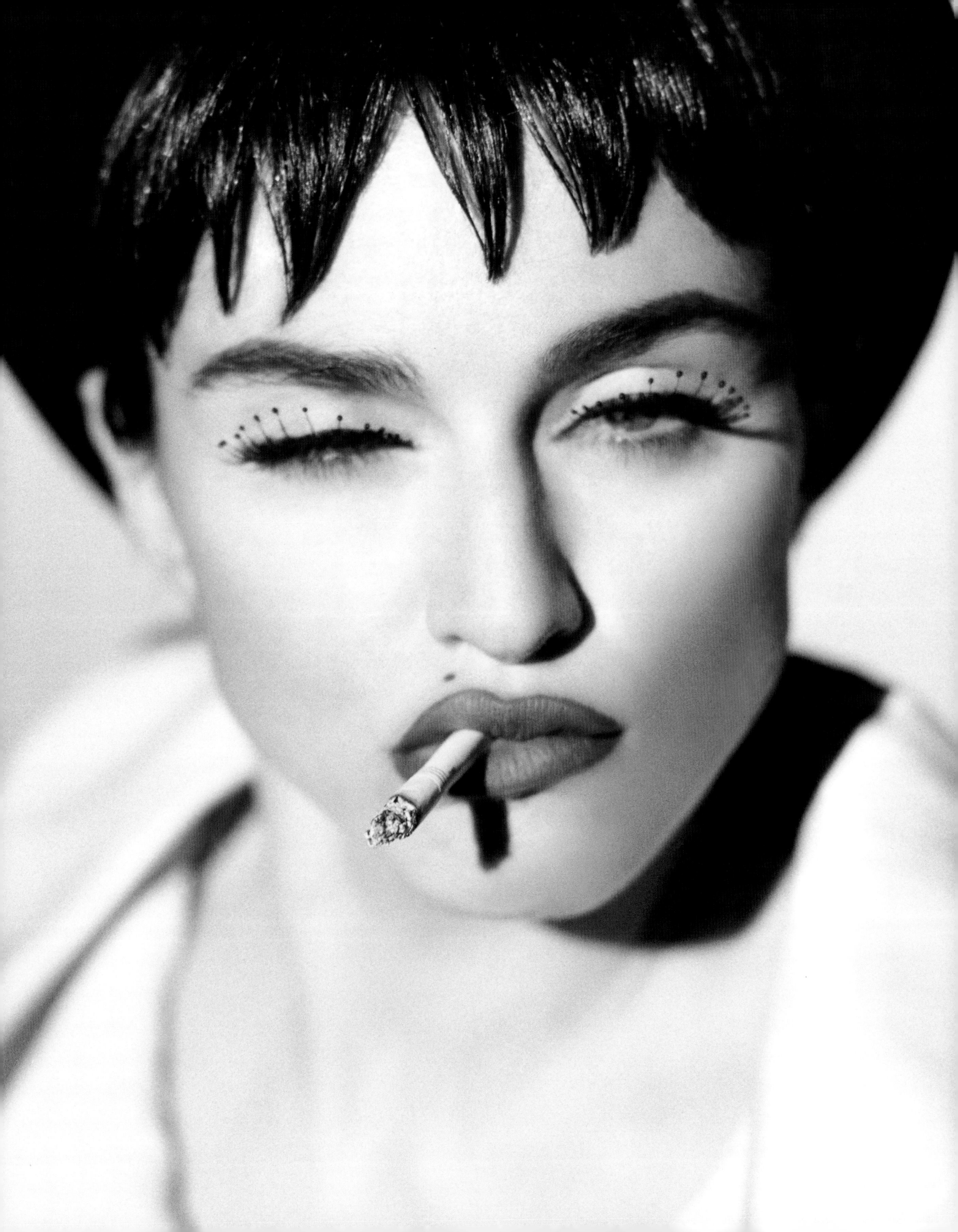

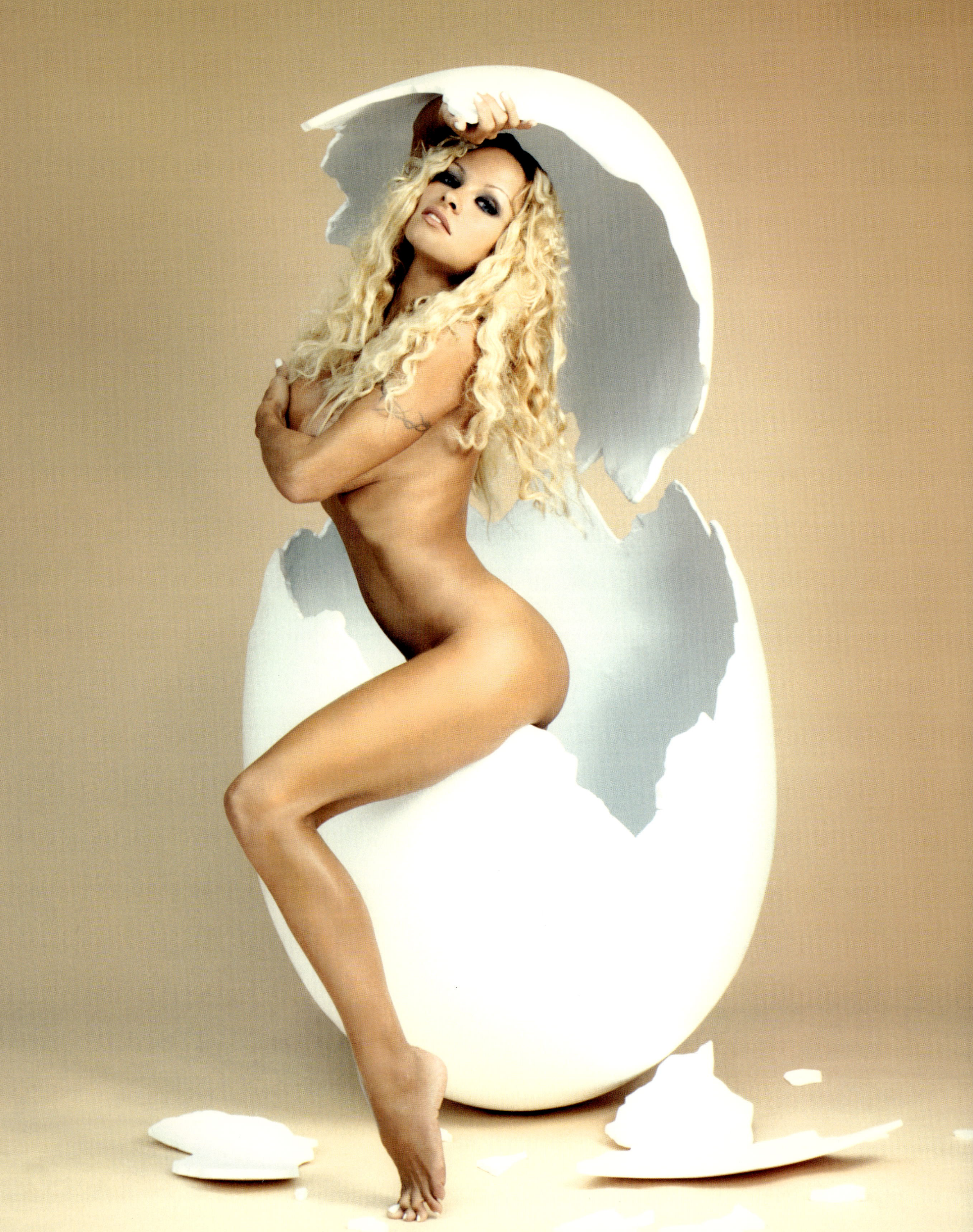

Pamela Anderson David LaChapelle

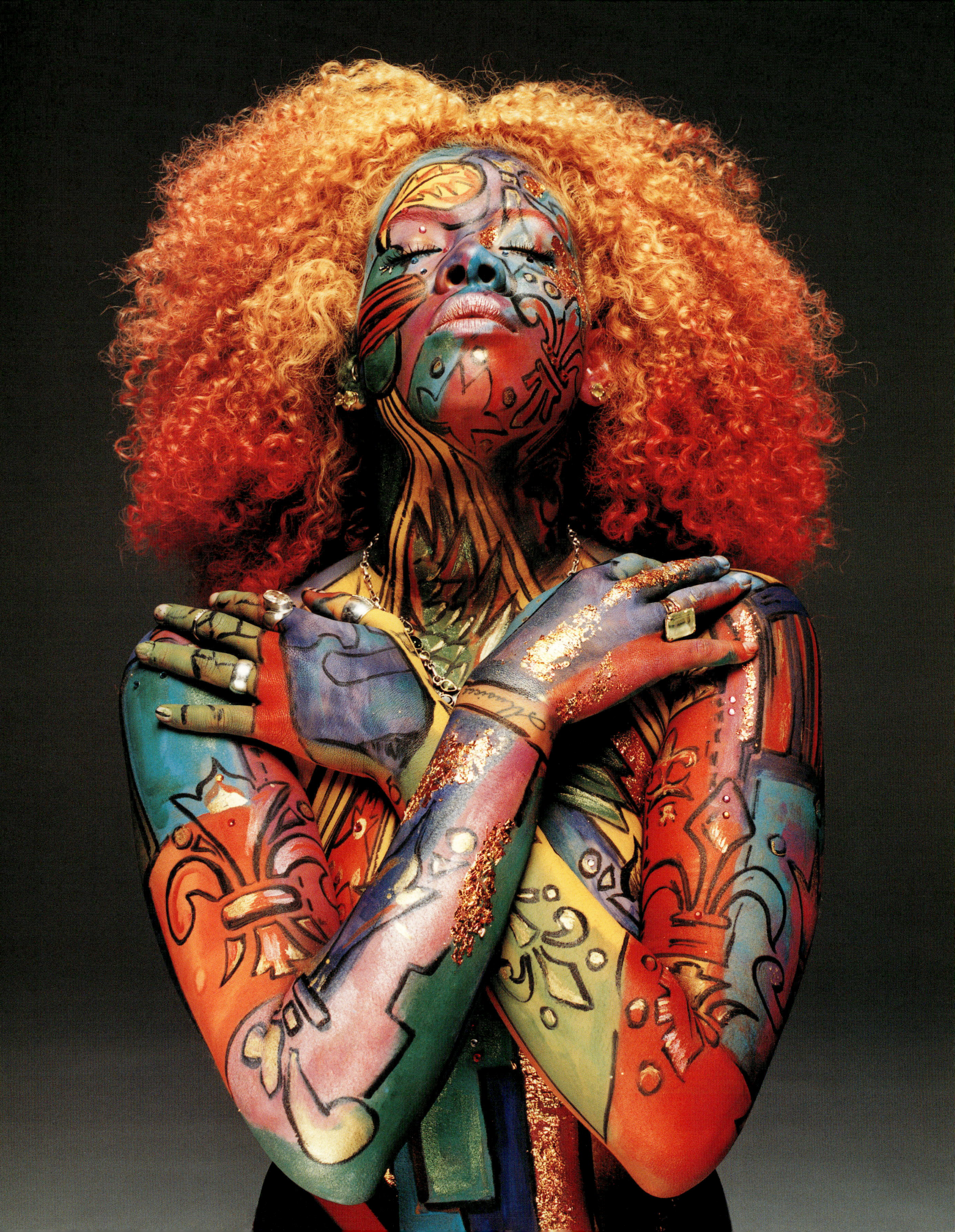

Kelis Jonathan Mannion

[overleaf] Lauren Gott Matthew Rolston

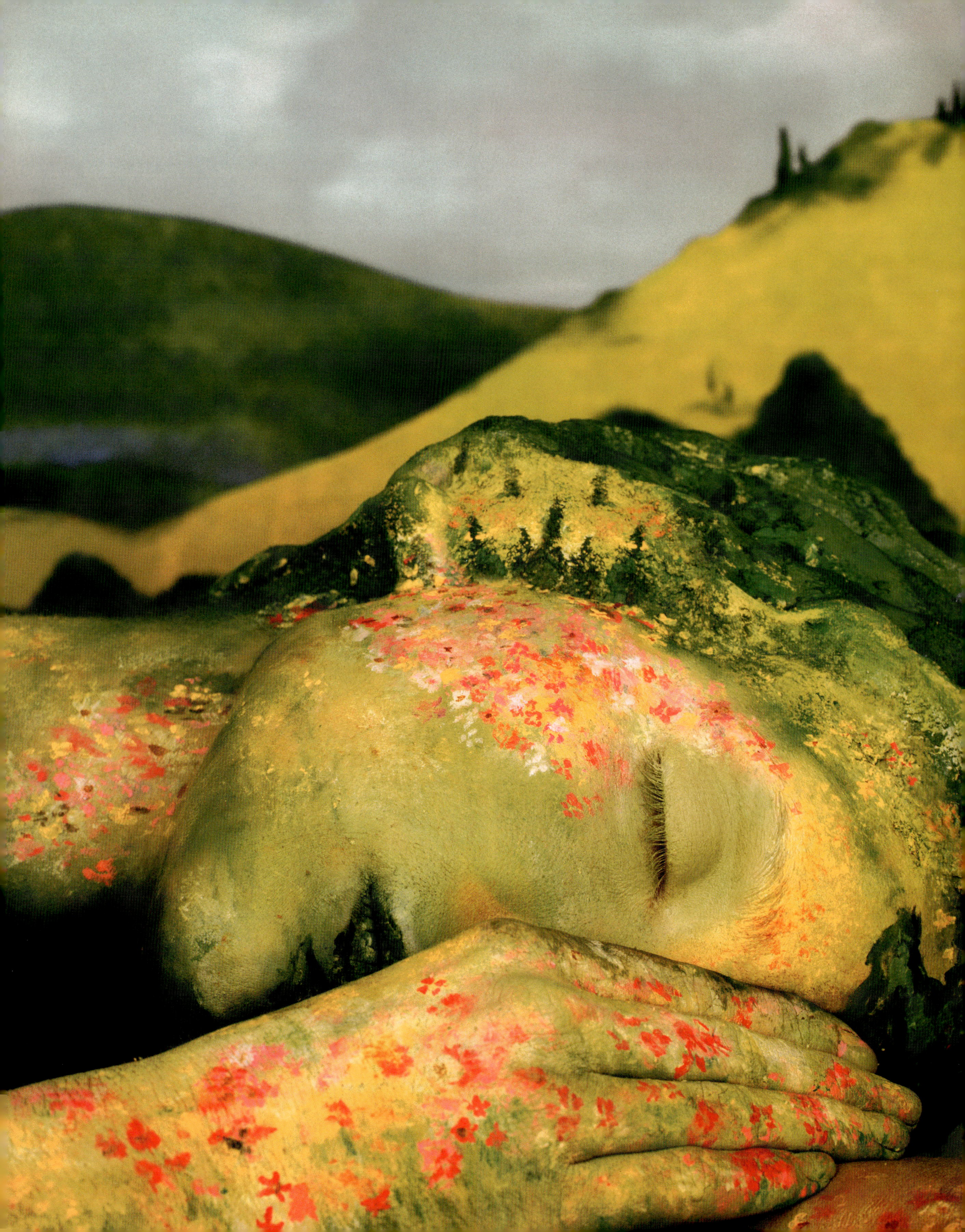

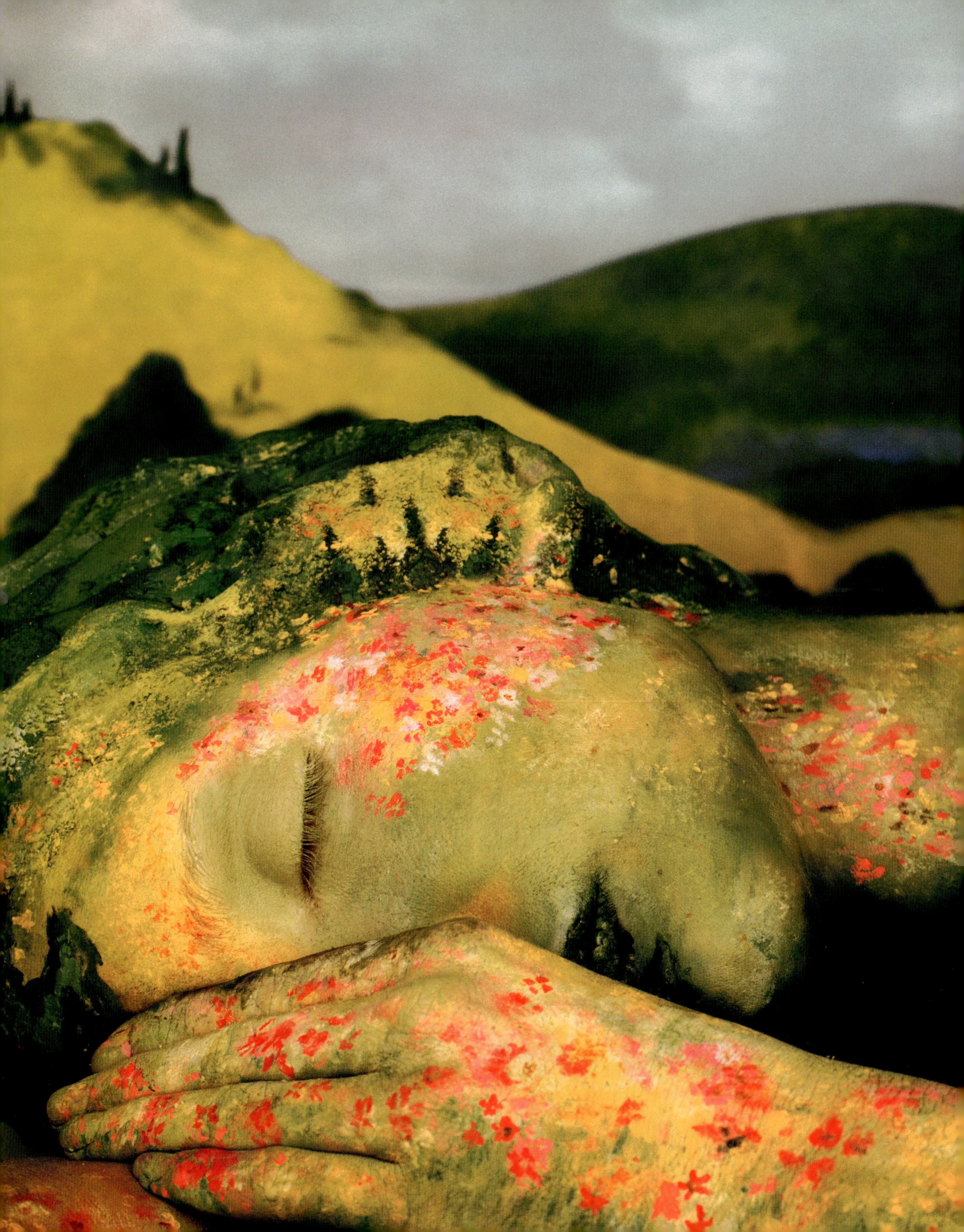

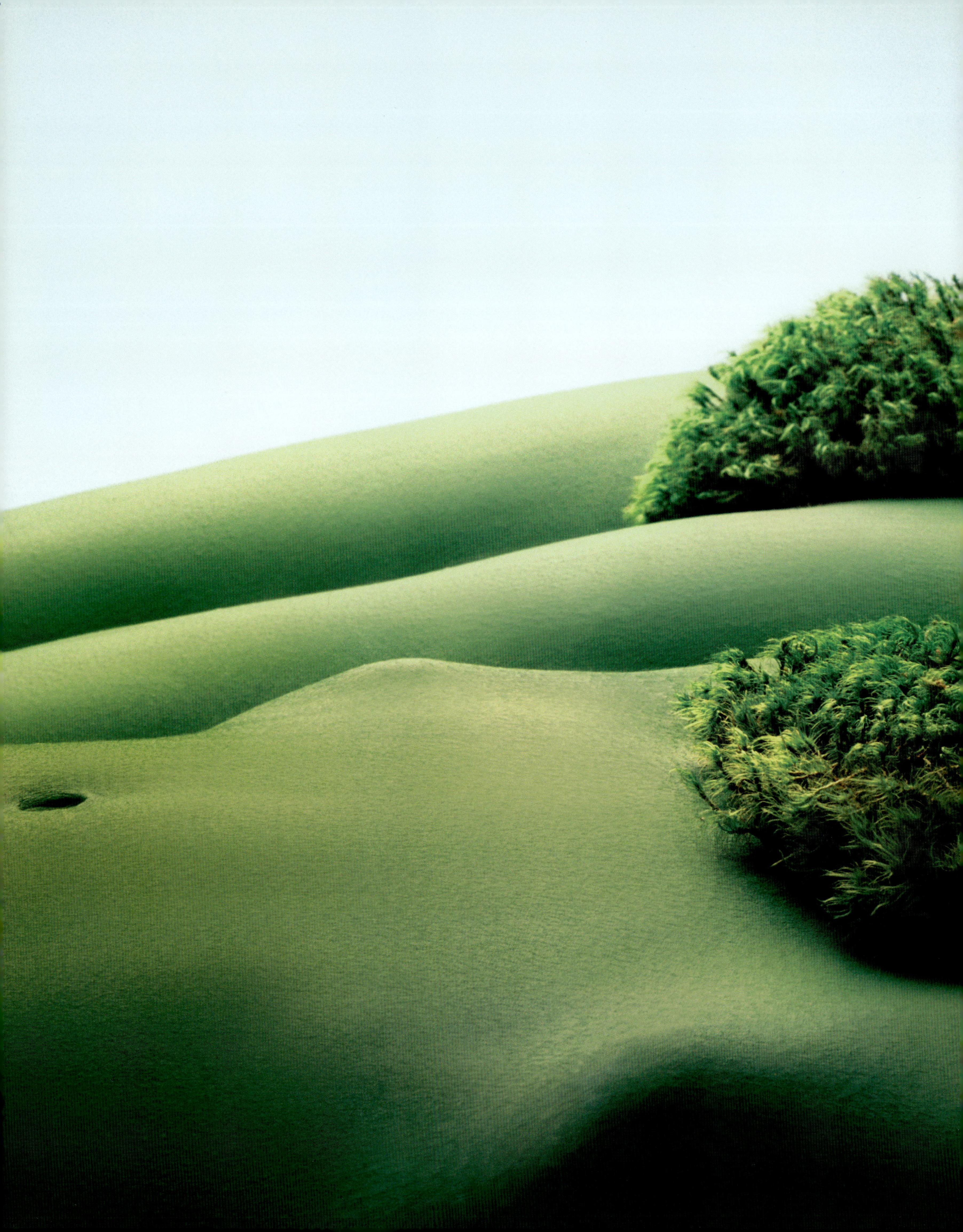

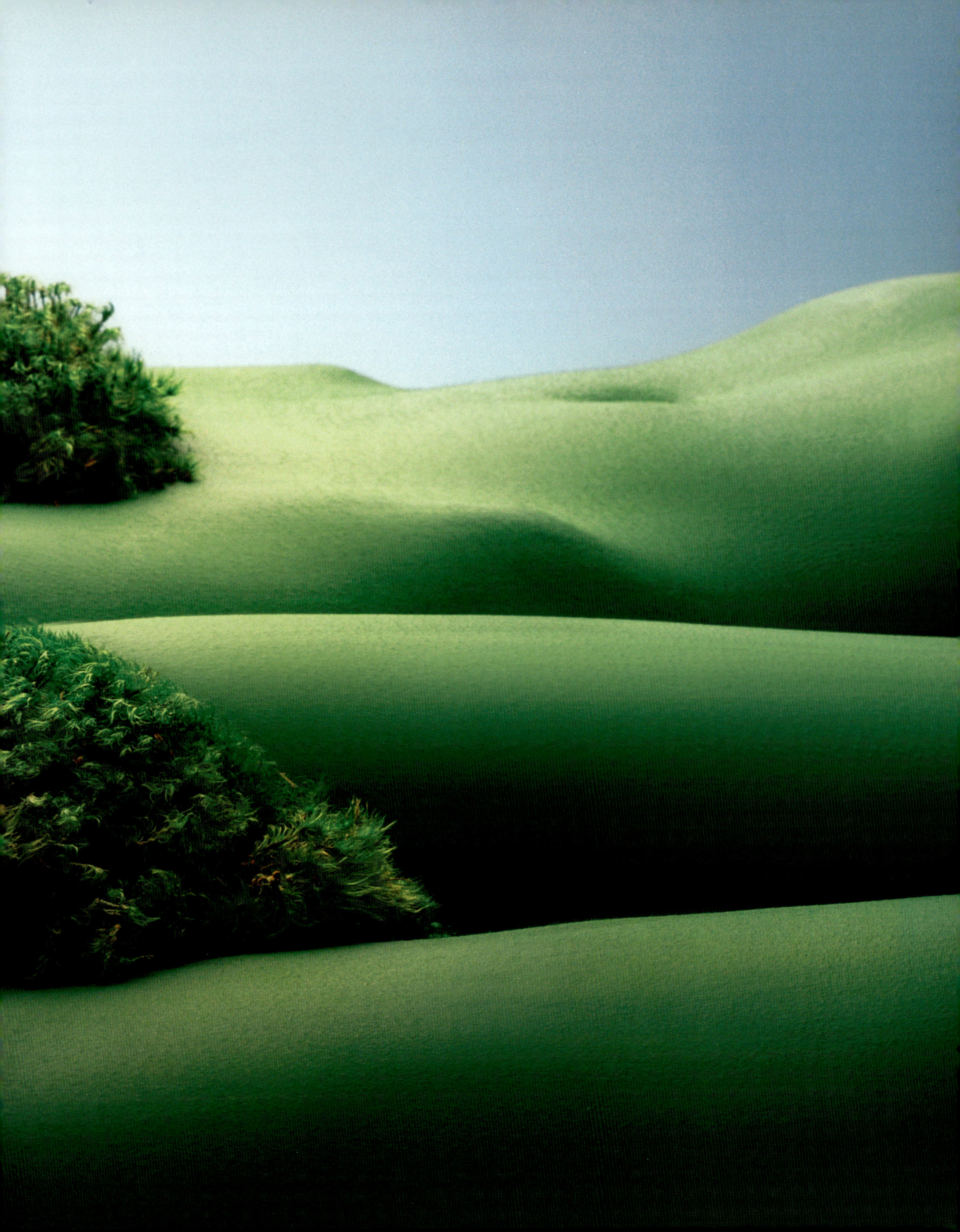

[previous] Eva Mueller

Yana Alberto Tolot

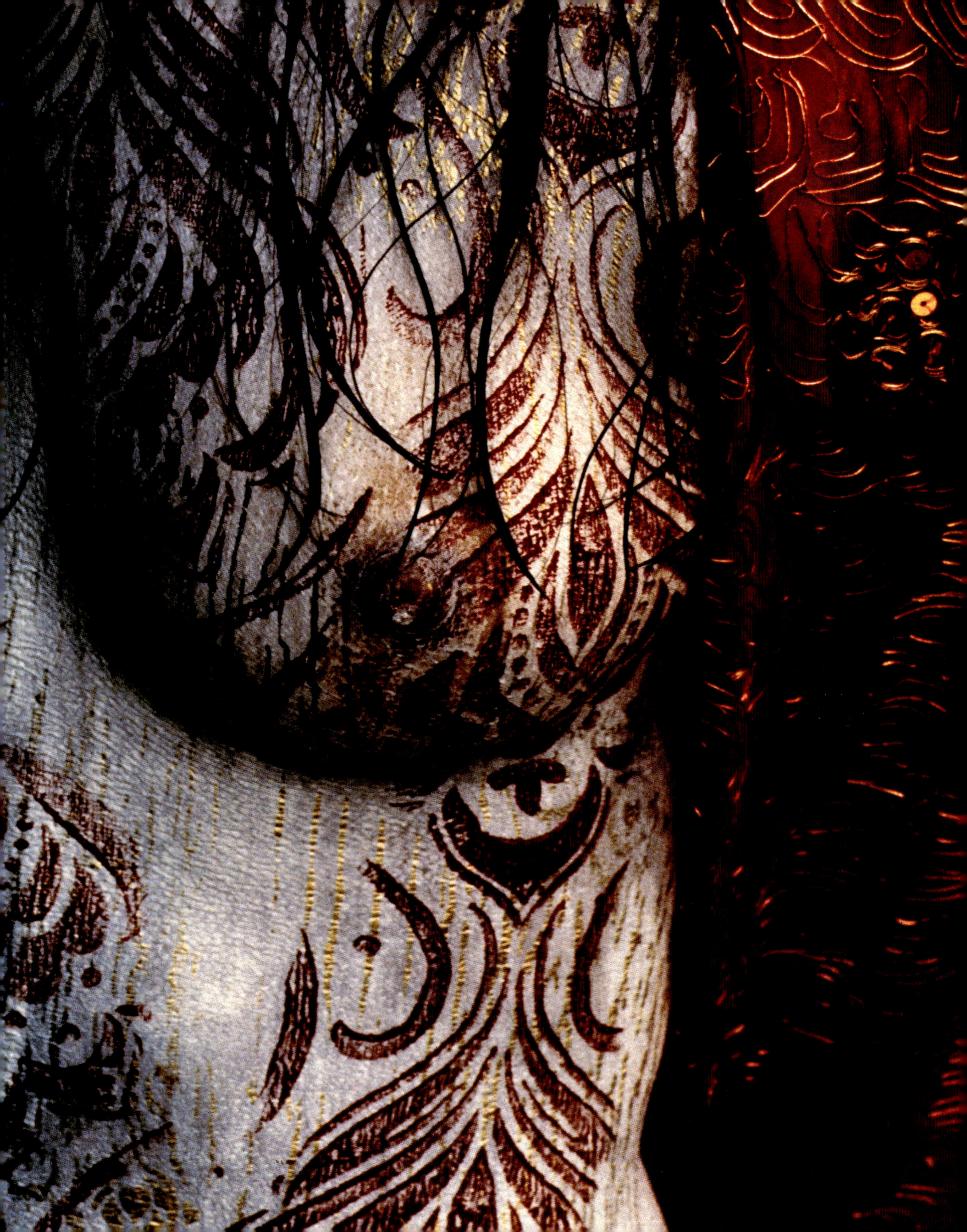

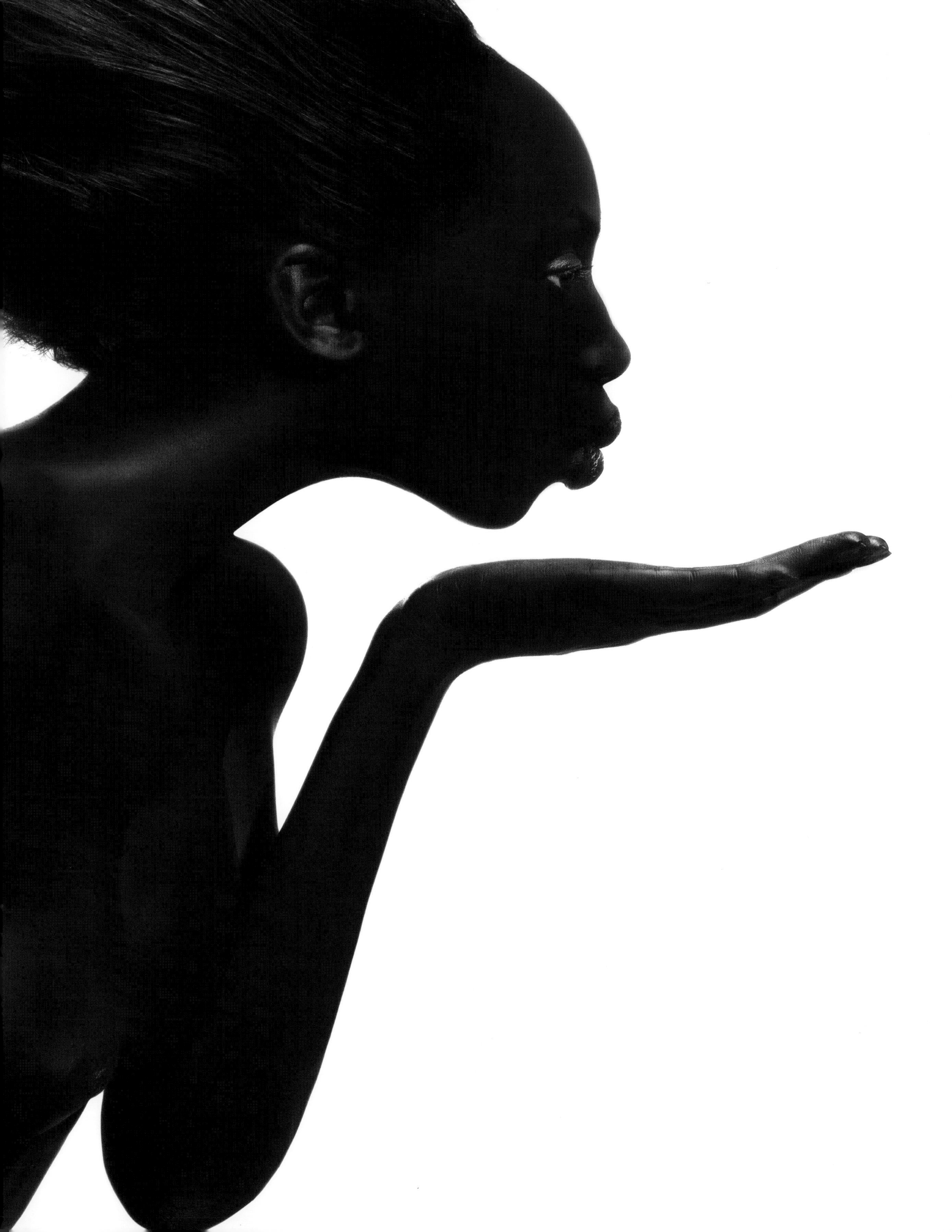

Suwana Joanne Gair

Suwana Joanne Gair

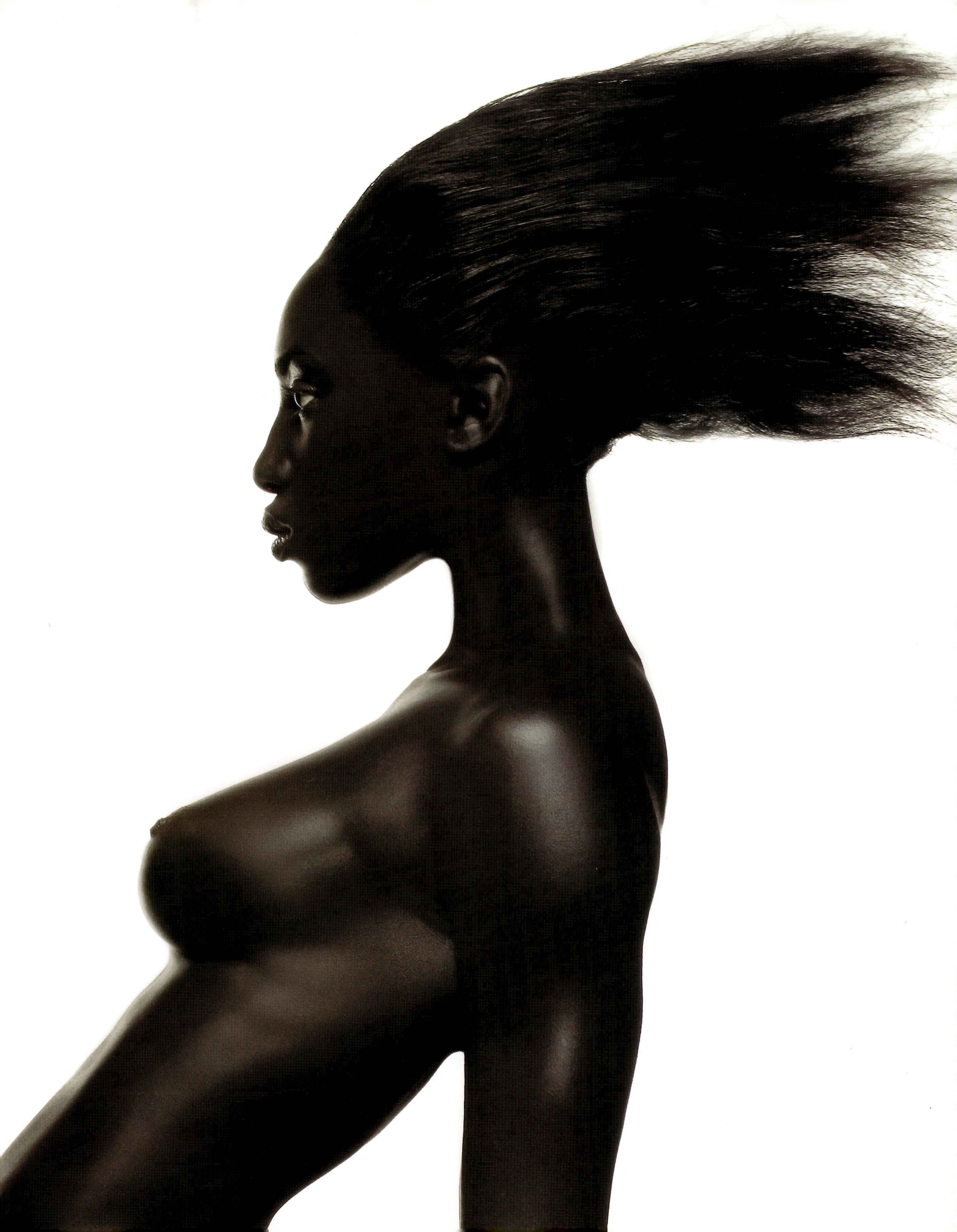

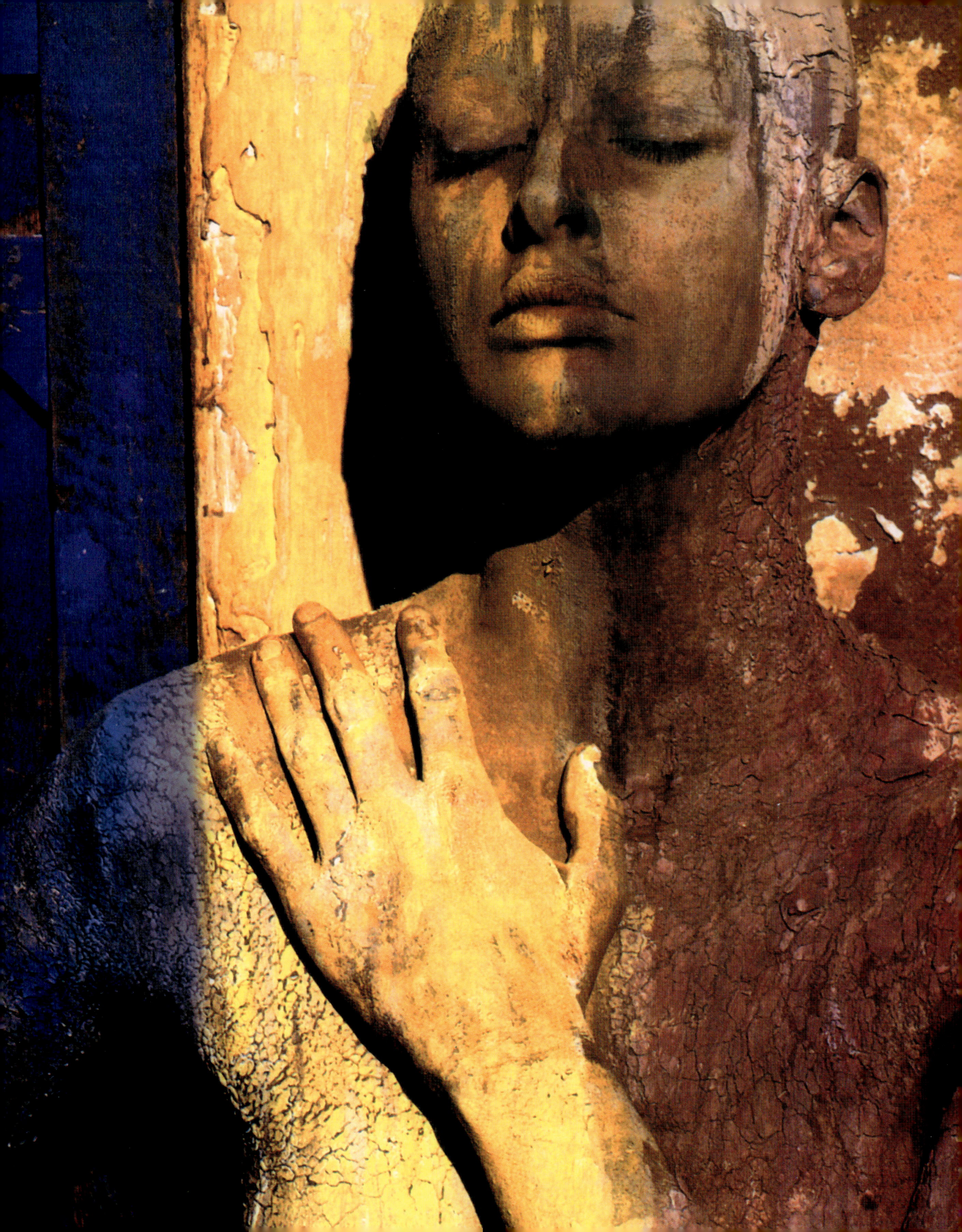

Broūn

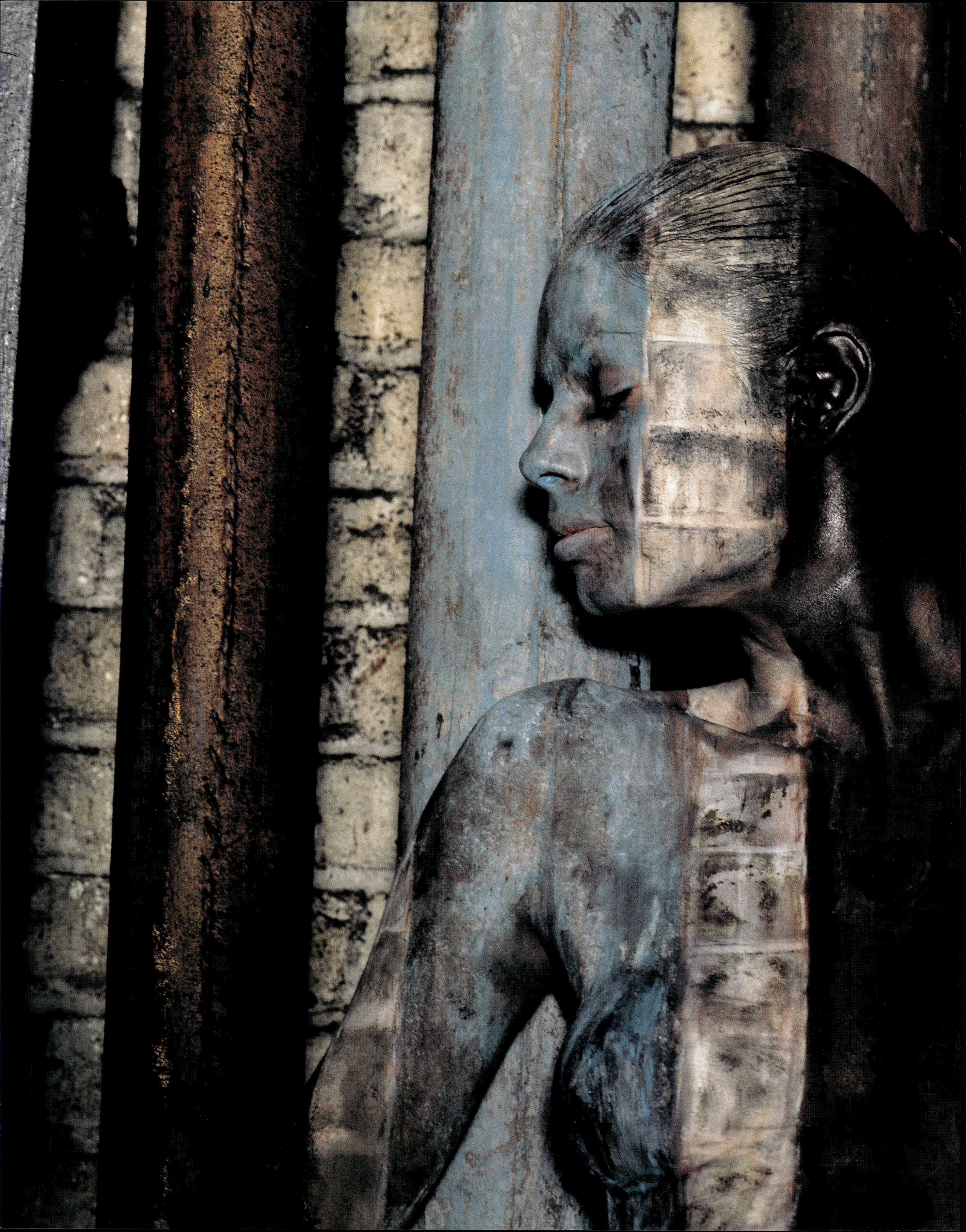

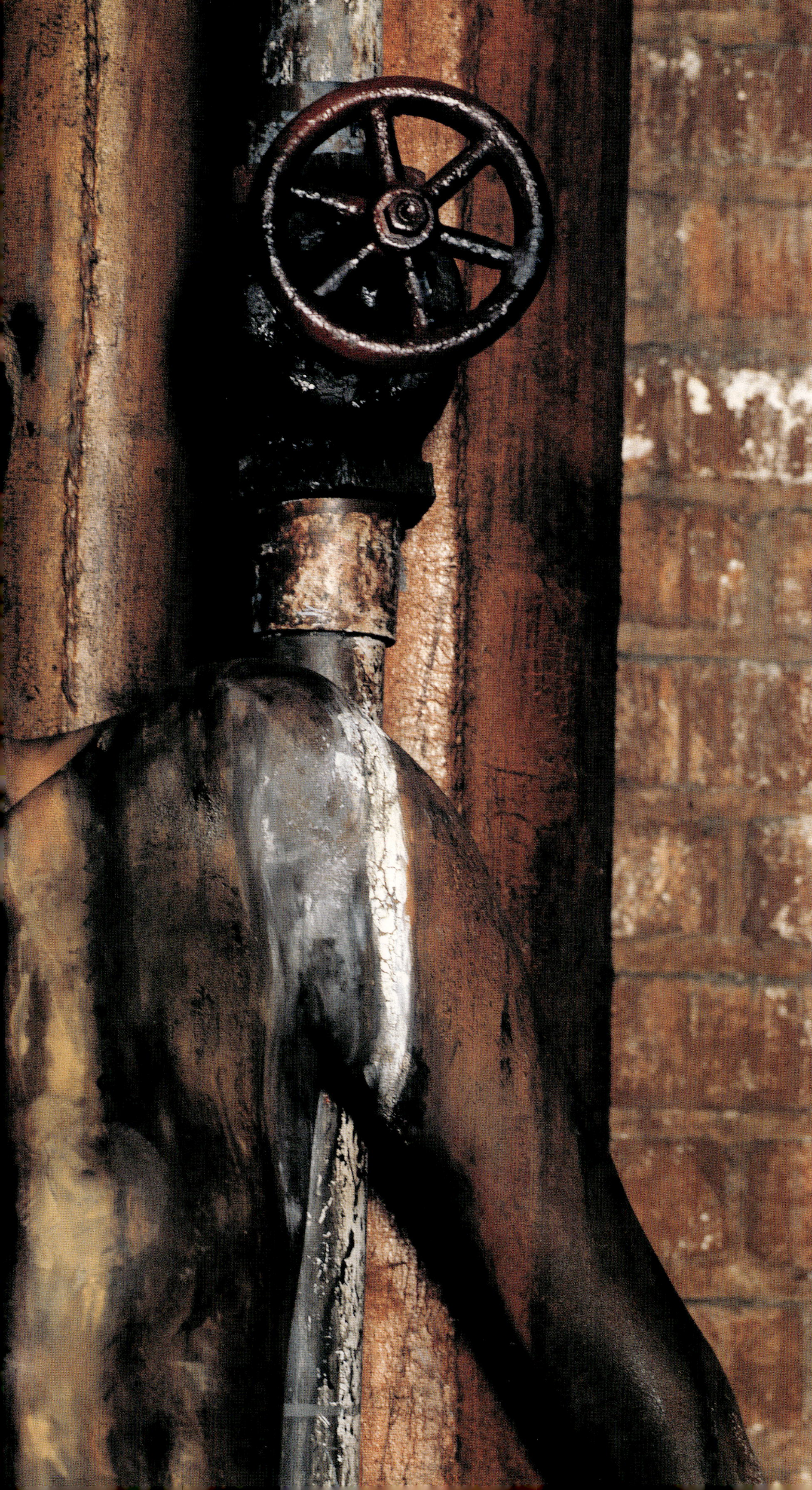

Broūn

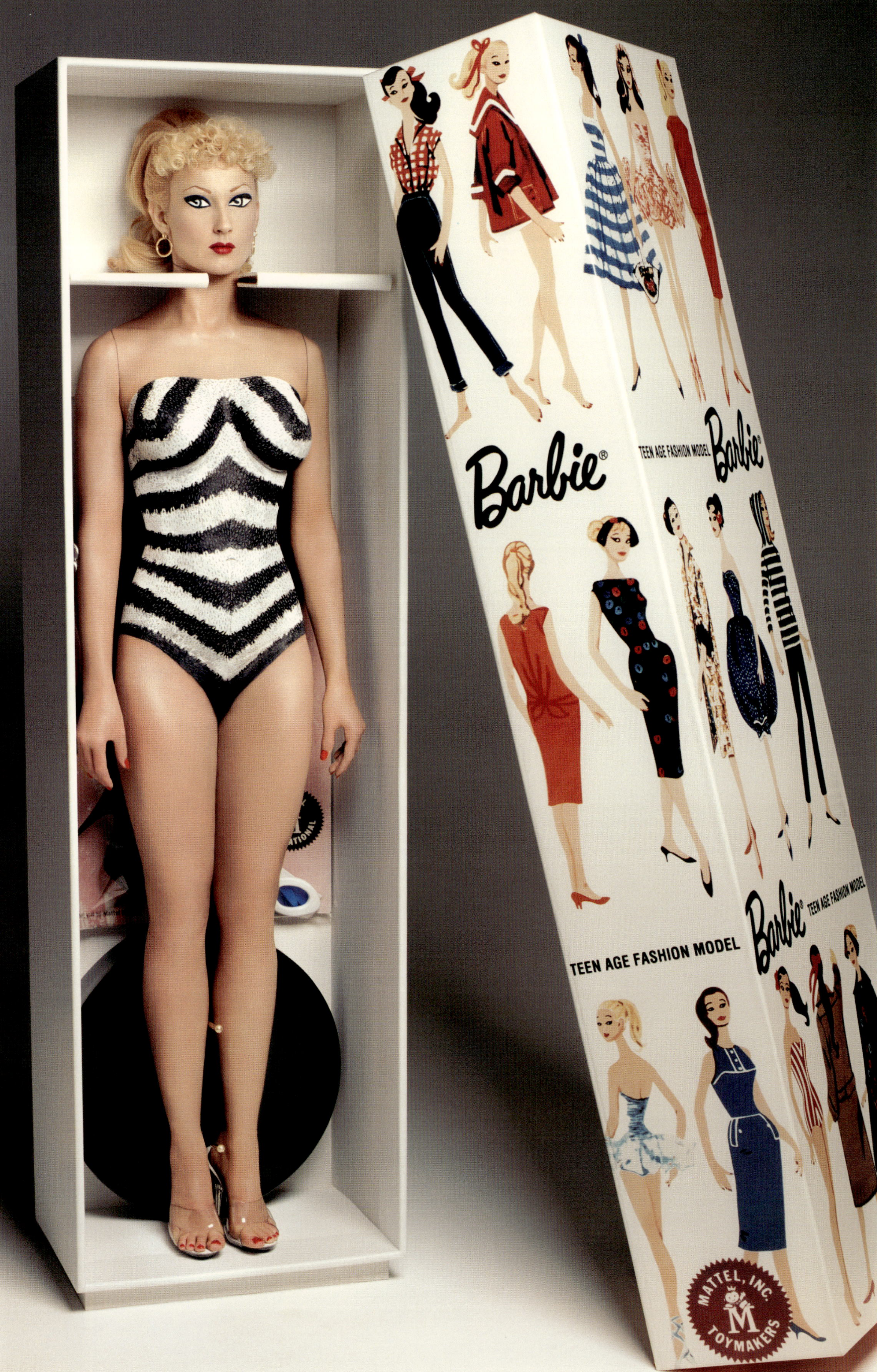
Barbie®
TEEN AGE FASHION MODEL Barbie®
Barbie® TEEN AGE FASHION MODEL
TEEN AGE FASHION MODEL
MATTEL, INC. M TOYMAKERS

Demi Moore Matthew Rolston

Demi Moore Matthew Rolston

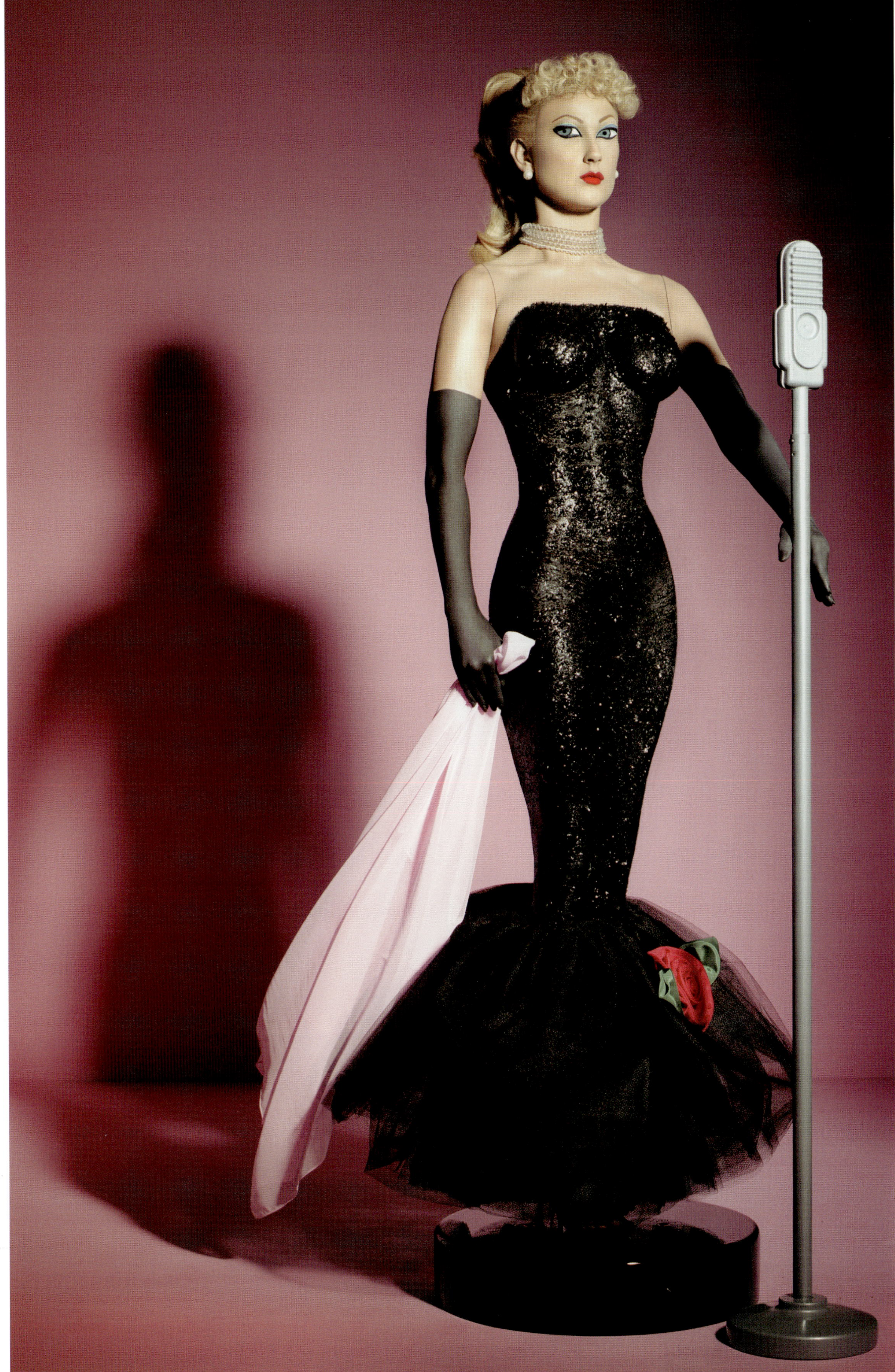

Tiffany Green Dan Escobar

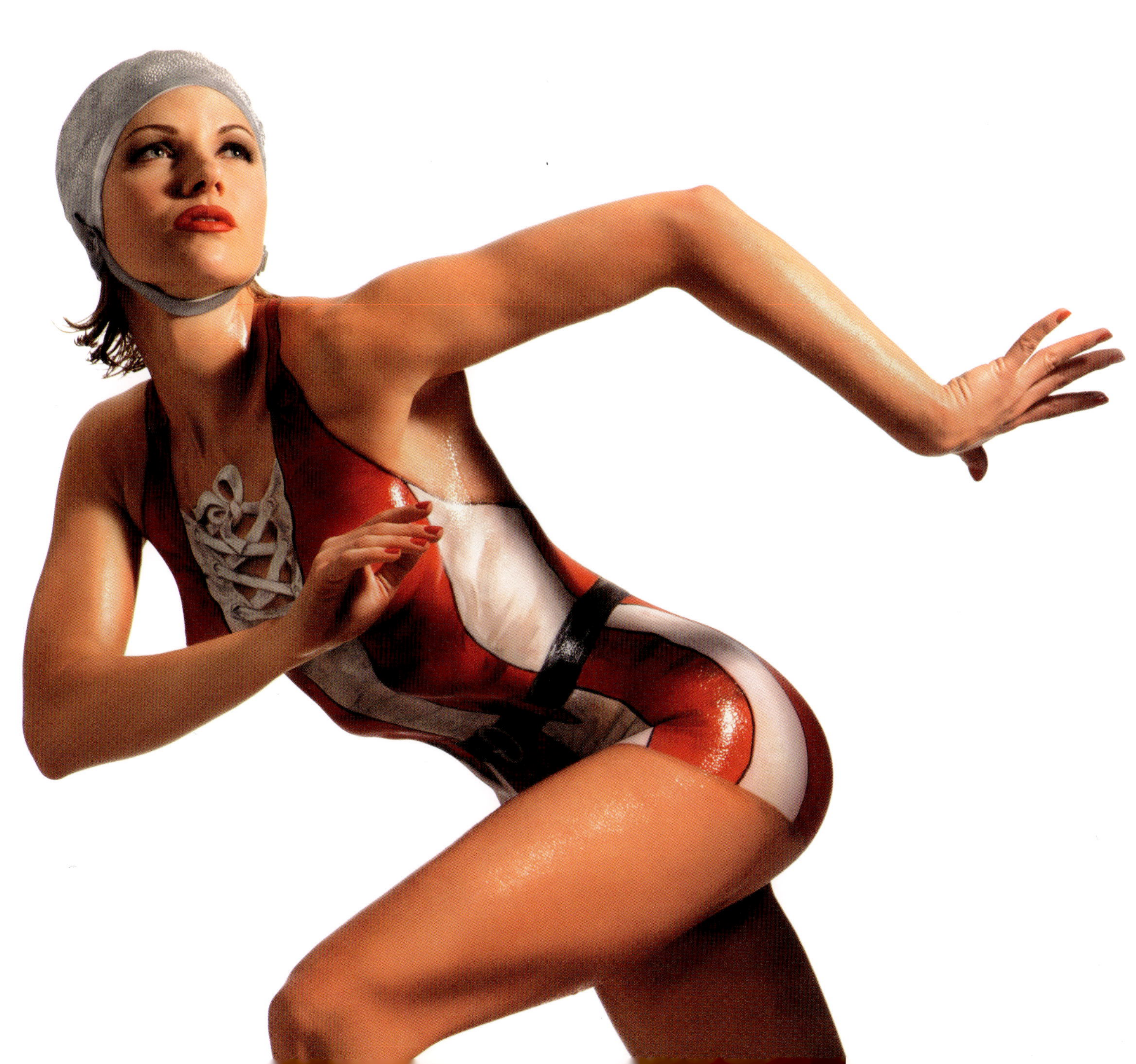

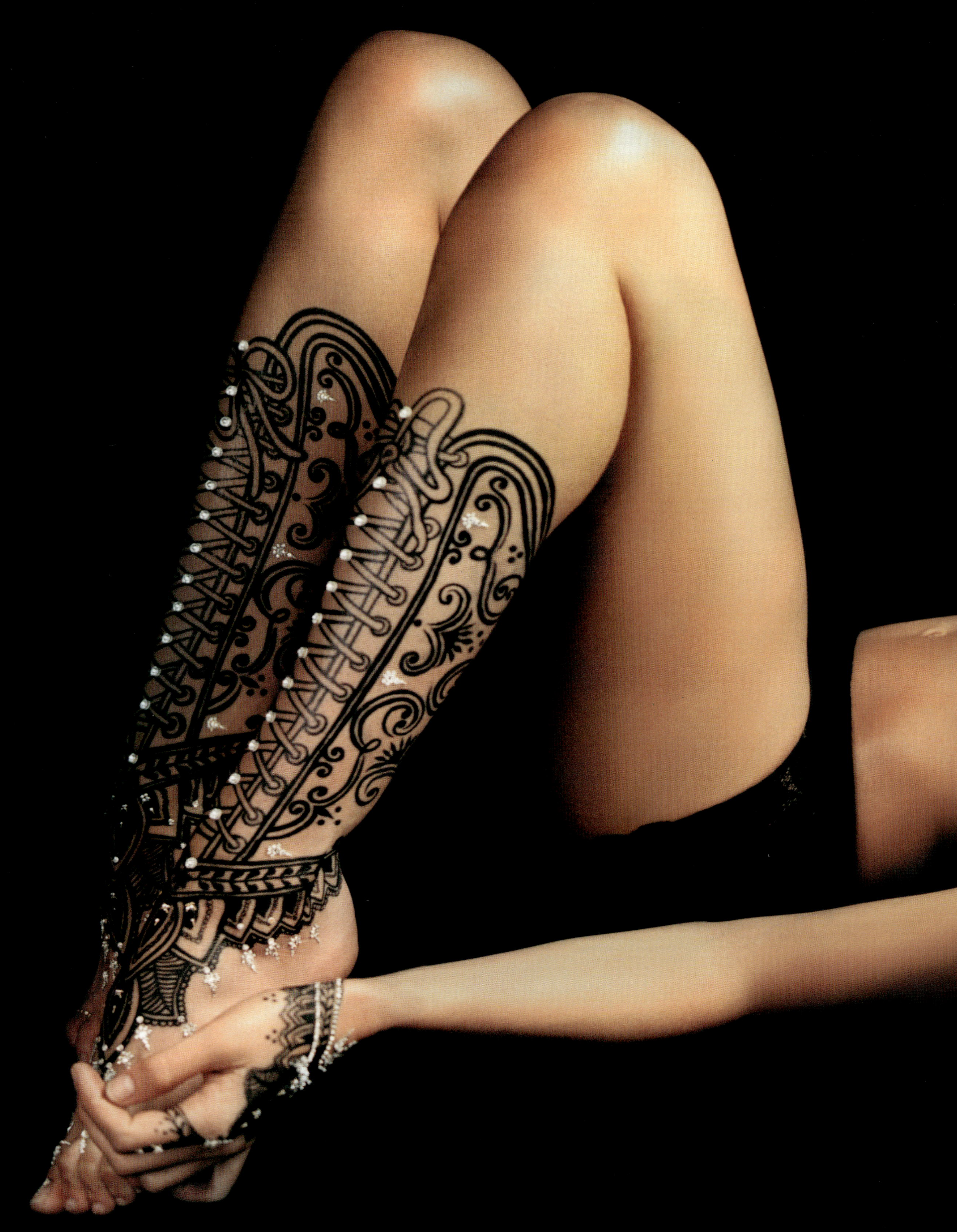

Libby McGinley   Tracy Bayne

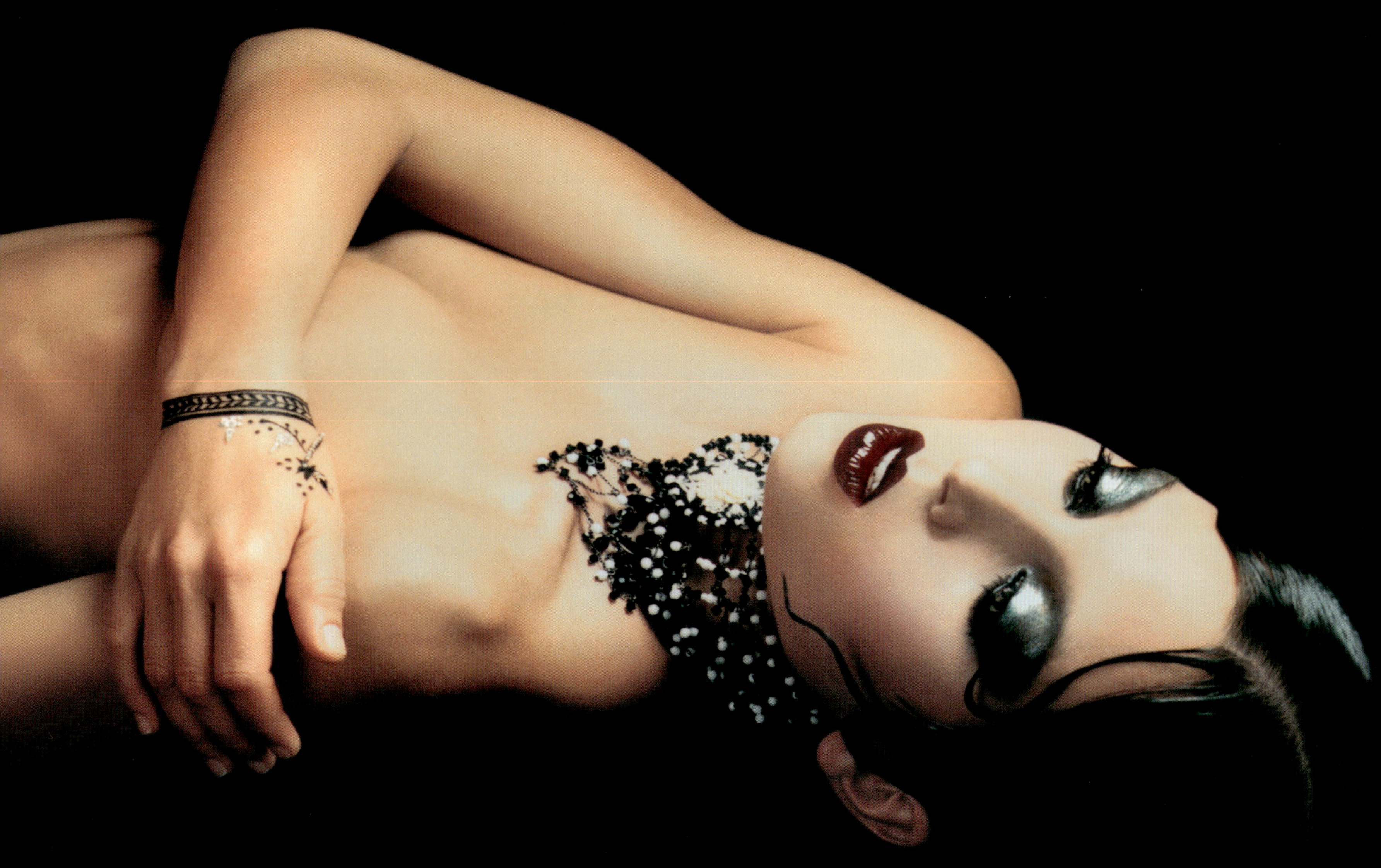

Libby McGinley Tracy Bayne

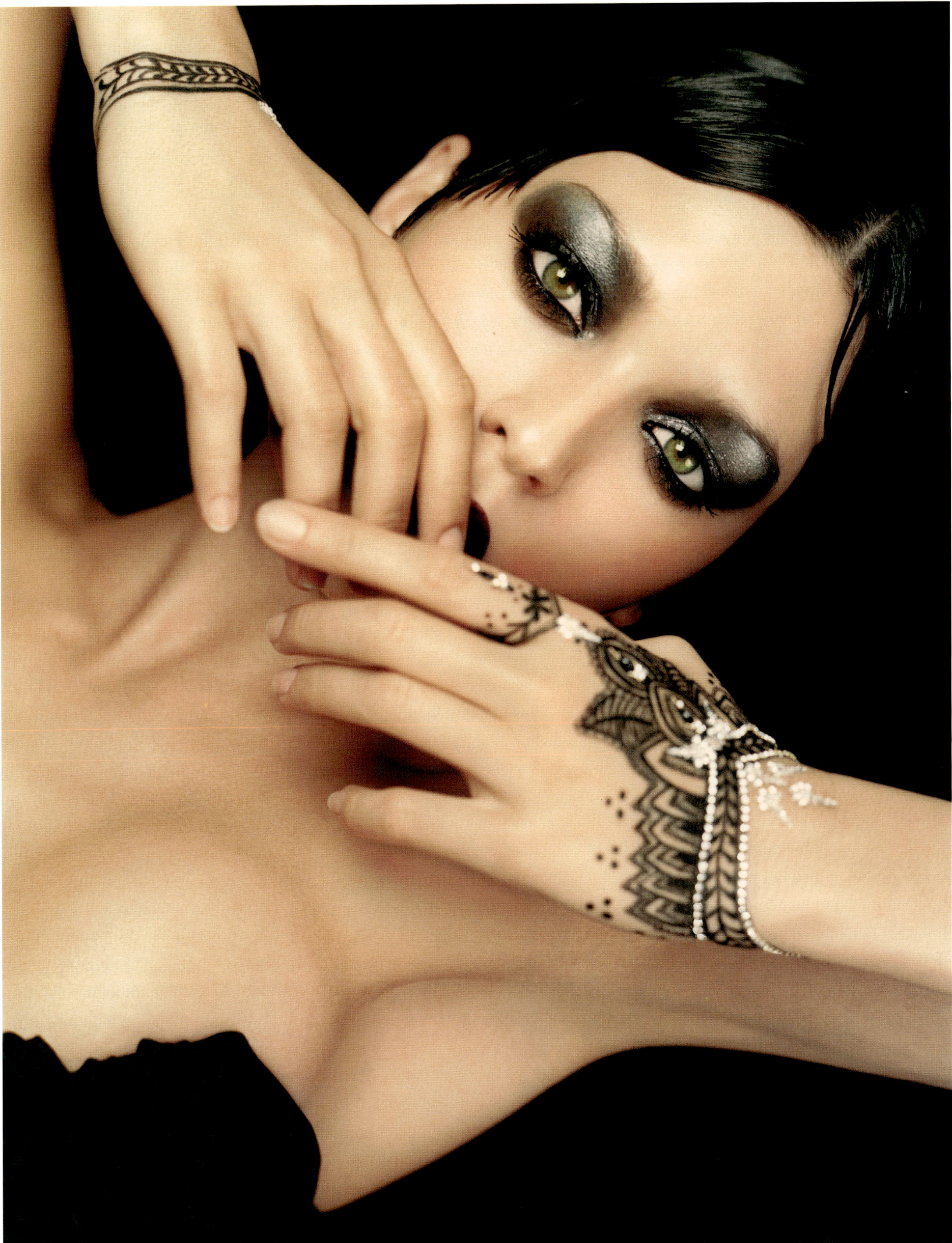

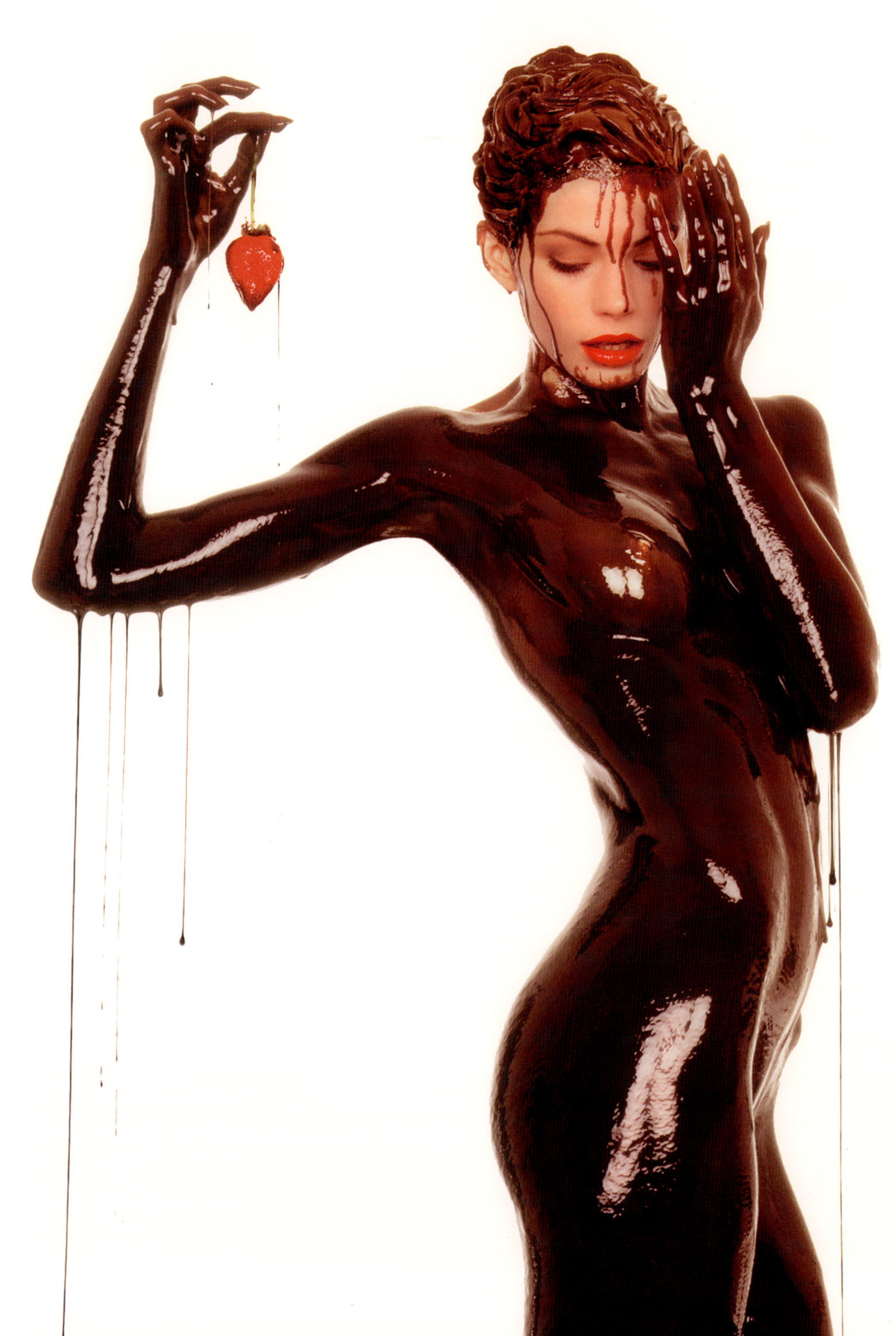

Howard Schatz

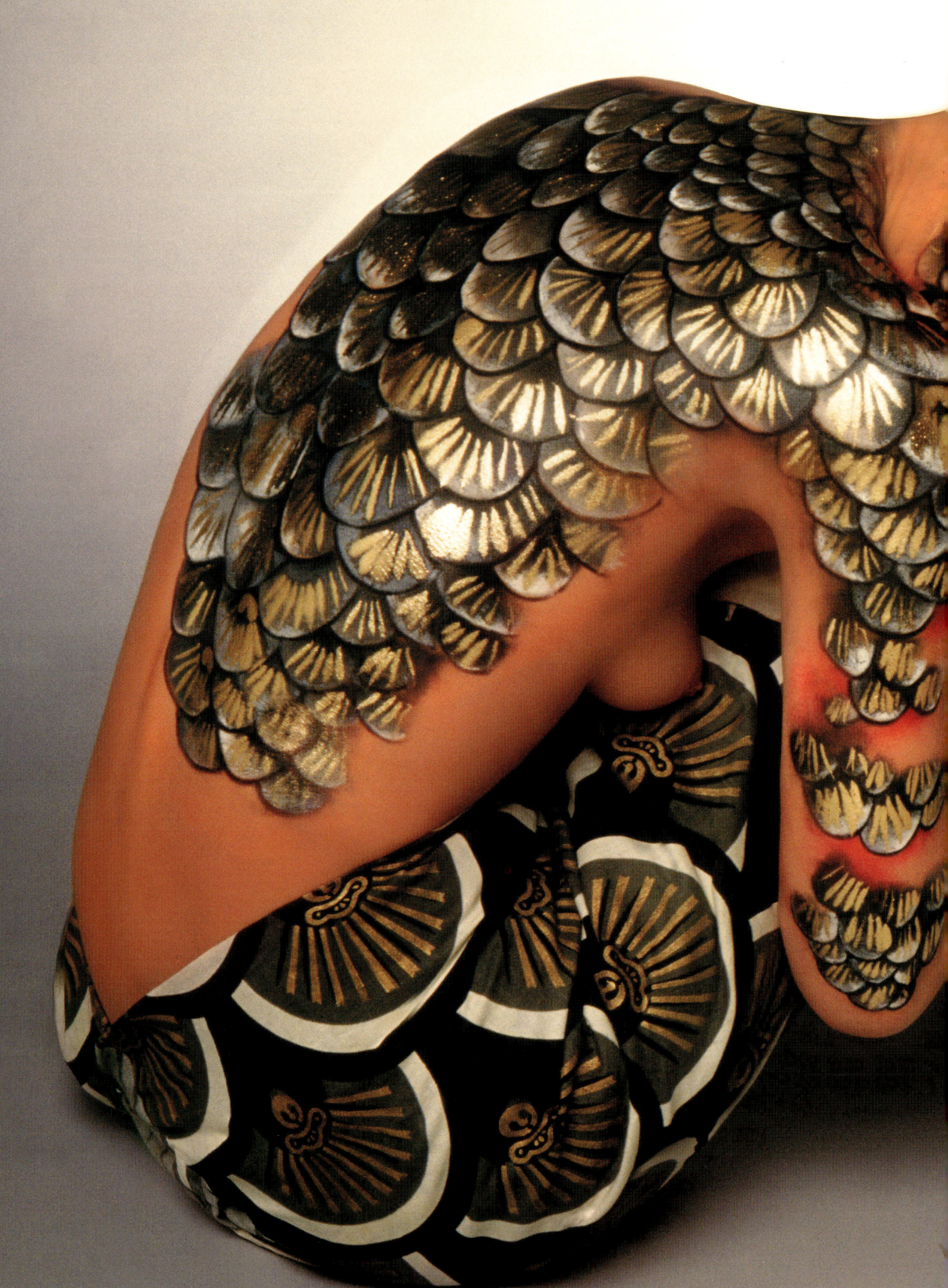

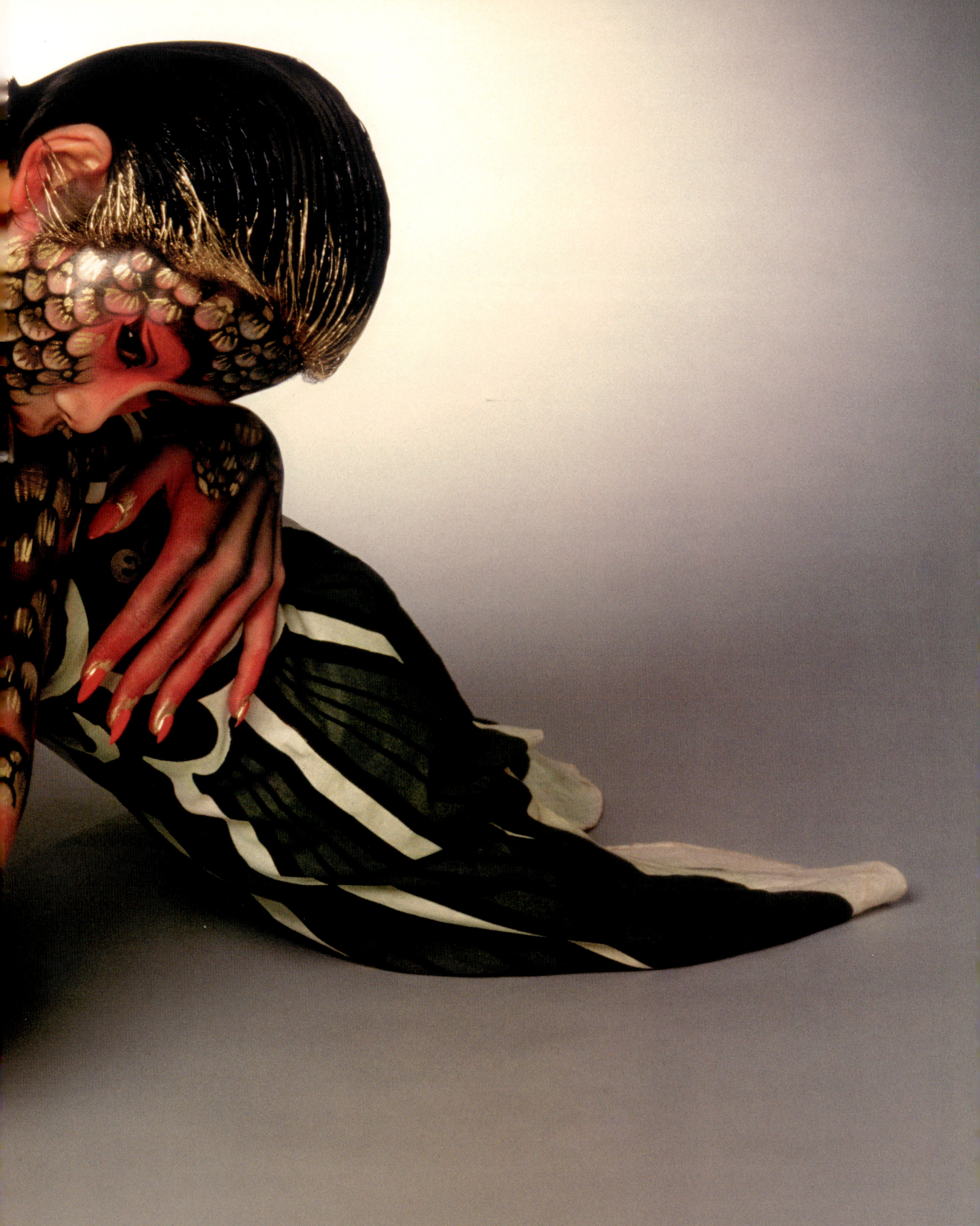

[previous] Geeling Ng Bob Watson

Alek Wek Herb Ritts

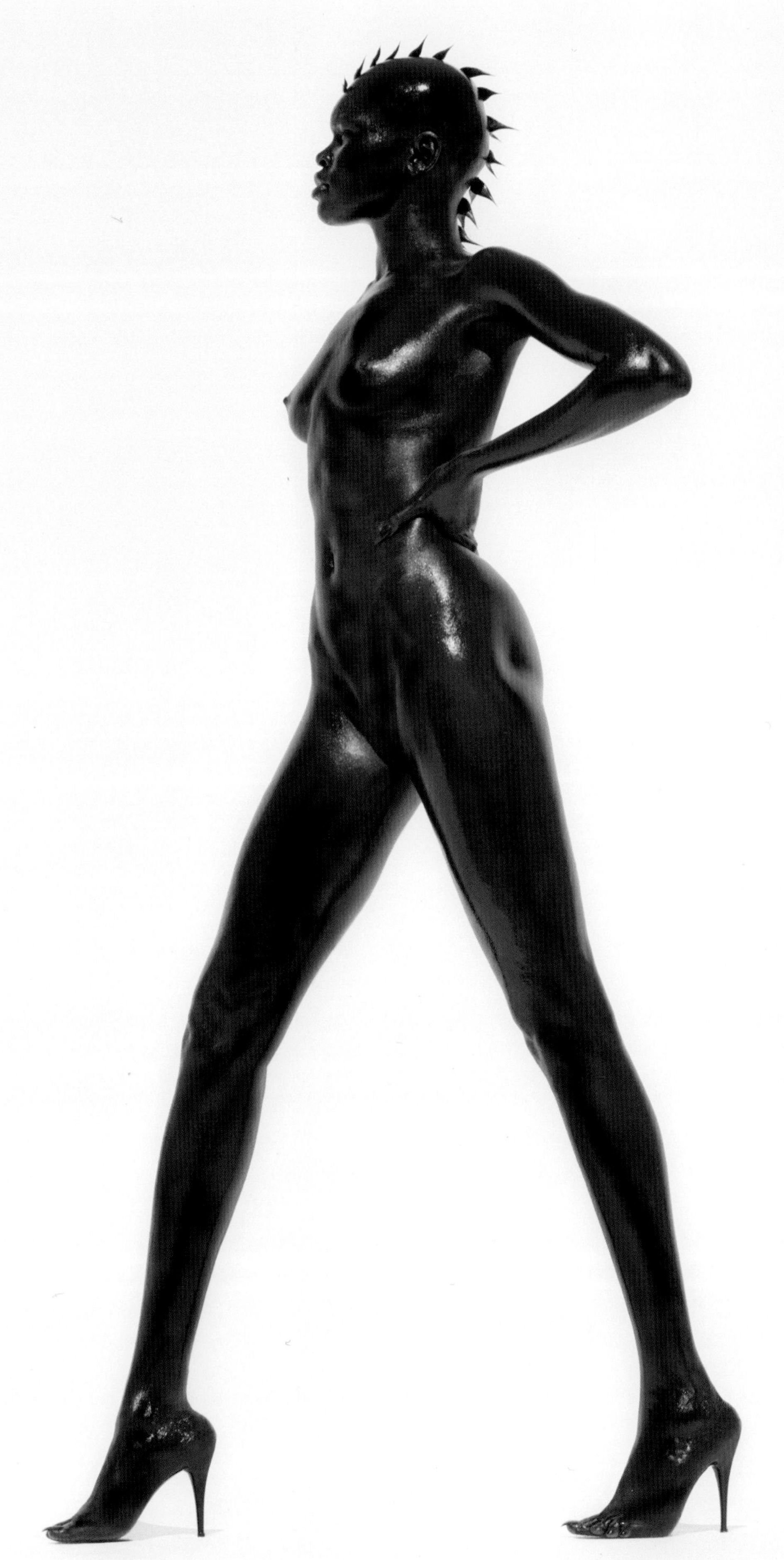

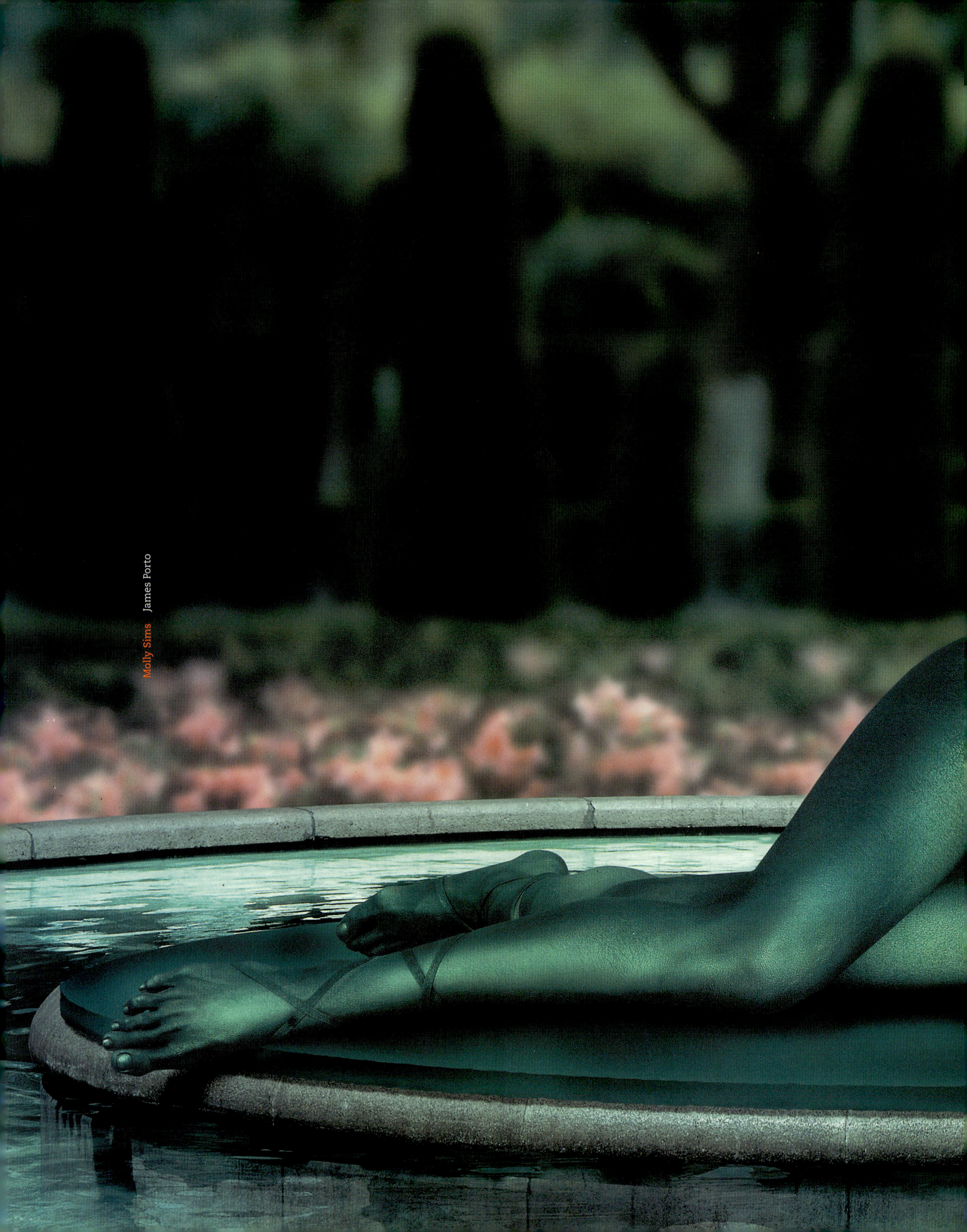

Molly Sims James Porto

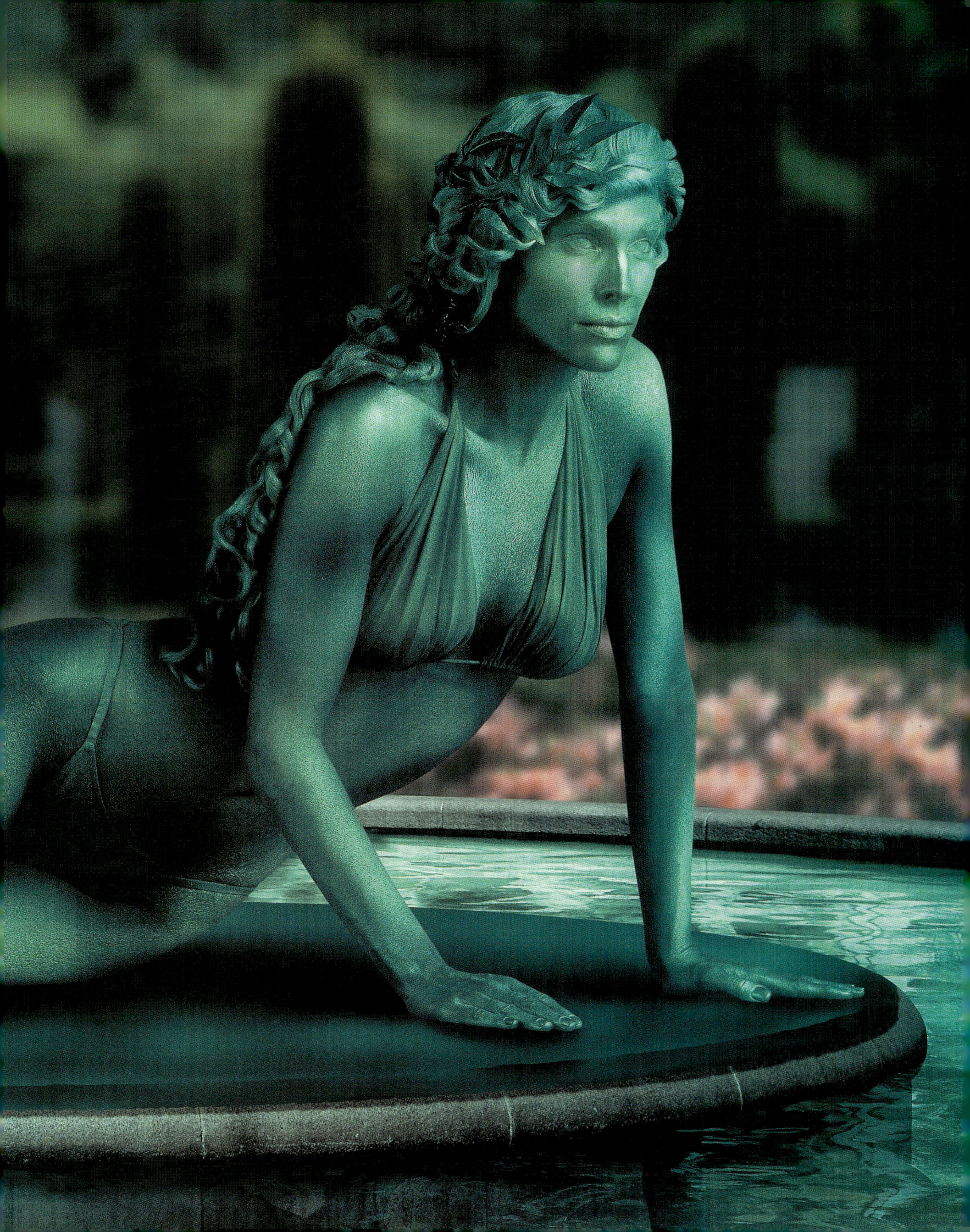

Sarah O'Hare Antoine Verglas

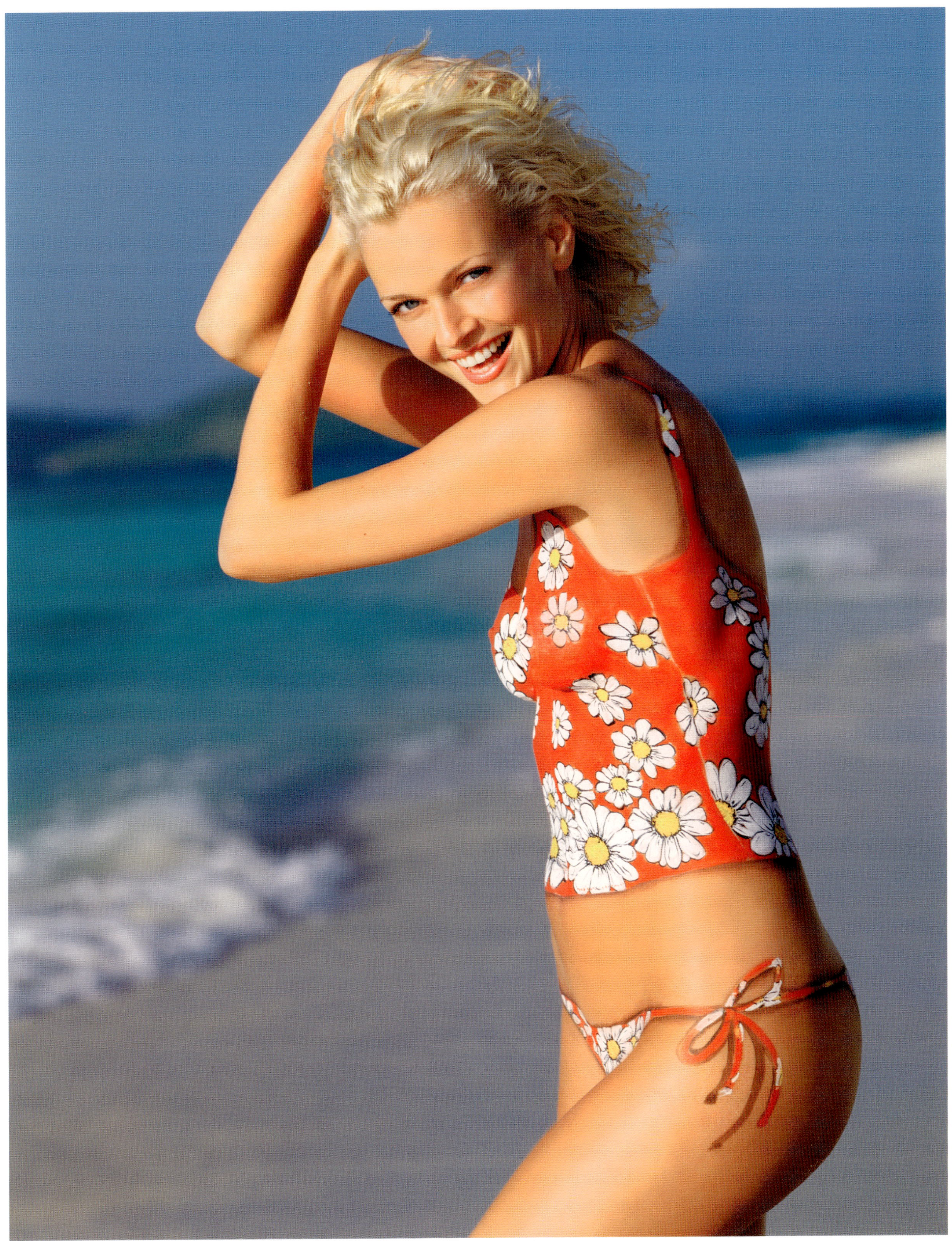

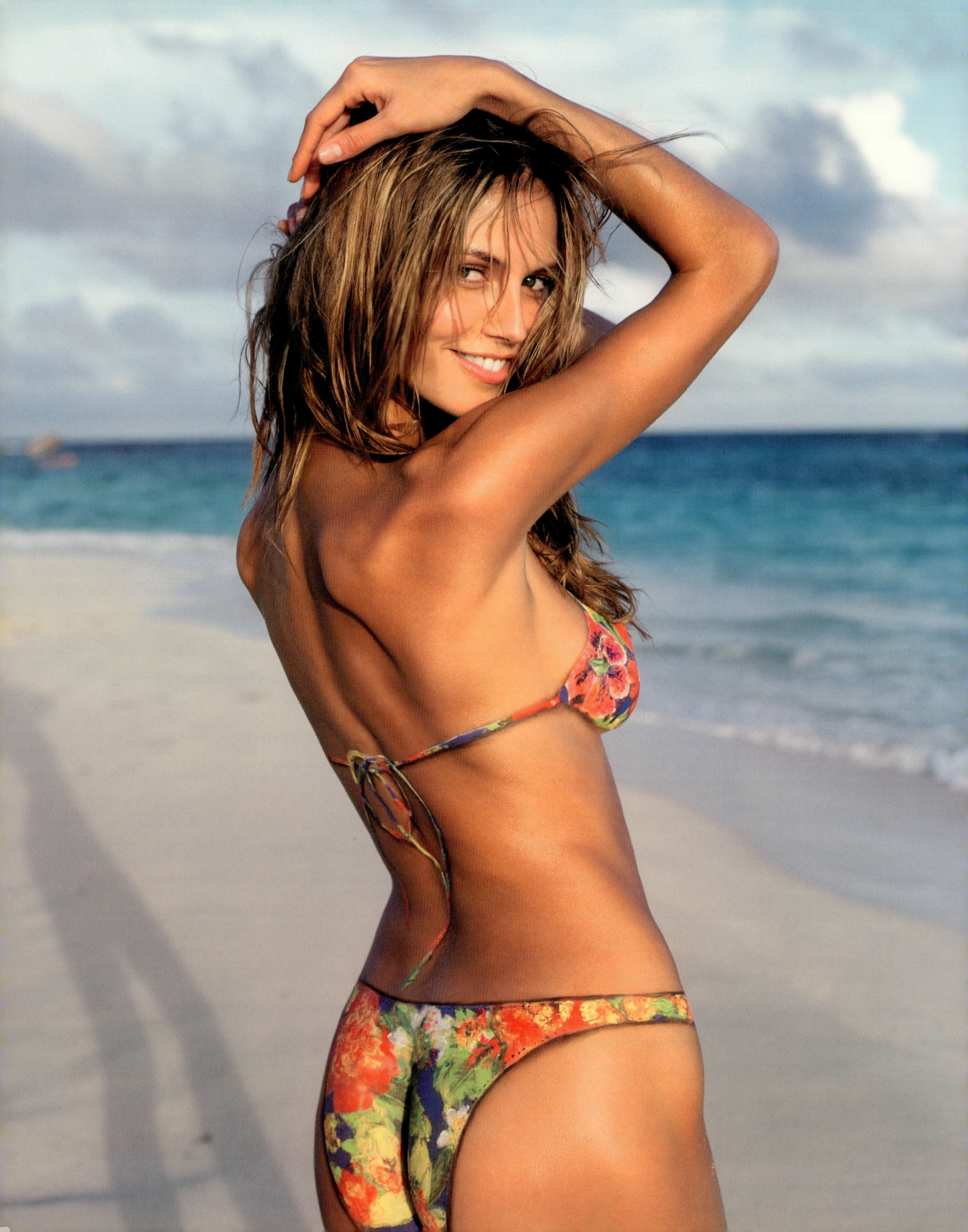

Heidi Klum   Antoine Verglas

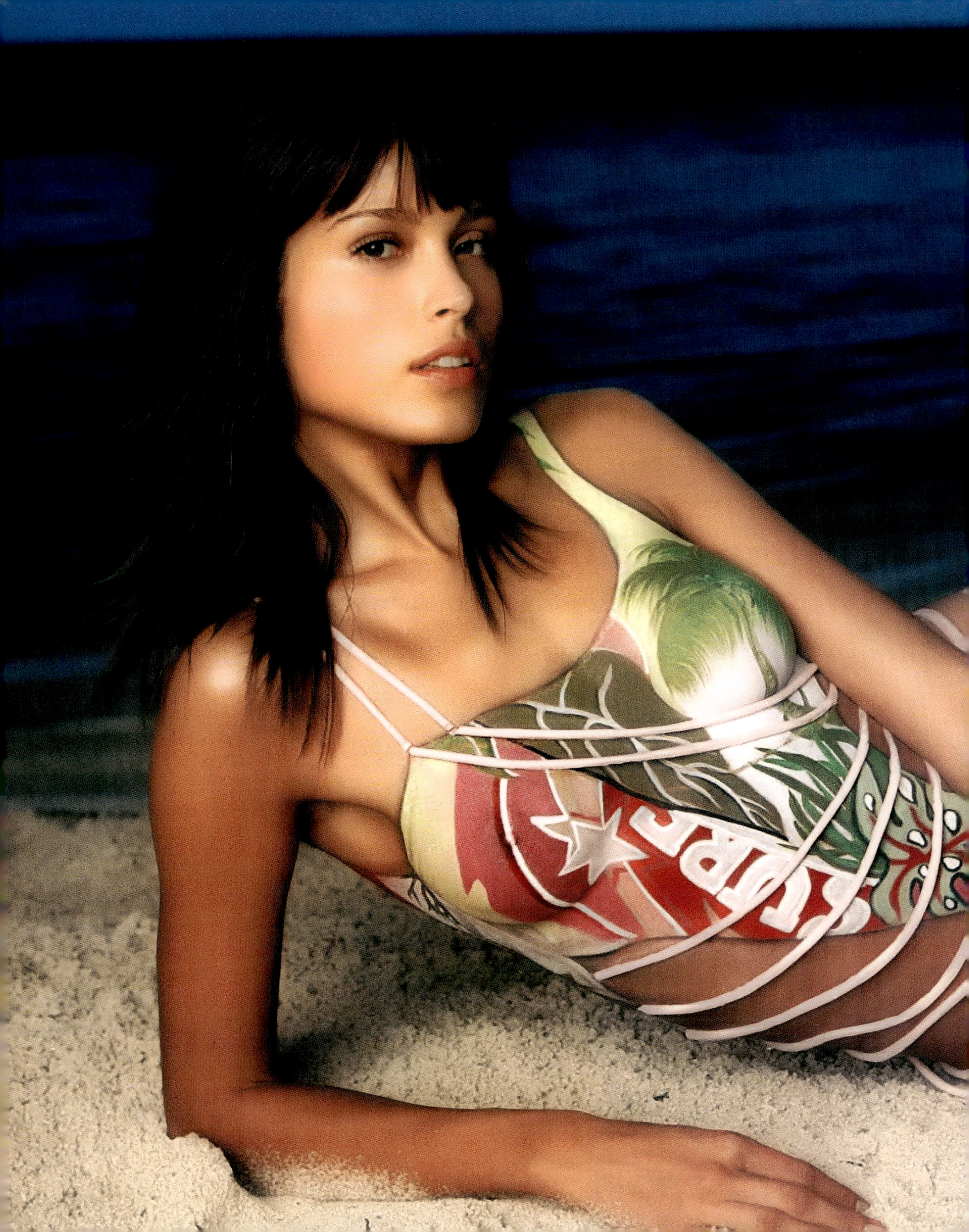

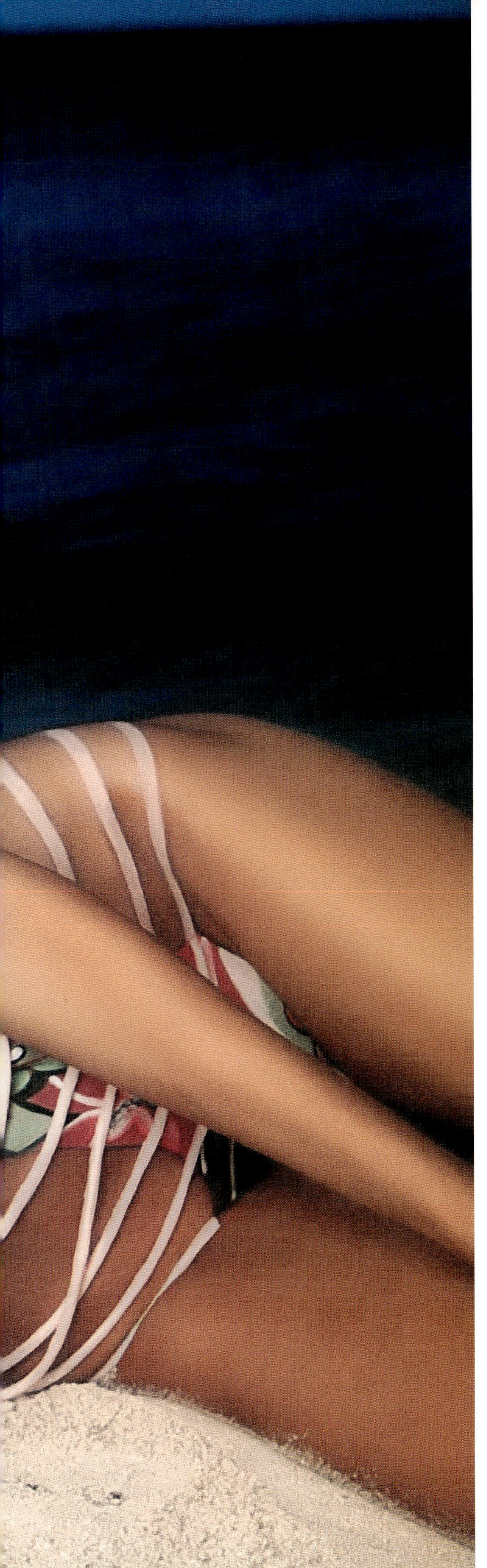

Petra Nemcova Steven White

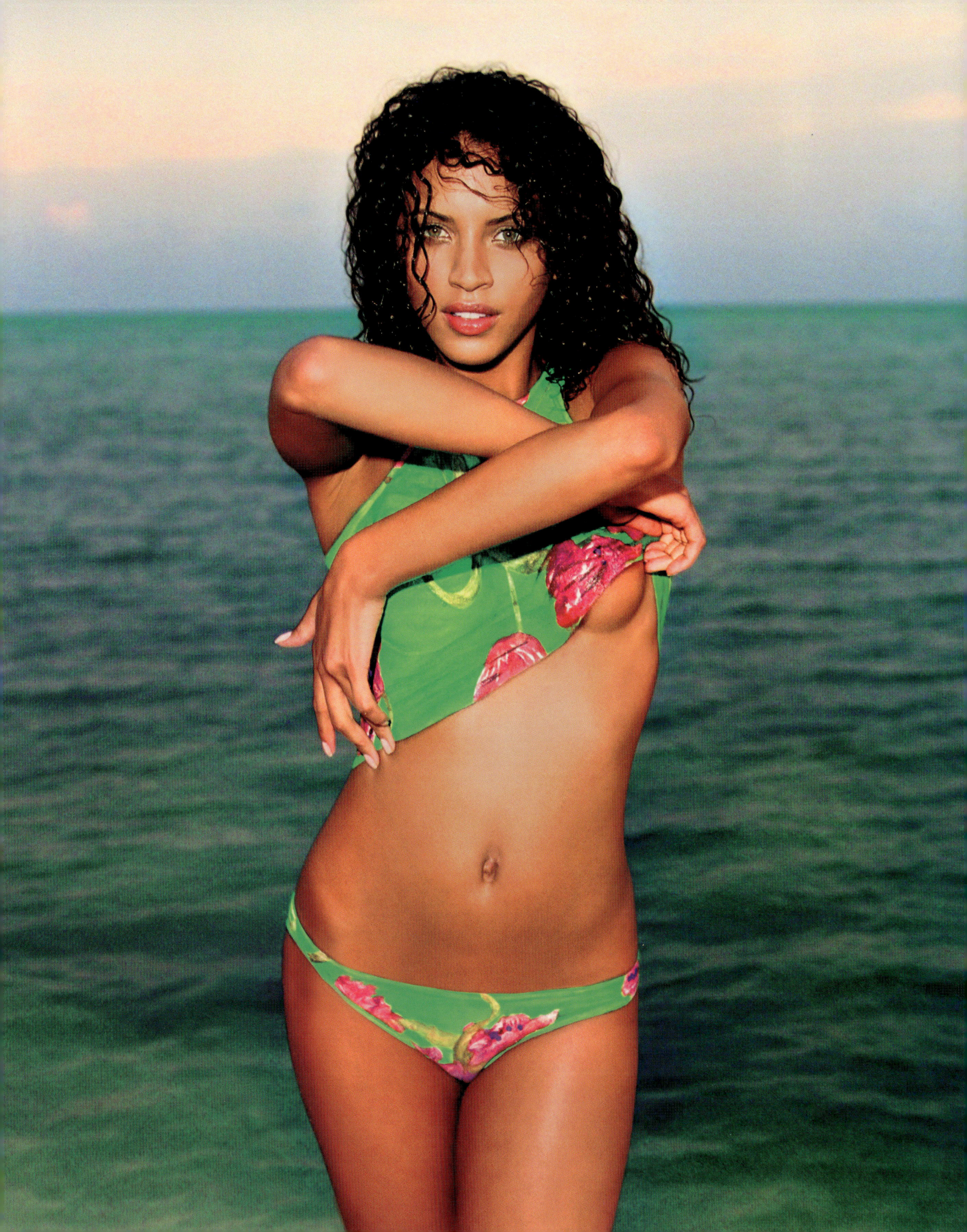

Noemie Lenoir Steven White

[overleaf] Yamila Diaz-Rahi Antoine Verglas

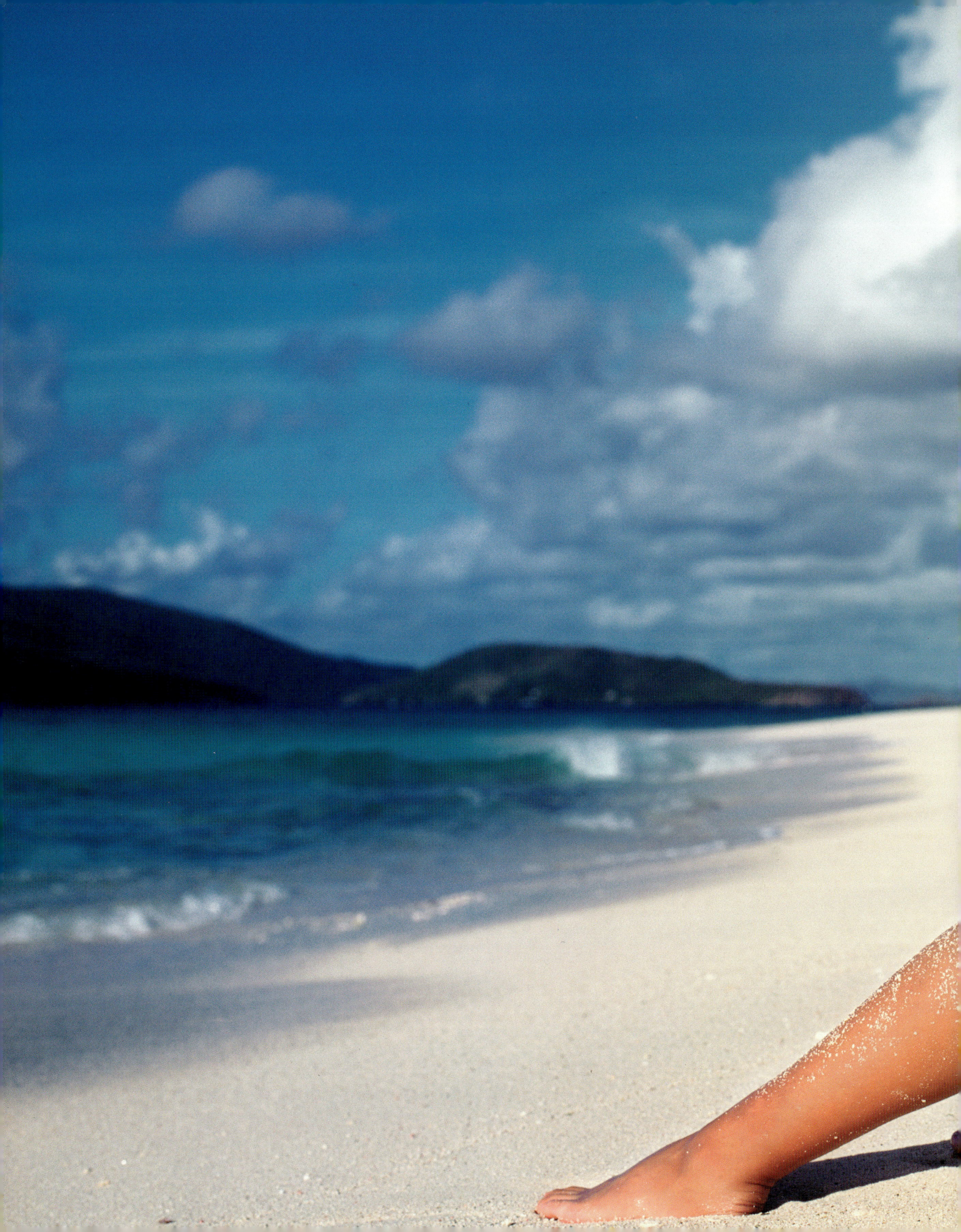

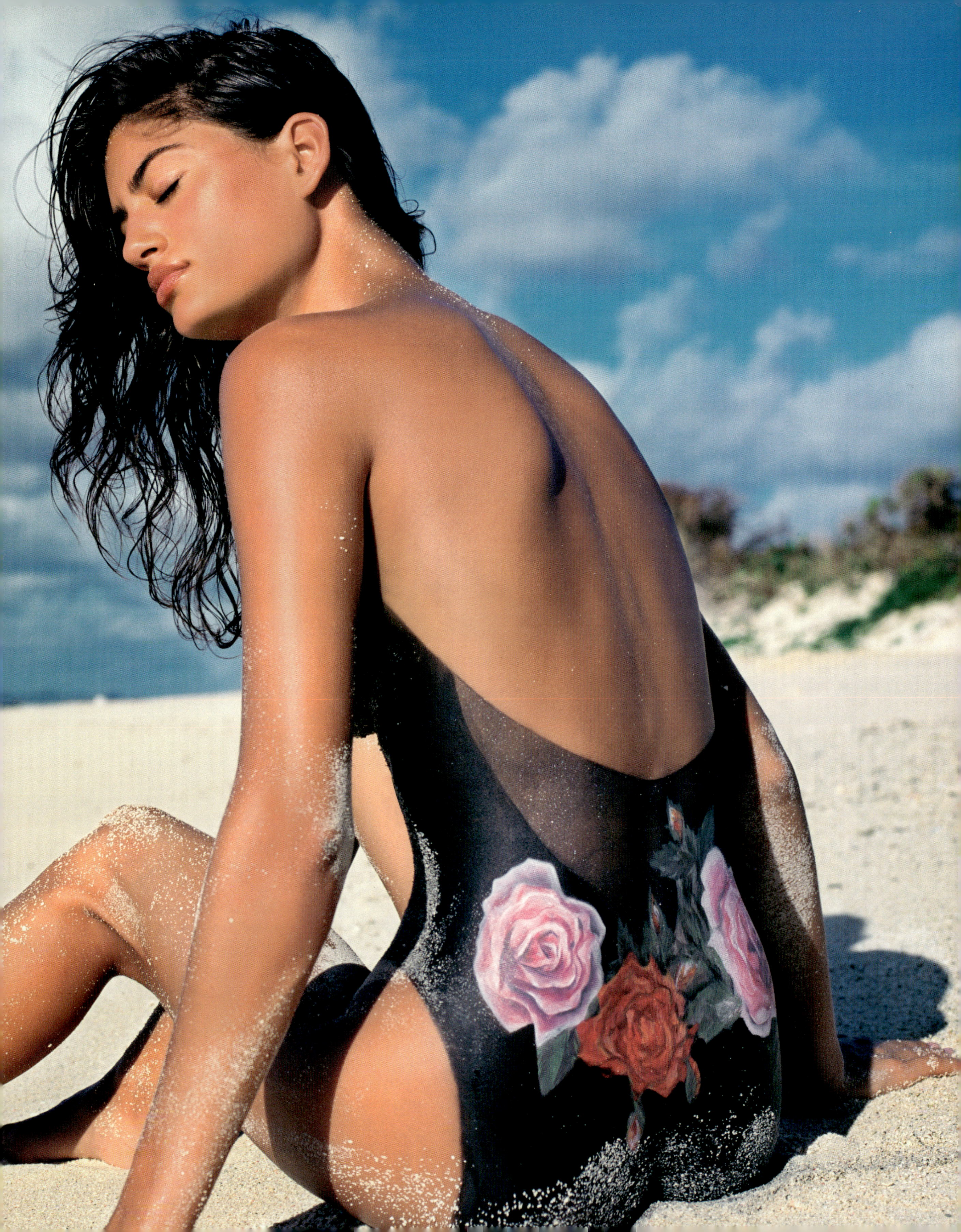

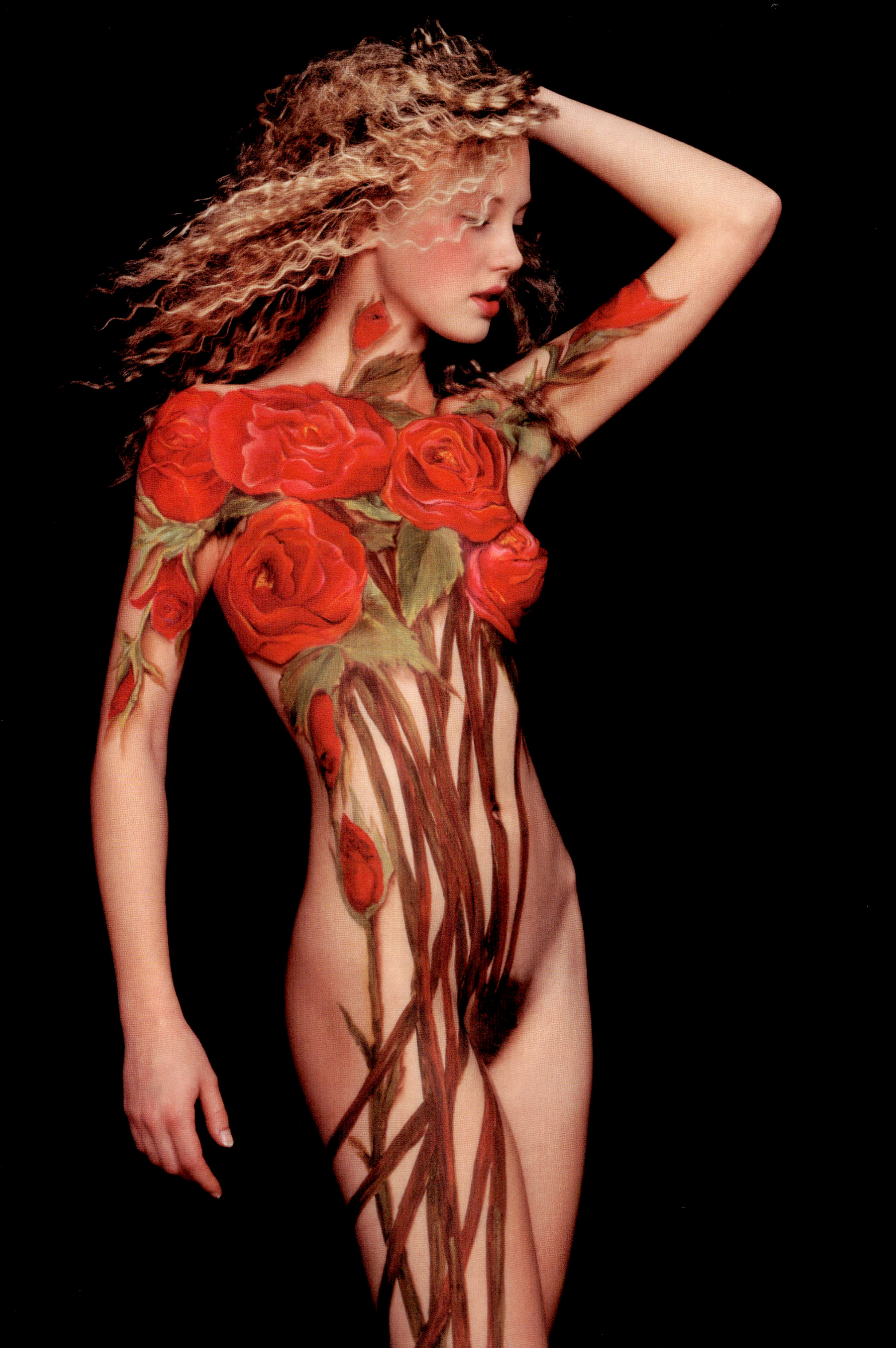

Howard Schatz

Demi Moore Peggy Sirota

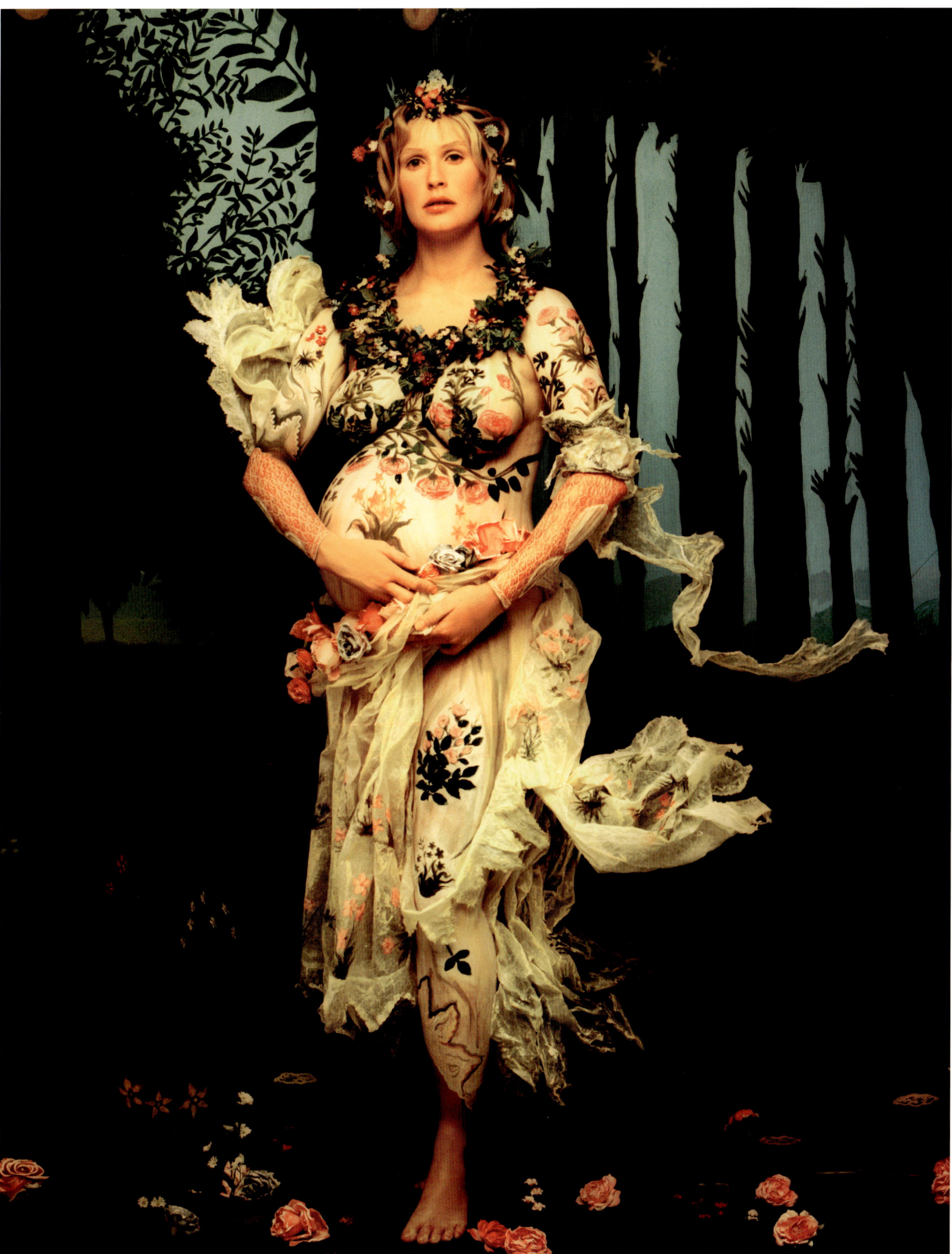

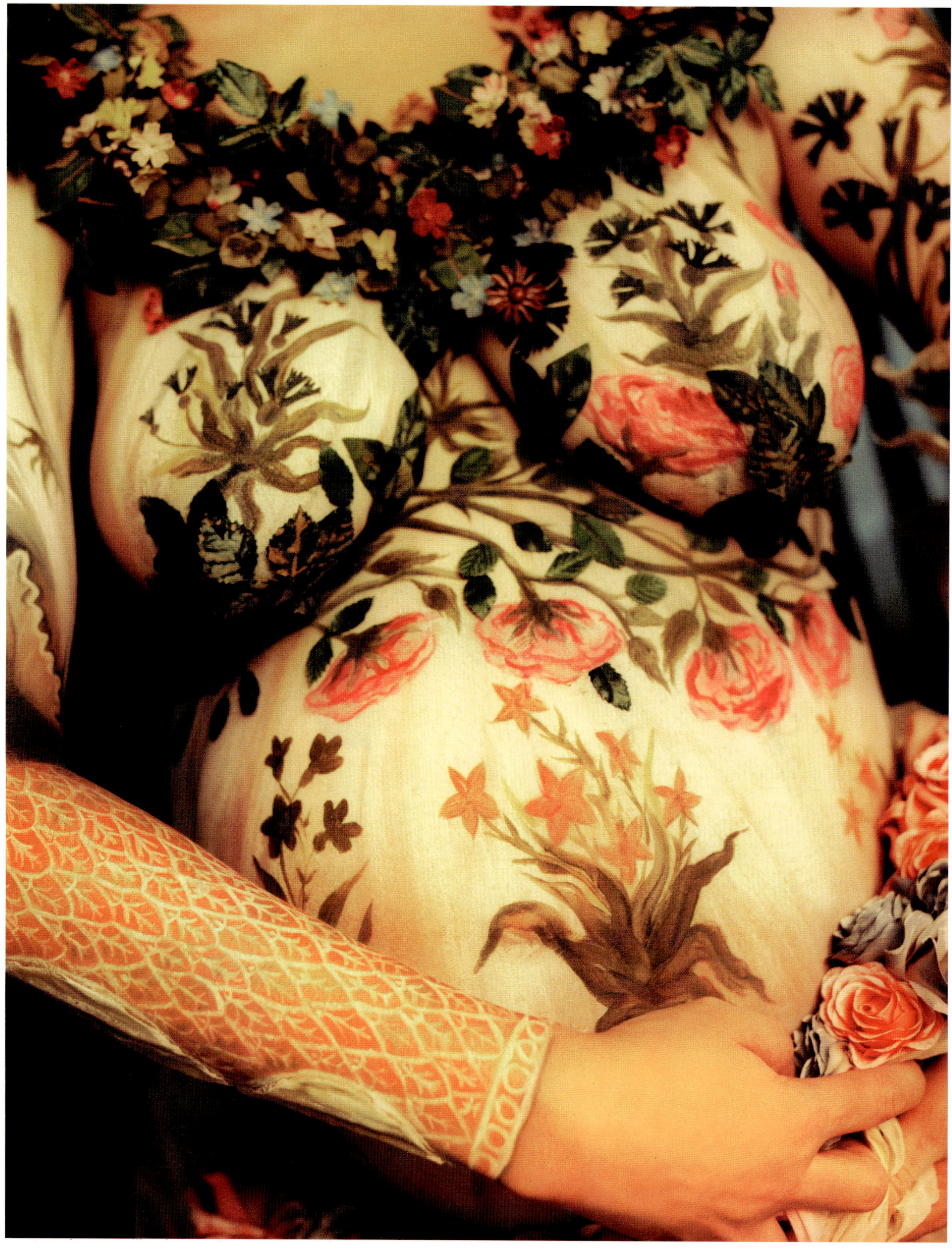

Demi Moore Peggy Sirota

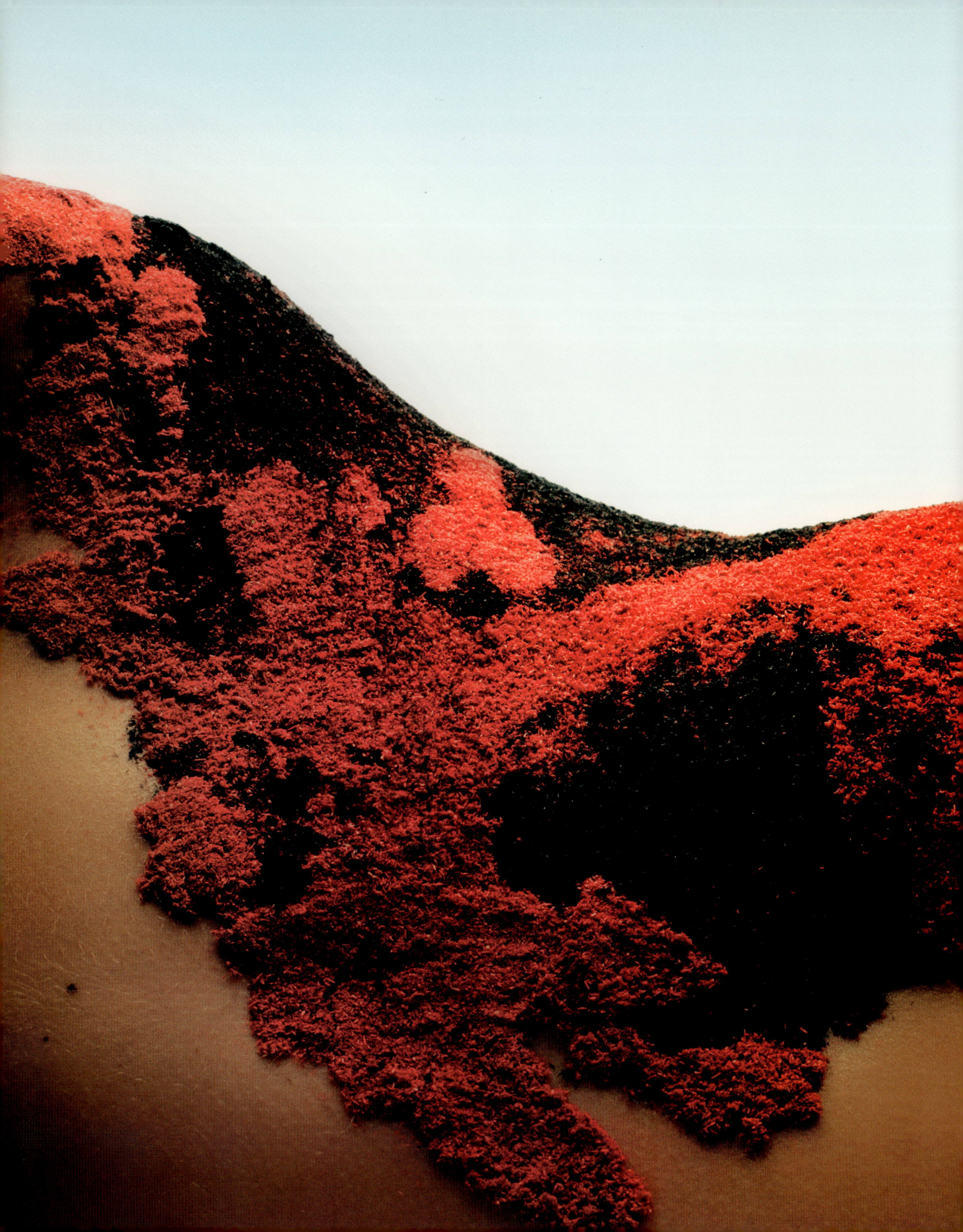

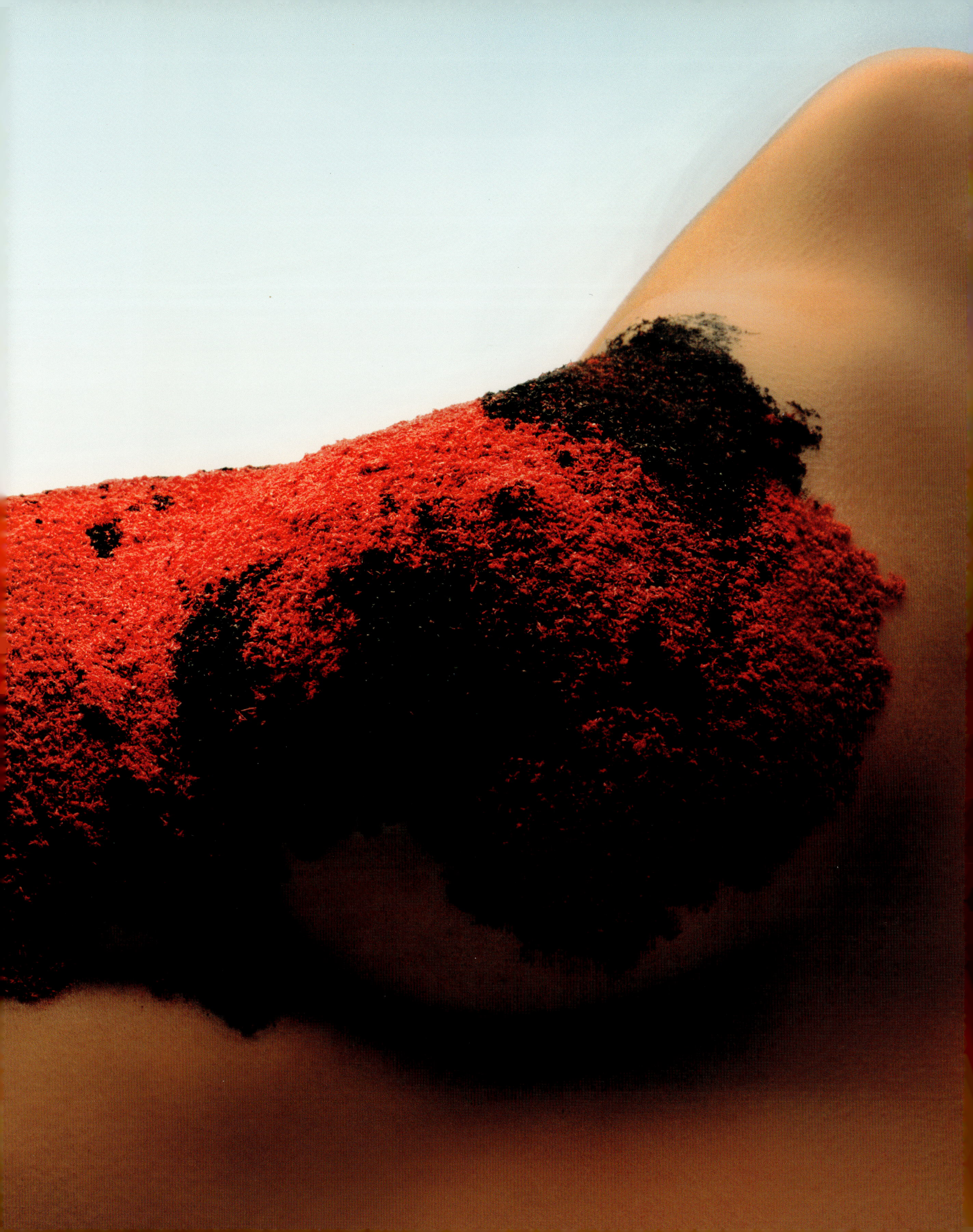

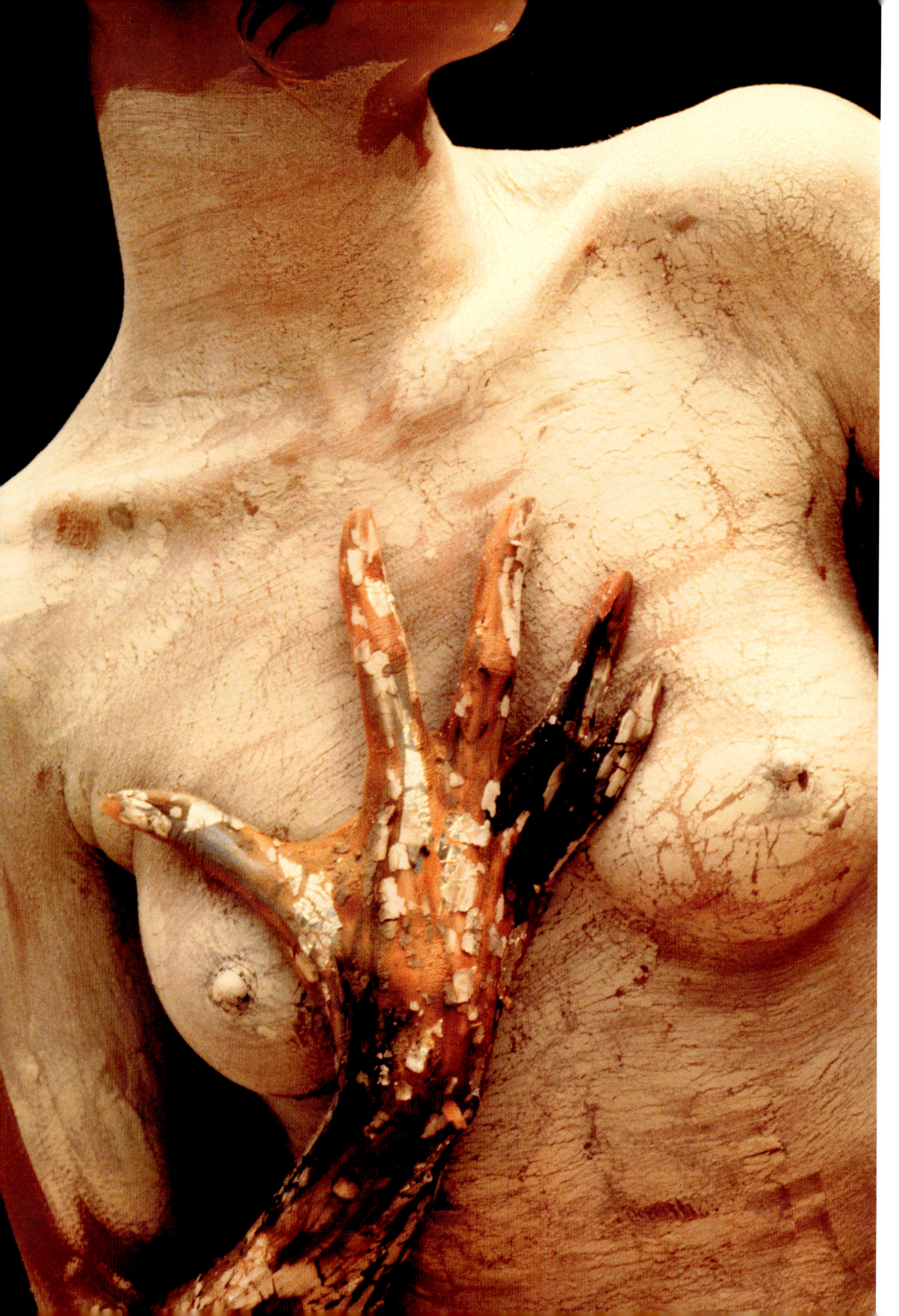

[previous] Eva Mueller

Mark Arbeit

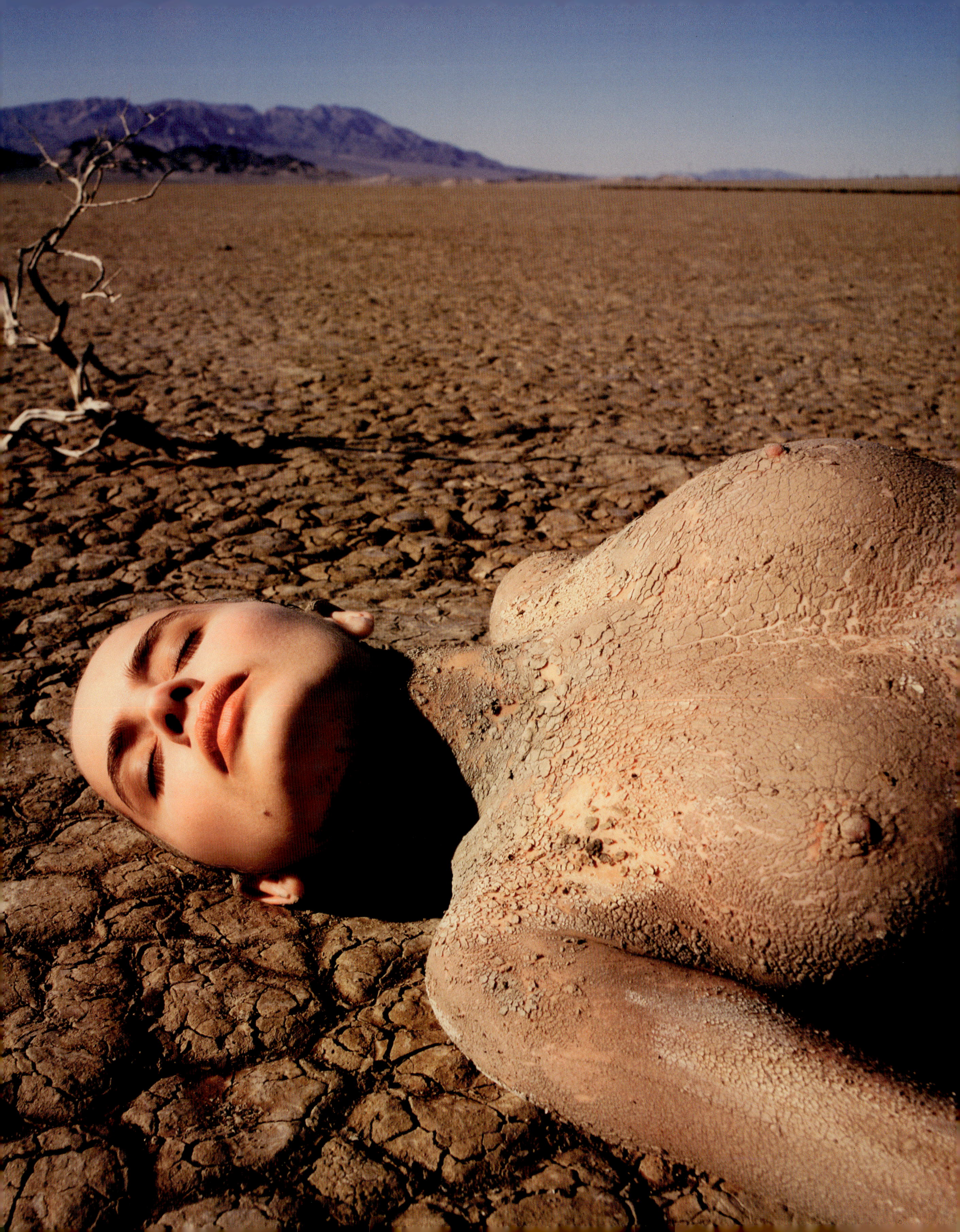

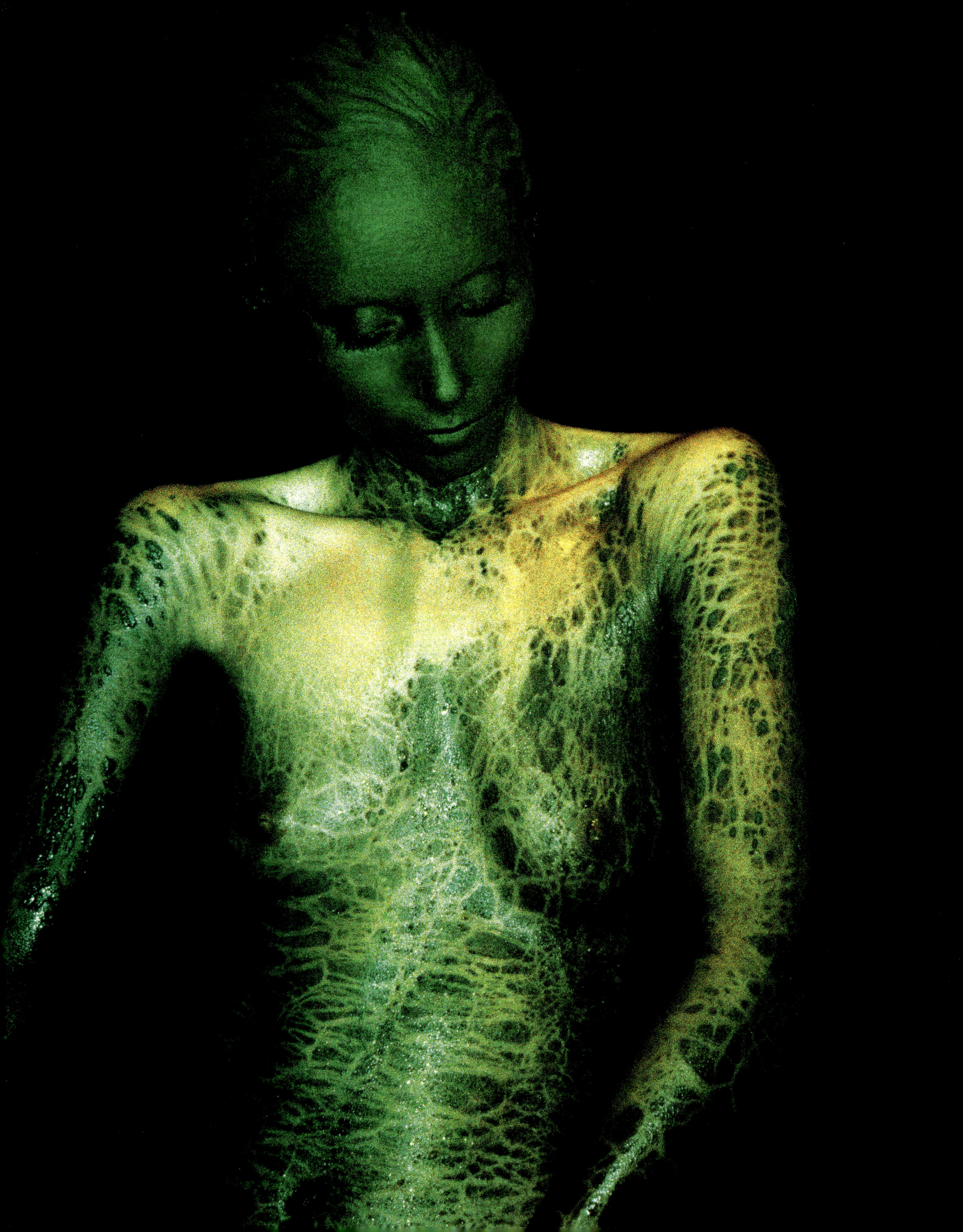

Tanya O   Joanne Gair

Joanne Gair

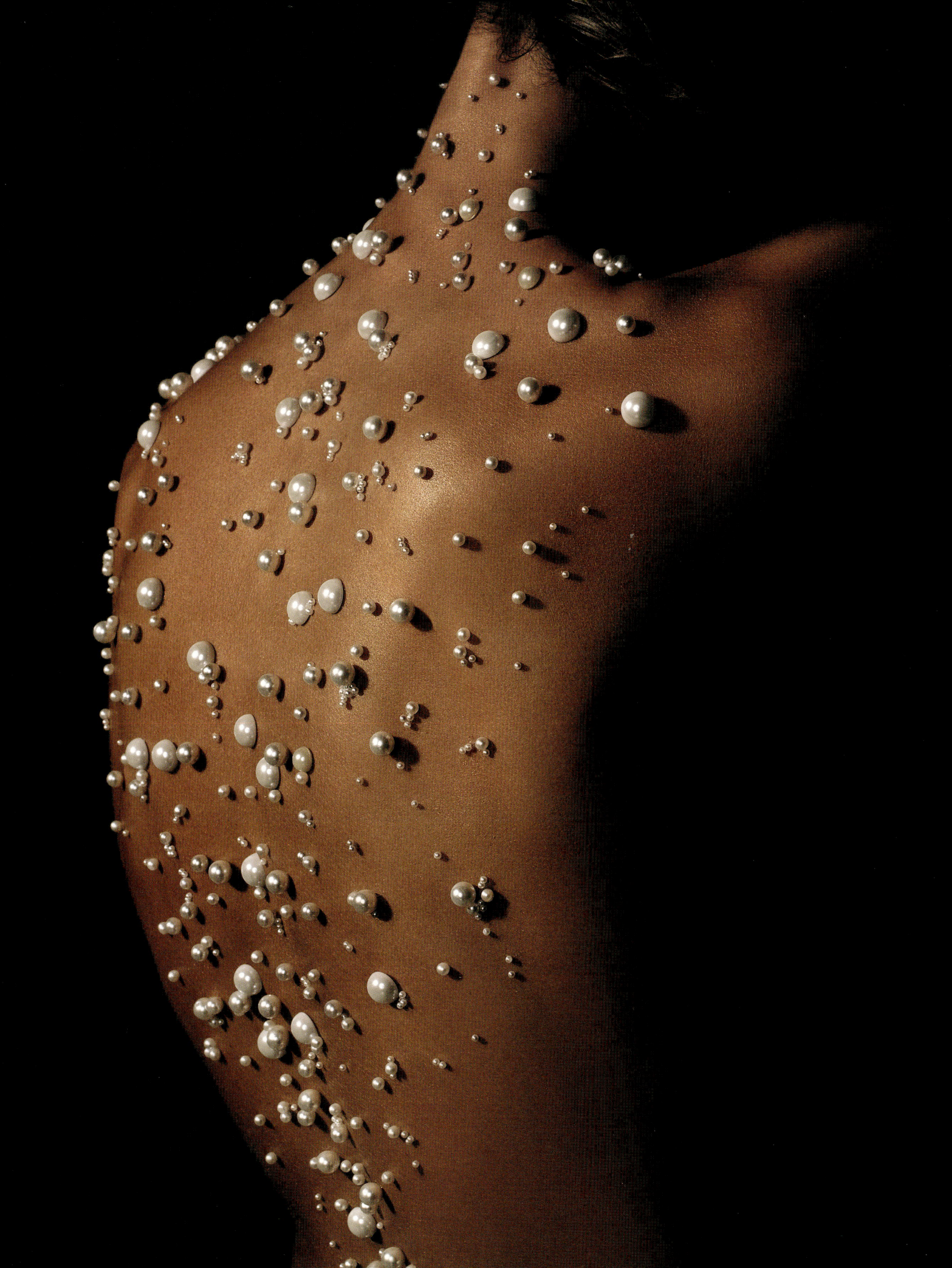

Yana Alberto Tolot

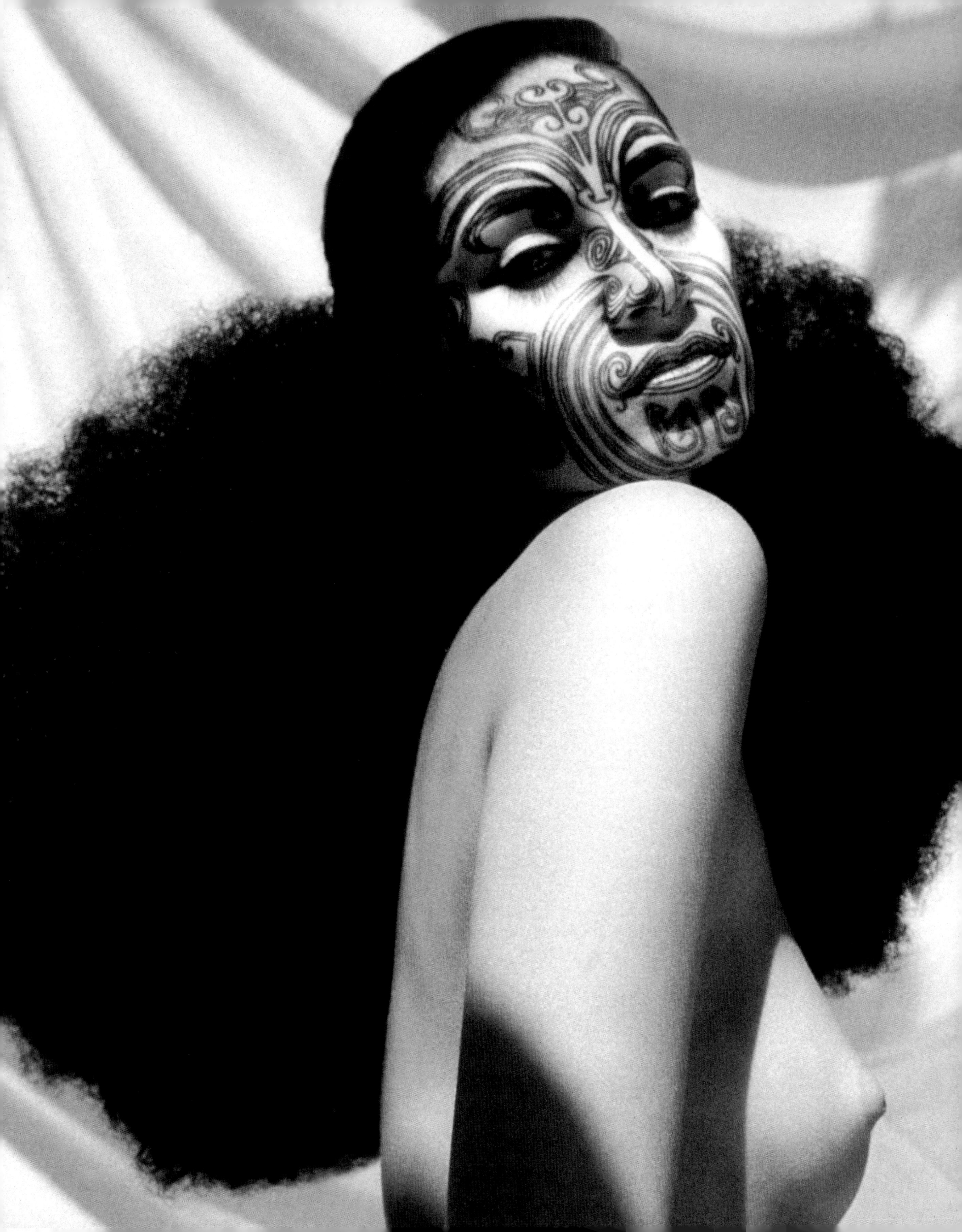

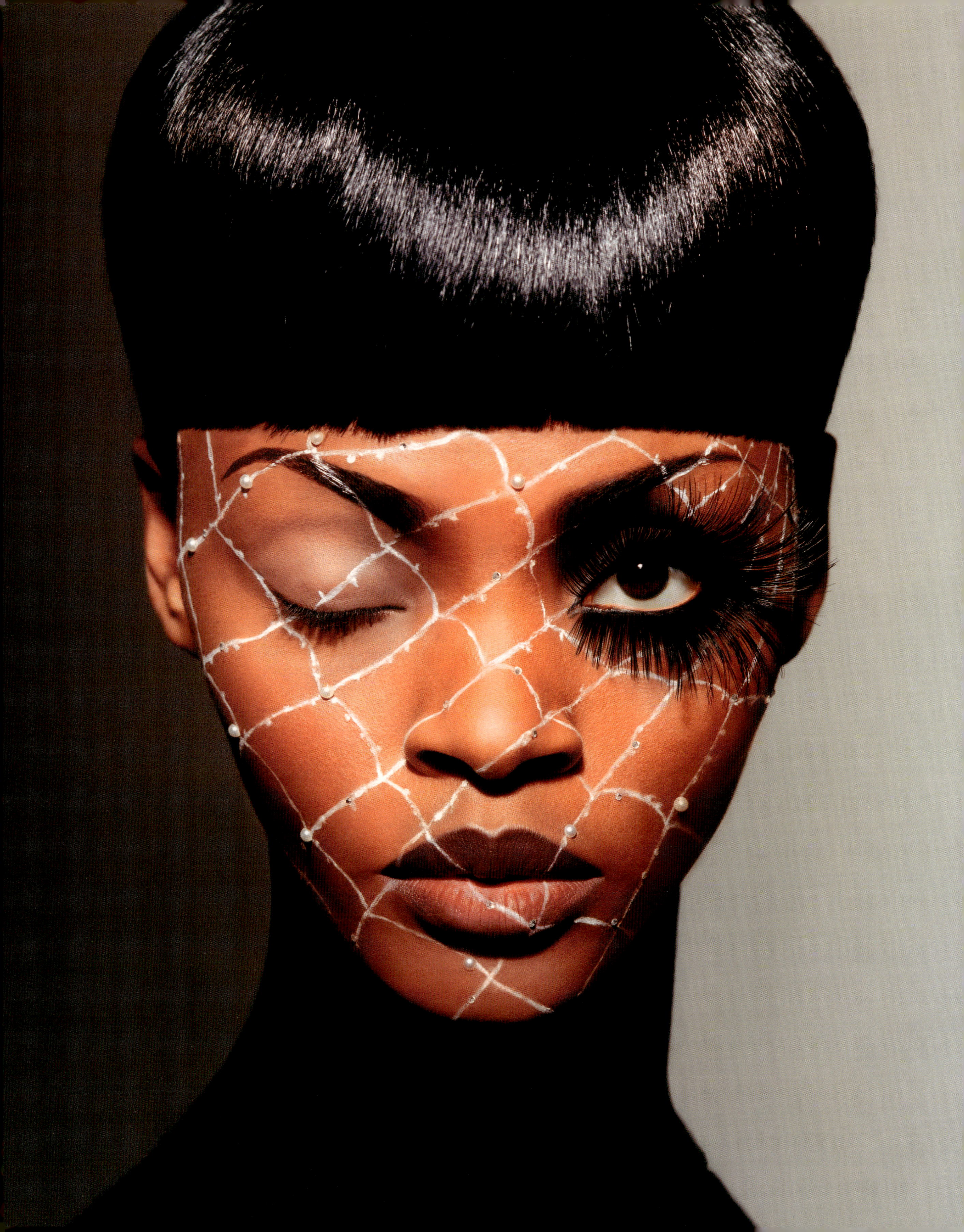

Lisa Butler   Matthew Rolston

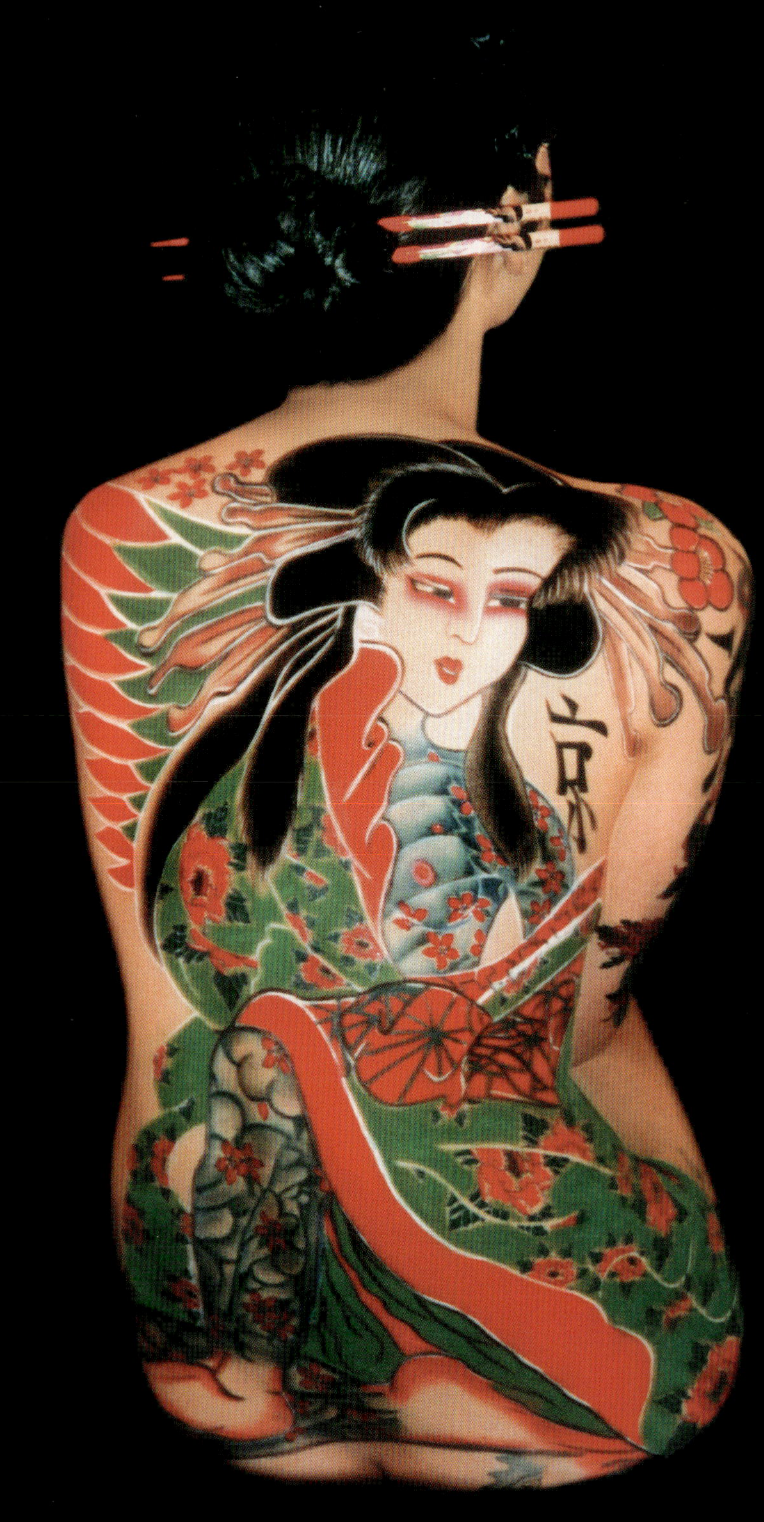
京

Michael Caulfield

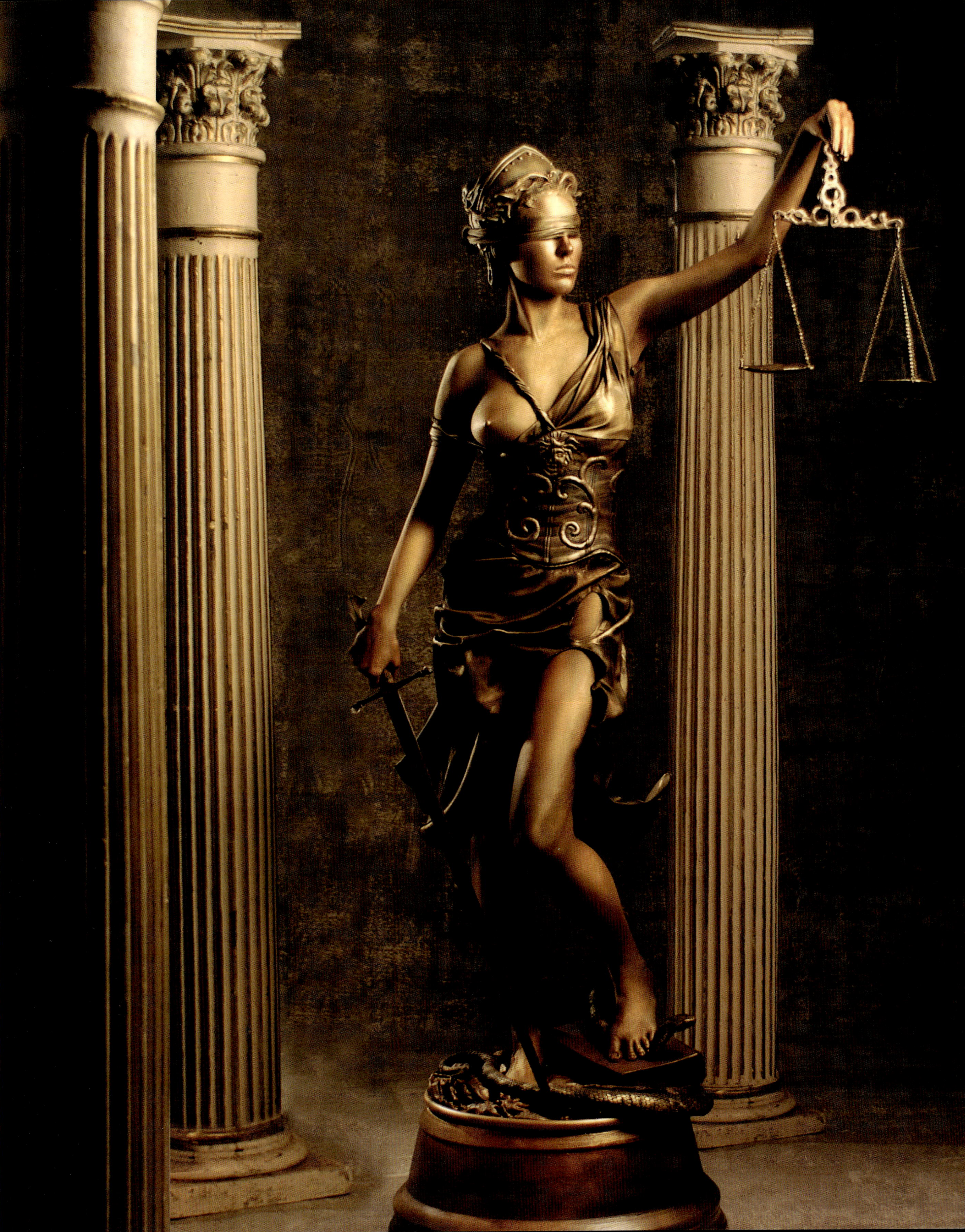

Emma Belcher Joanne Gair

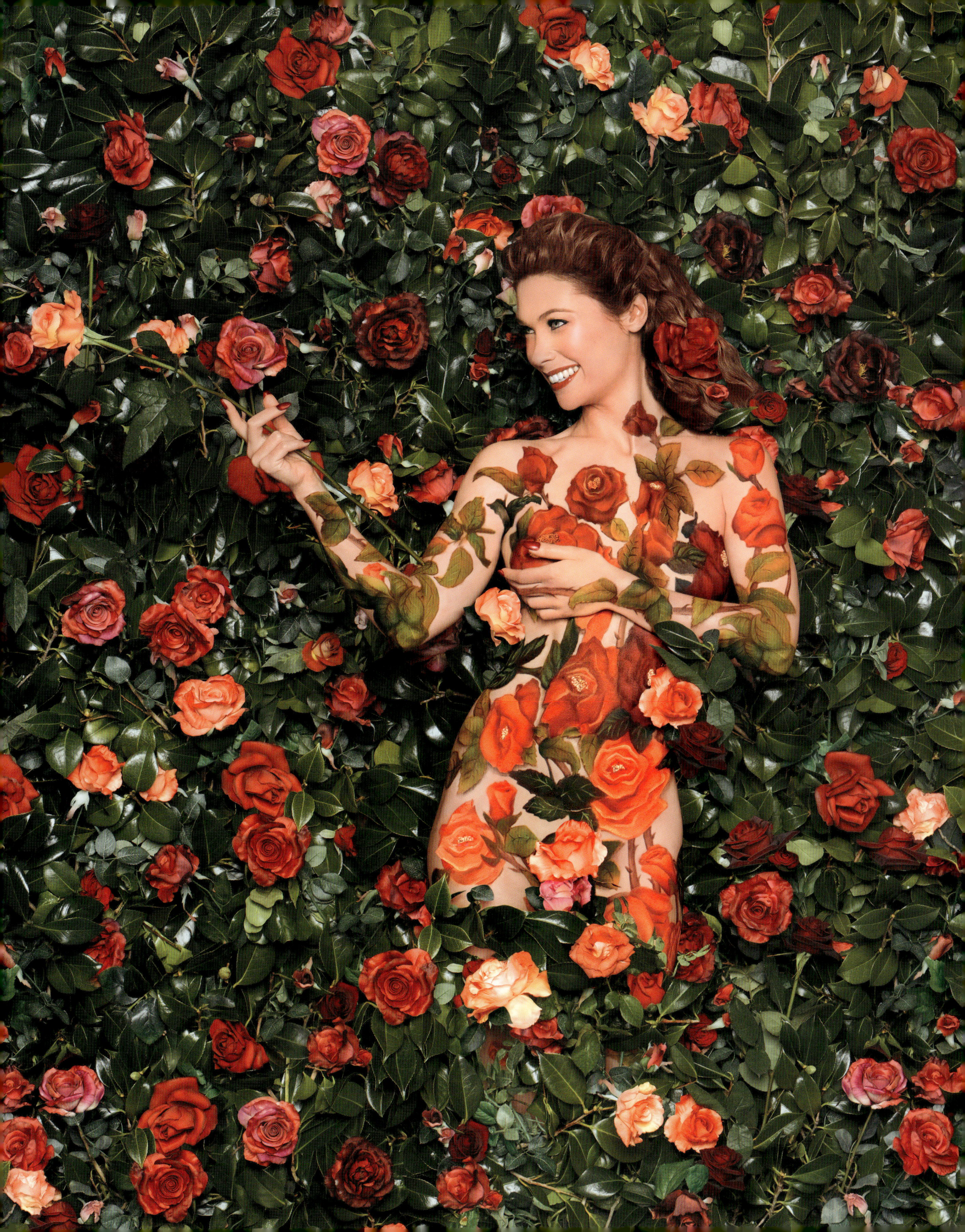

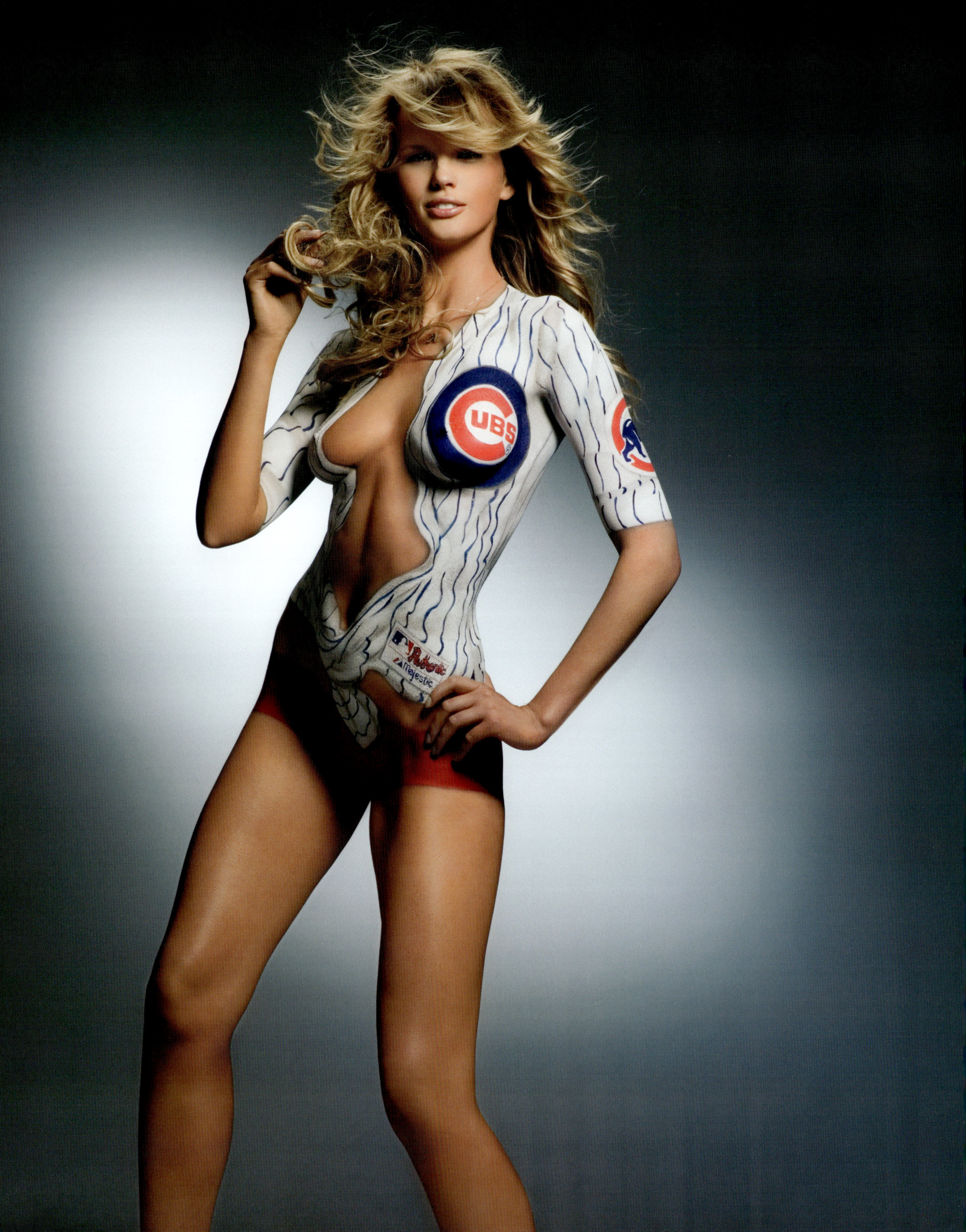
CUBS

Anne V Joanne Gair

[overleaf] Daniella Sarahyba Joanne Gair

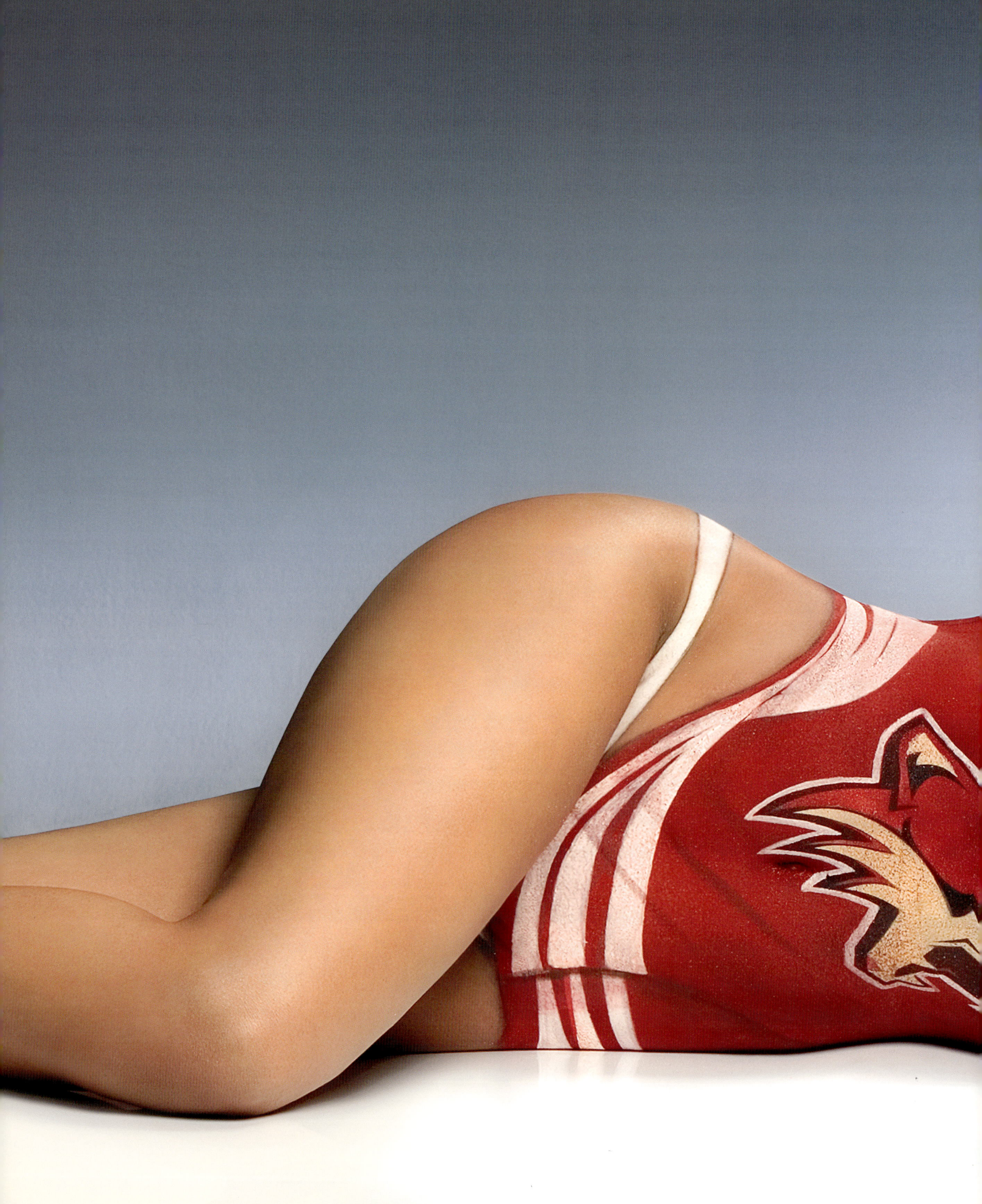

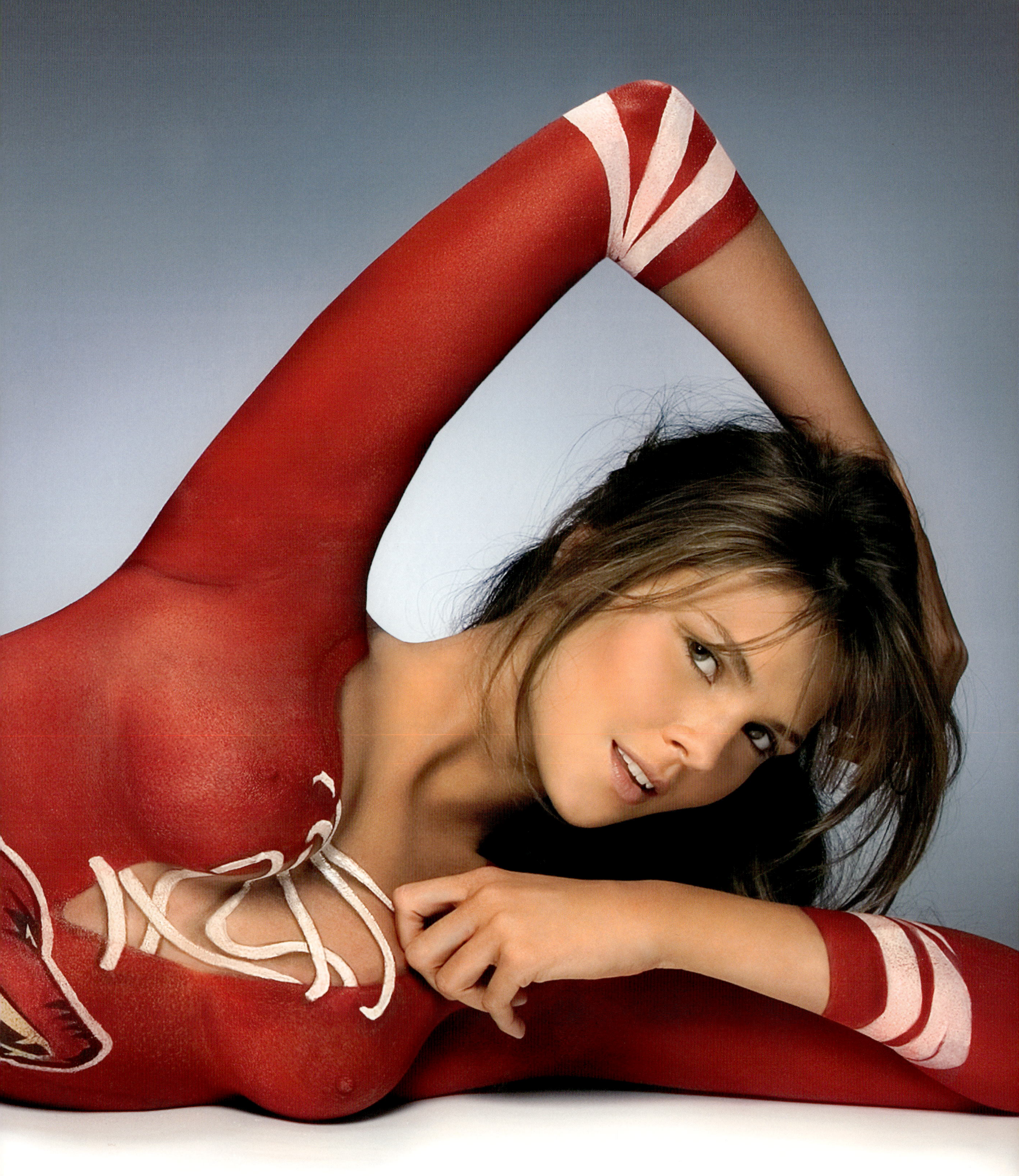

Phillip Dixon

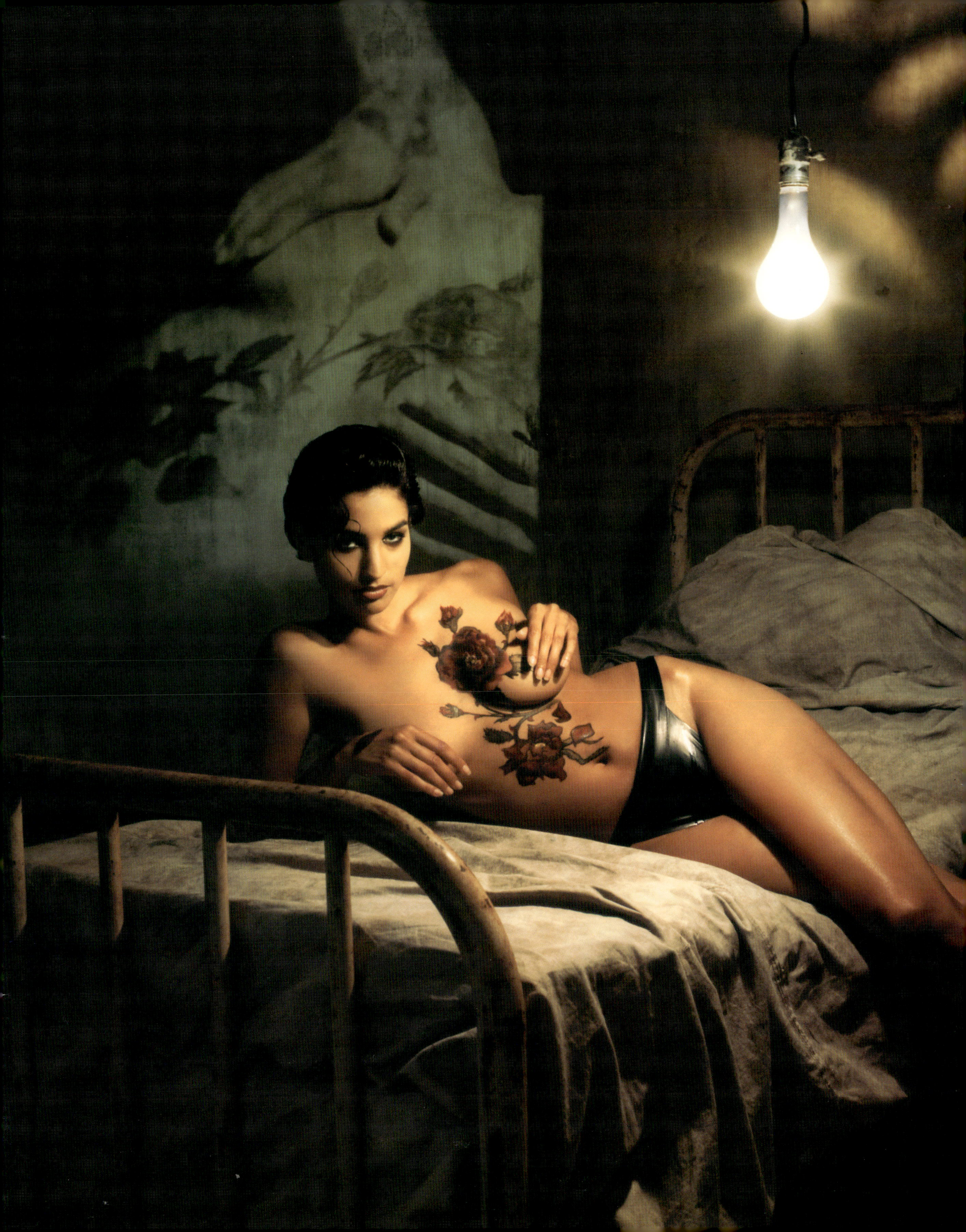

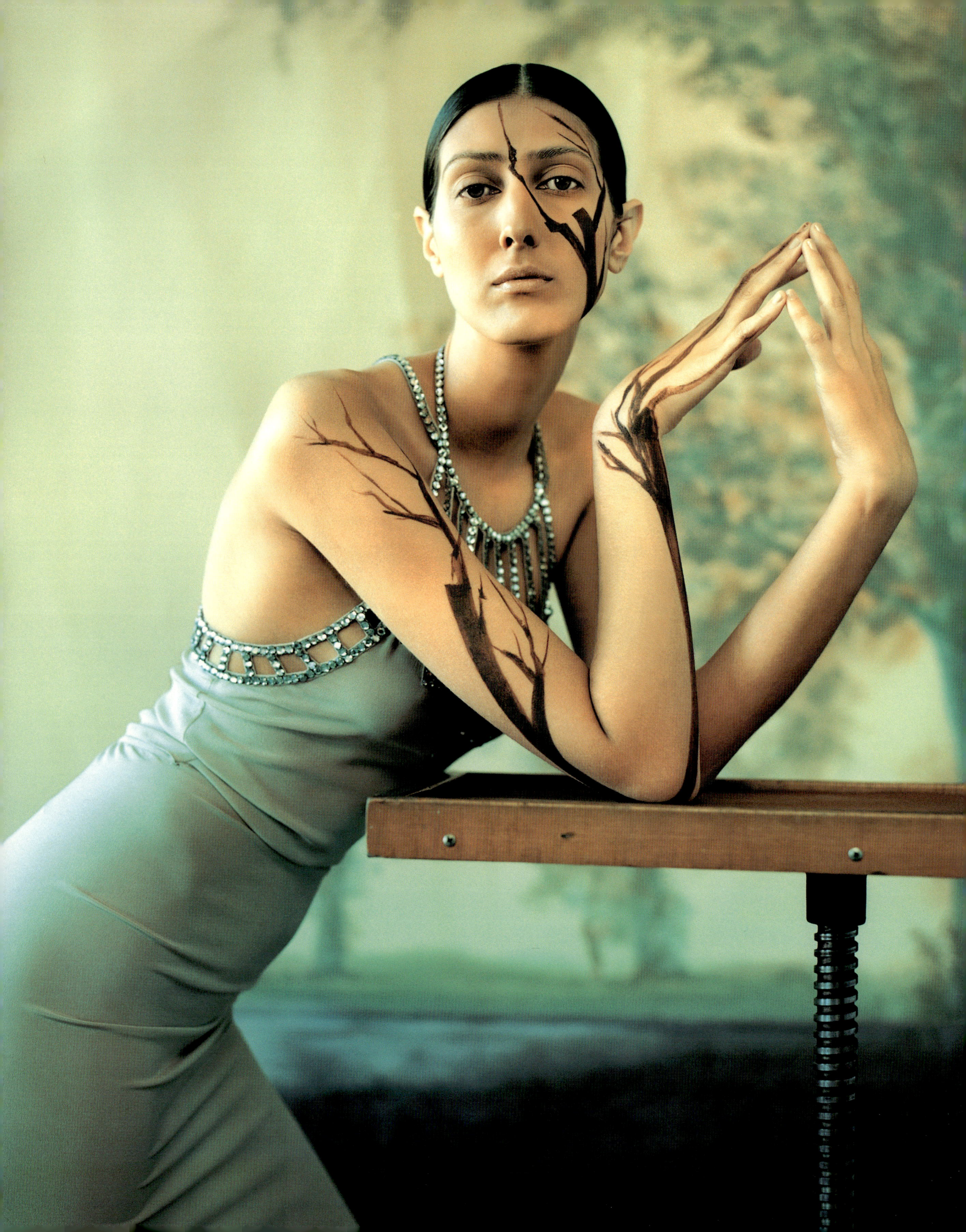

Ruven Afanador

Rachel Hunter Michael Zeppetello

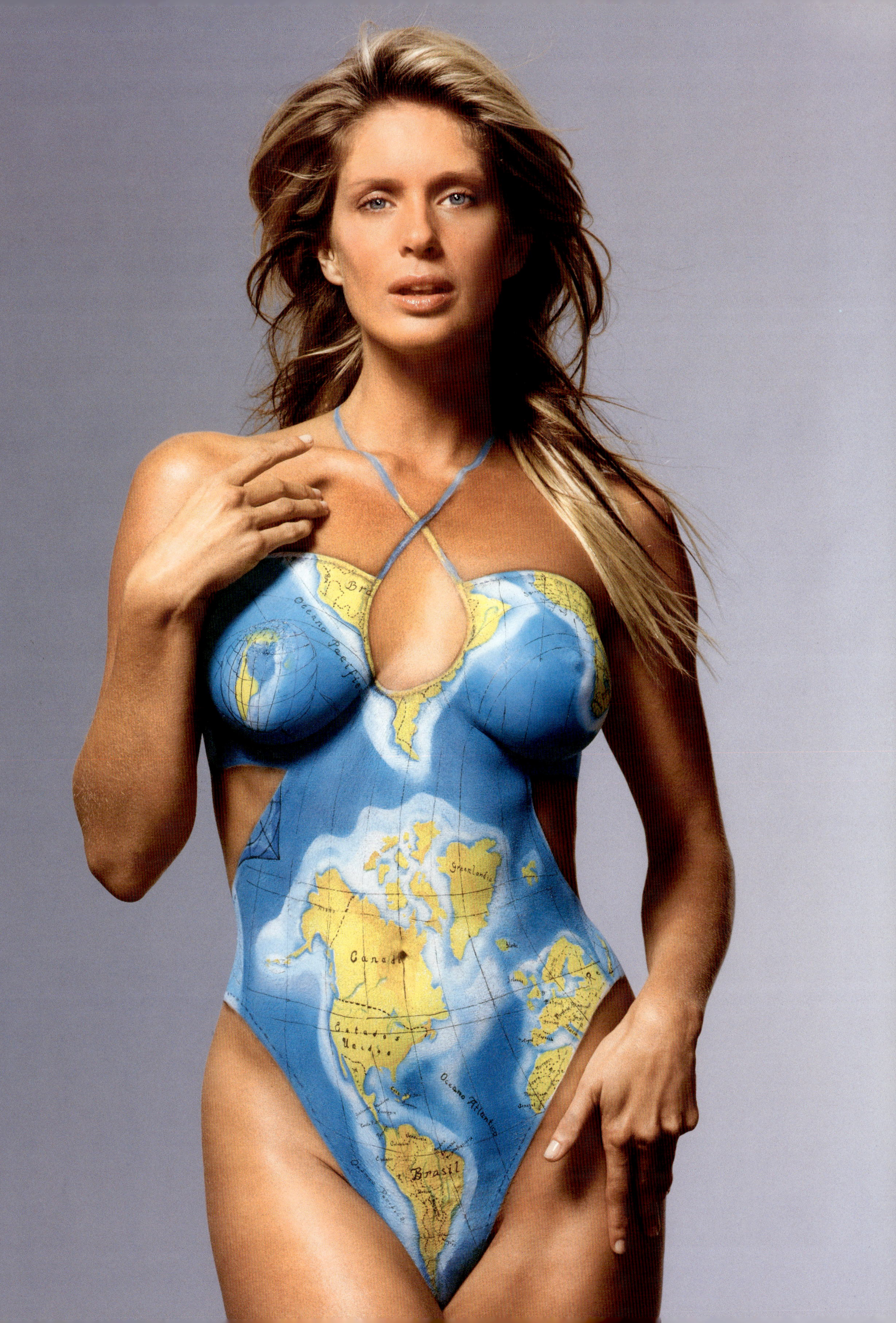
Oceano Pacifico
Greenlandia
Canada
Estados Unidos
Oceano Atlantico
Brasil
Oceano Pacifico

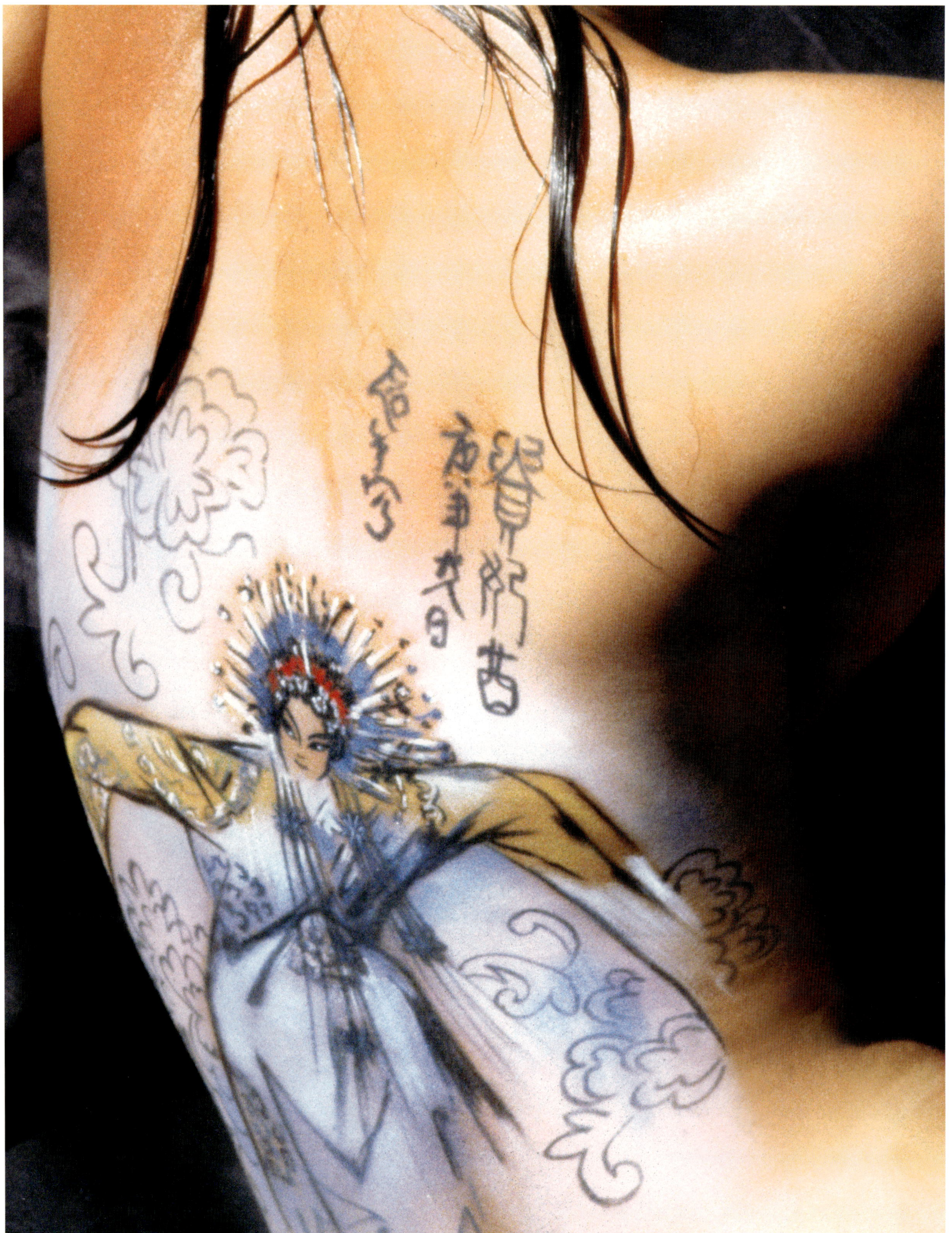

Yana Alberto Tolot

Torkil Gudnason

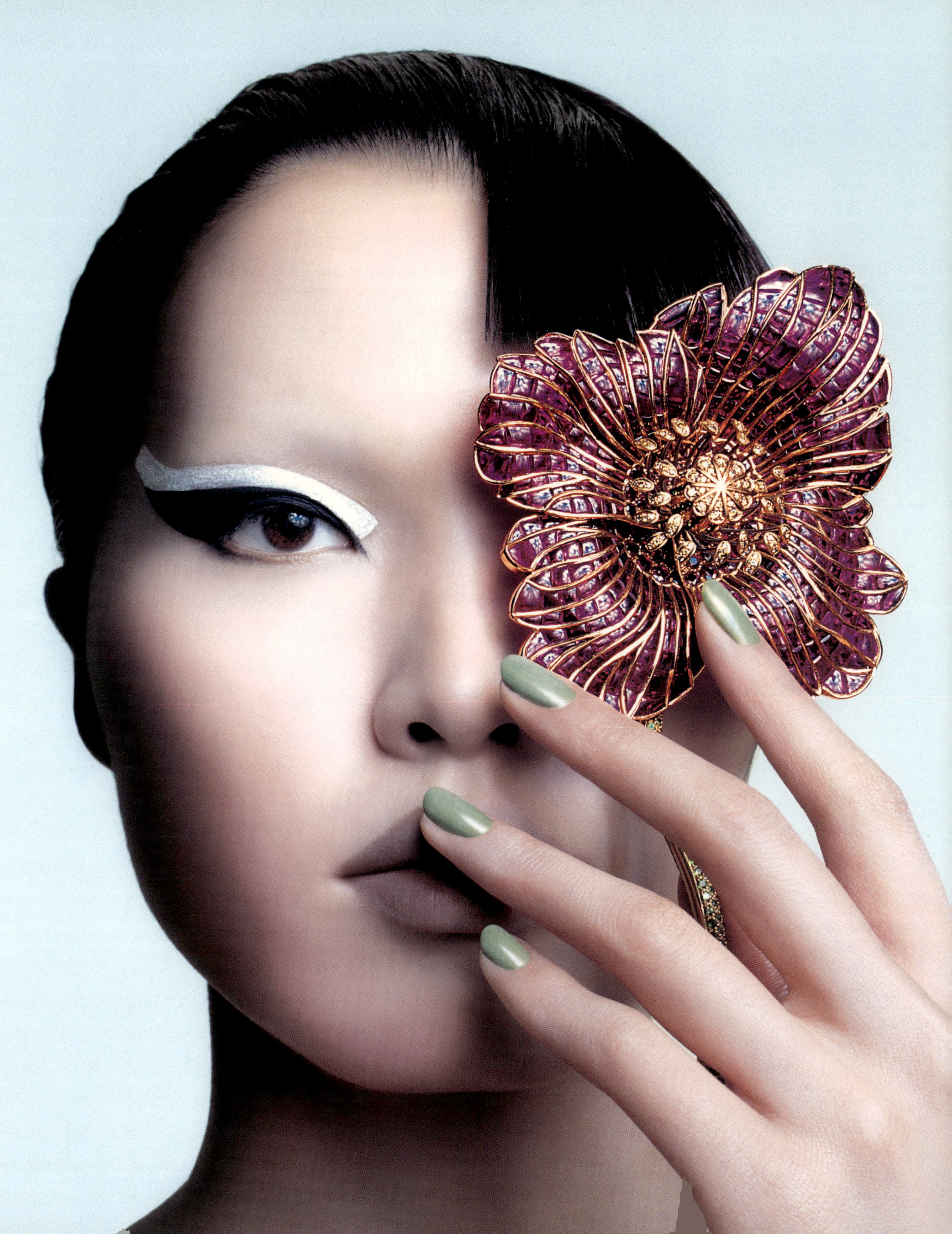

David Jacobson

[overleaf] Nadia Riza Joanne Gair

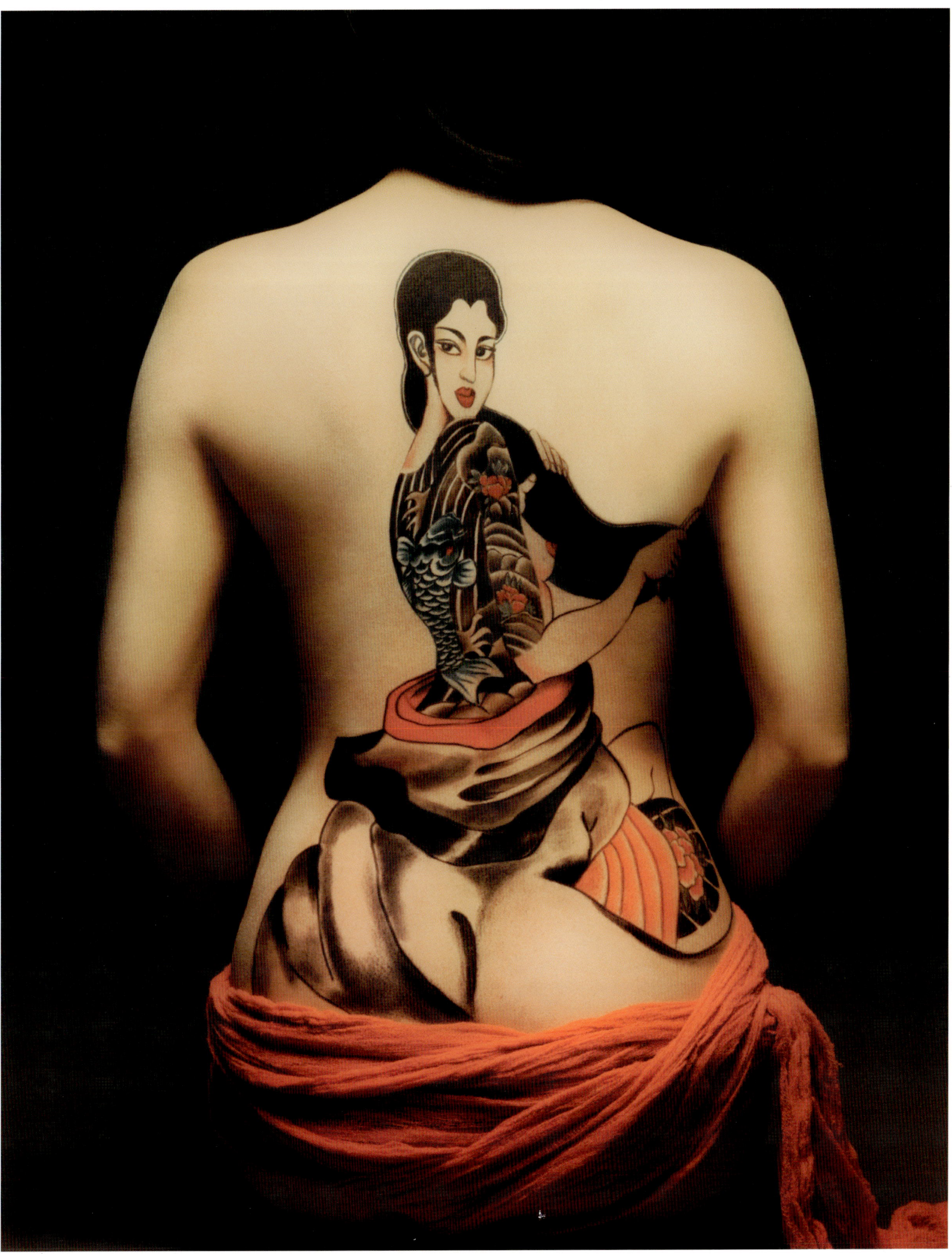

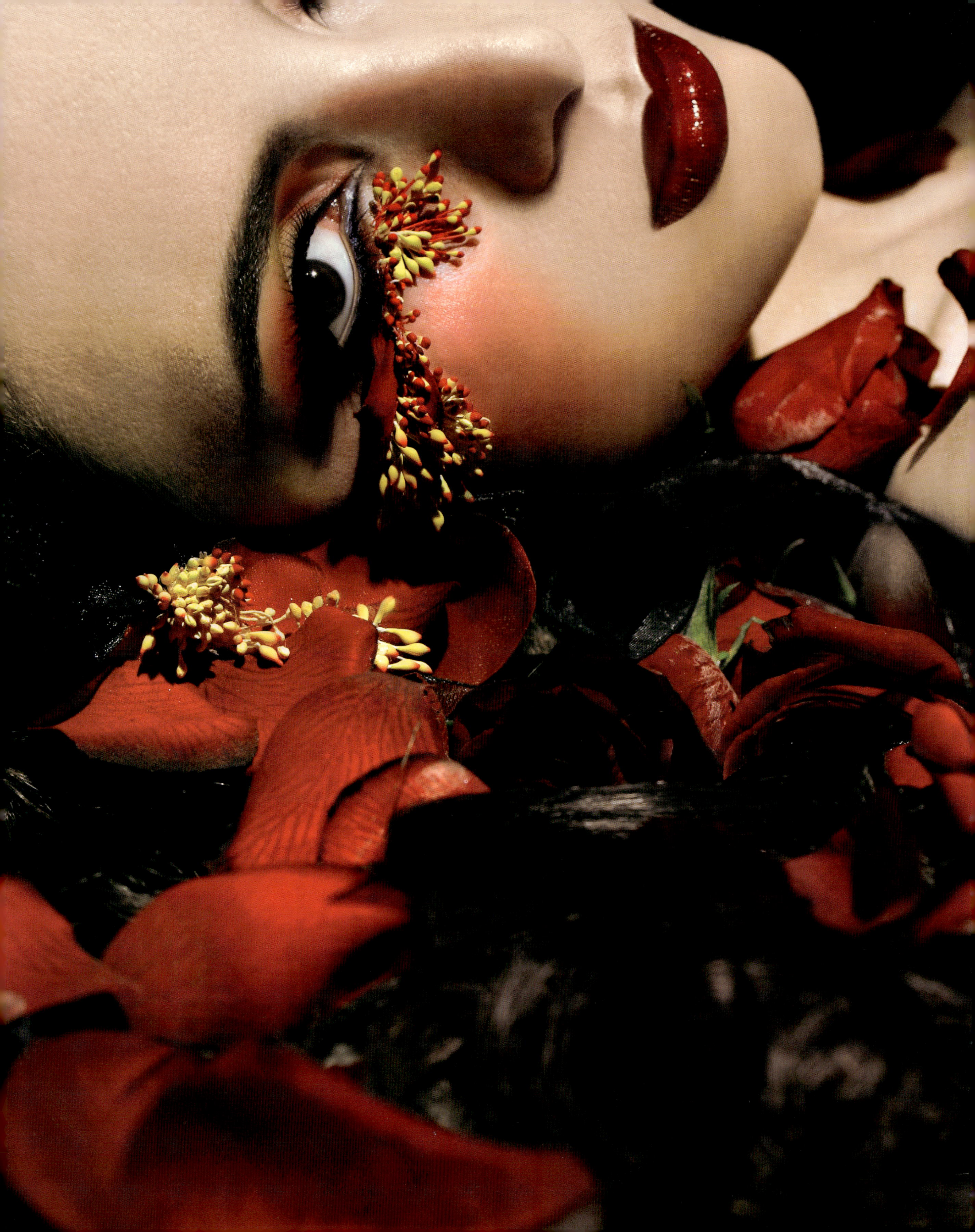

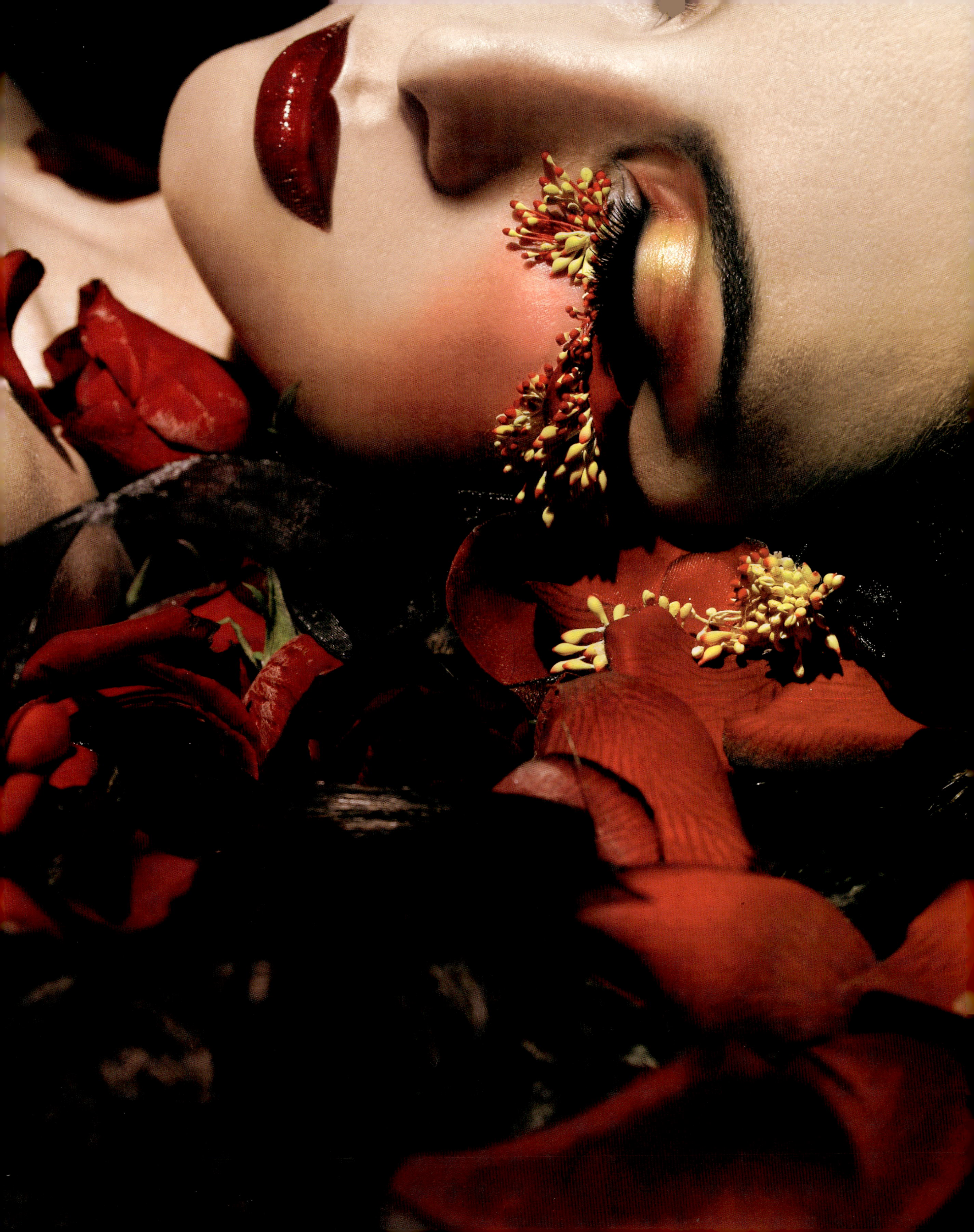

Mark Abrahams

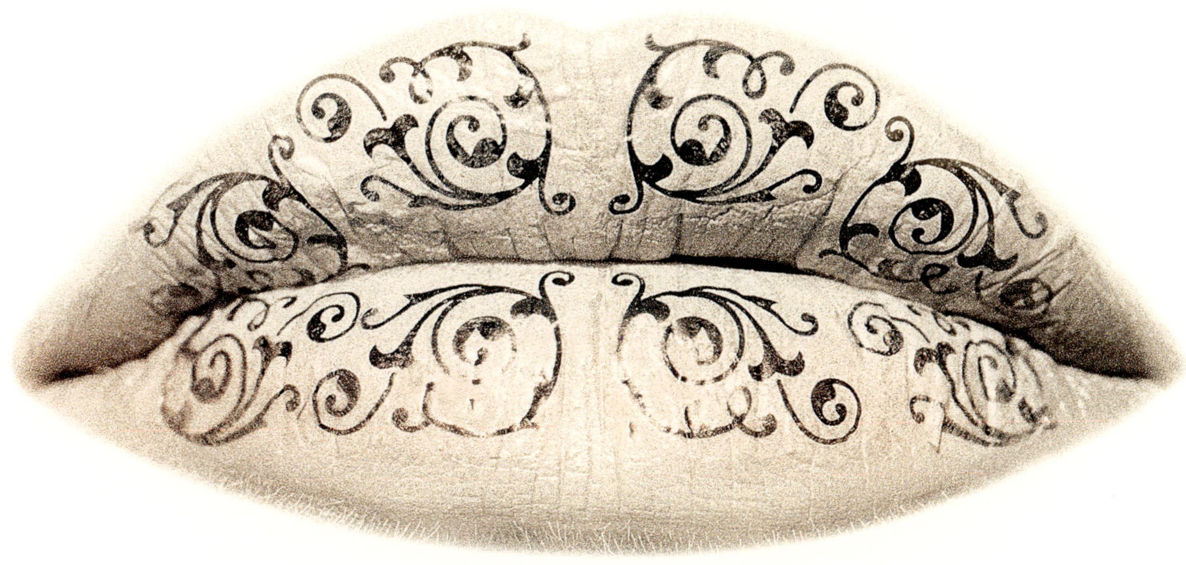

Eva Mueller

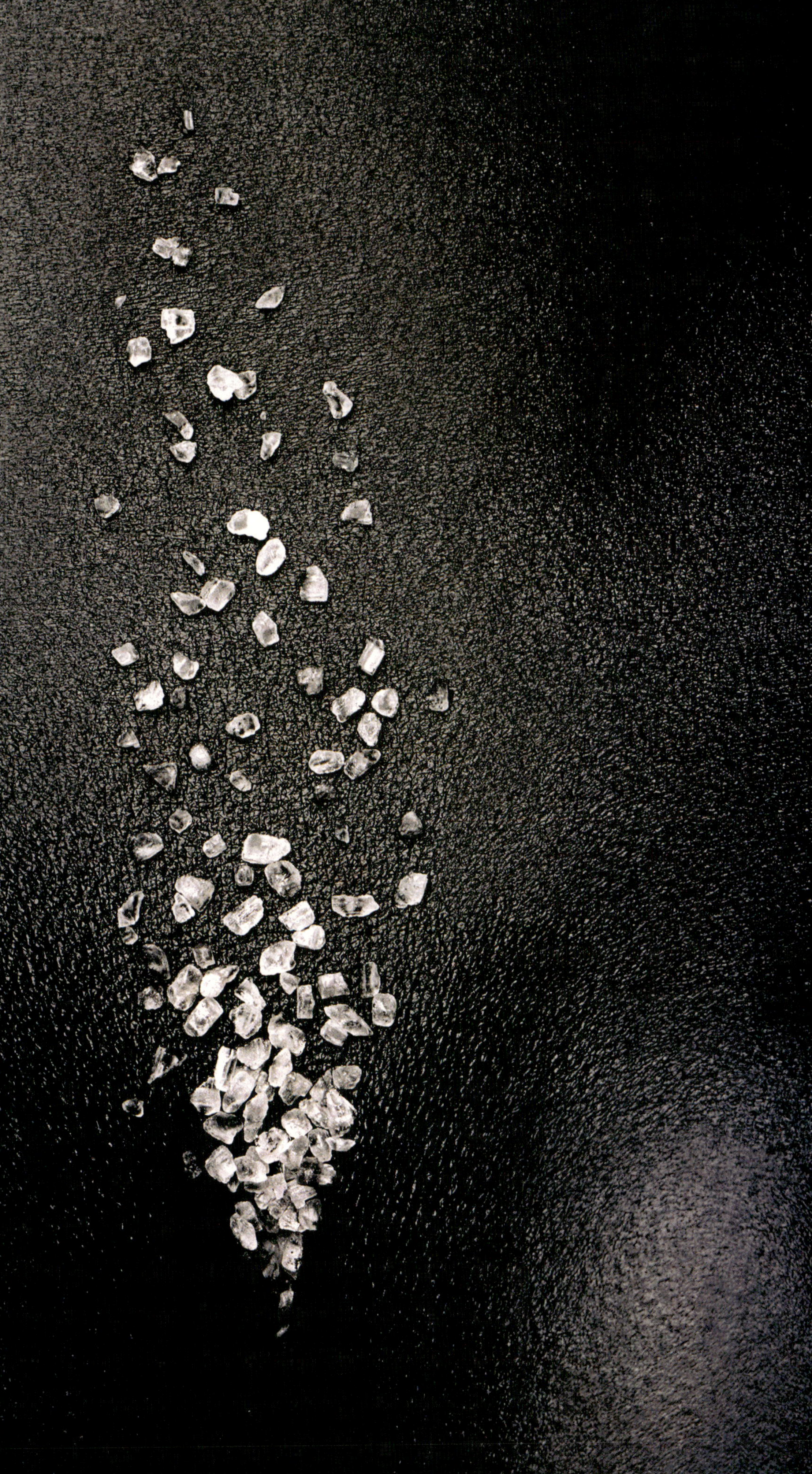

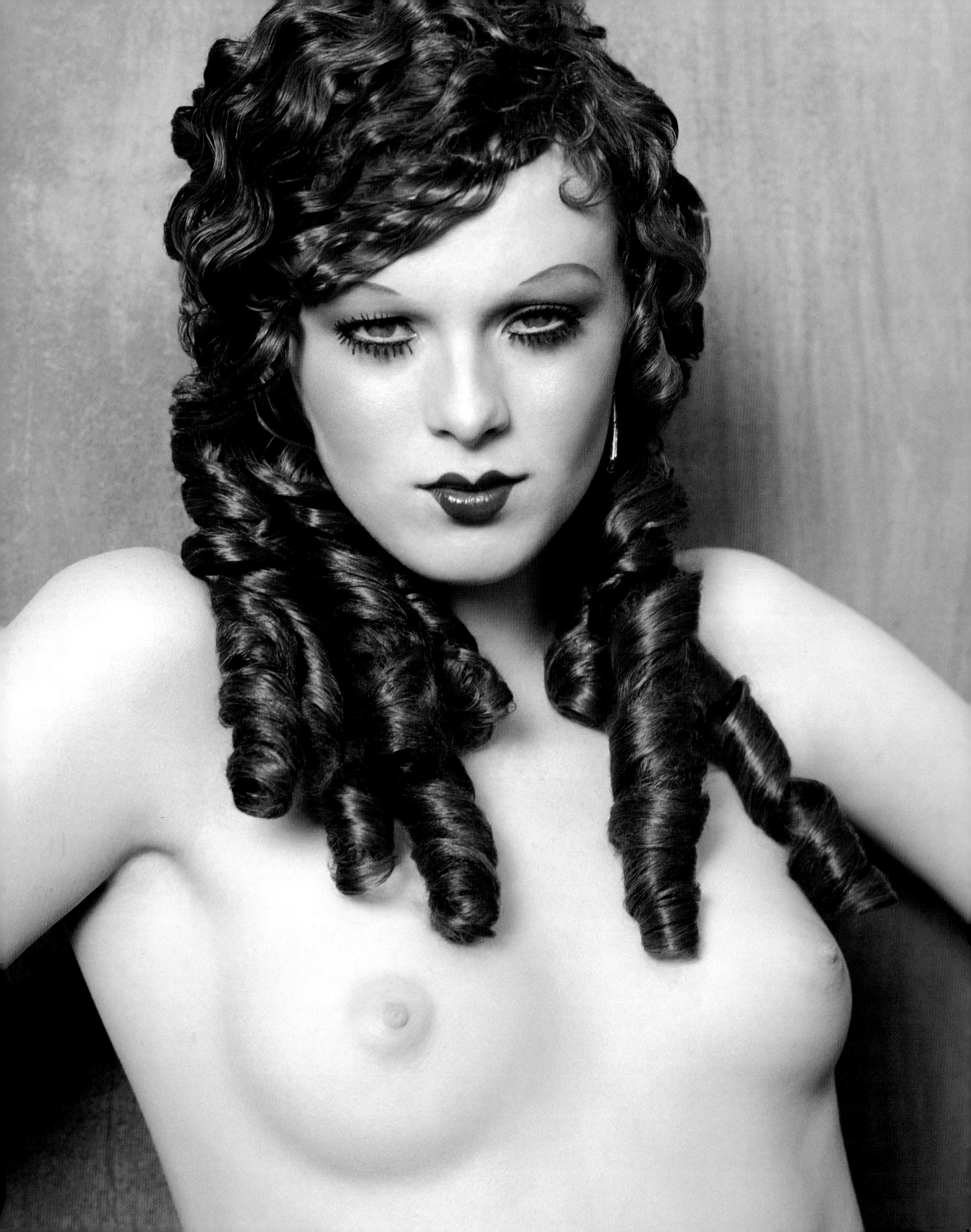

Karen Elson Herb Ritts

Carolyn Murphy Herb Ritts

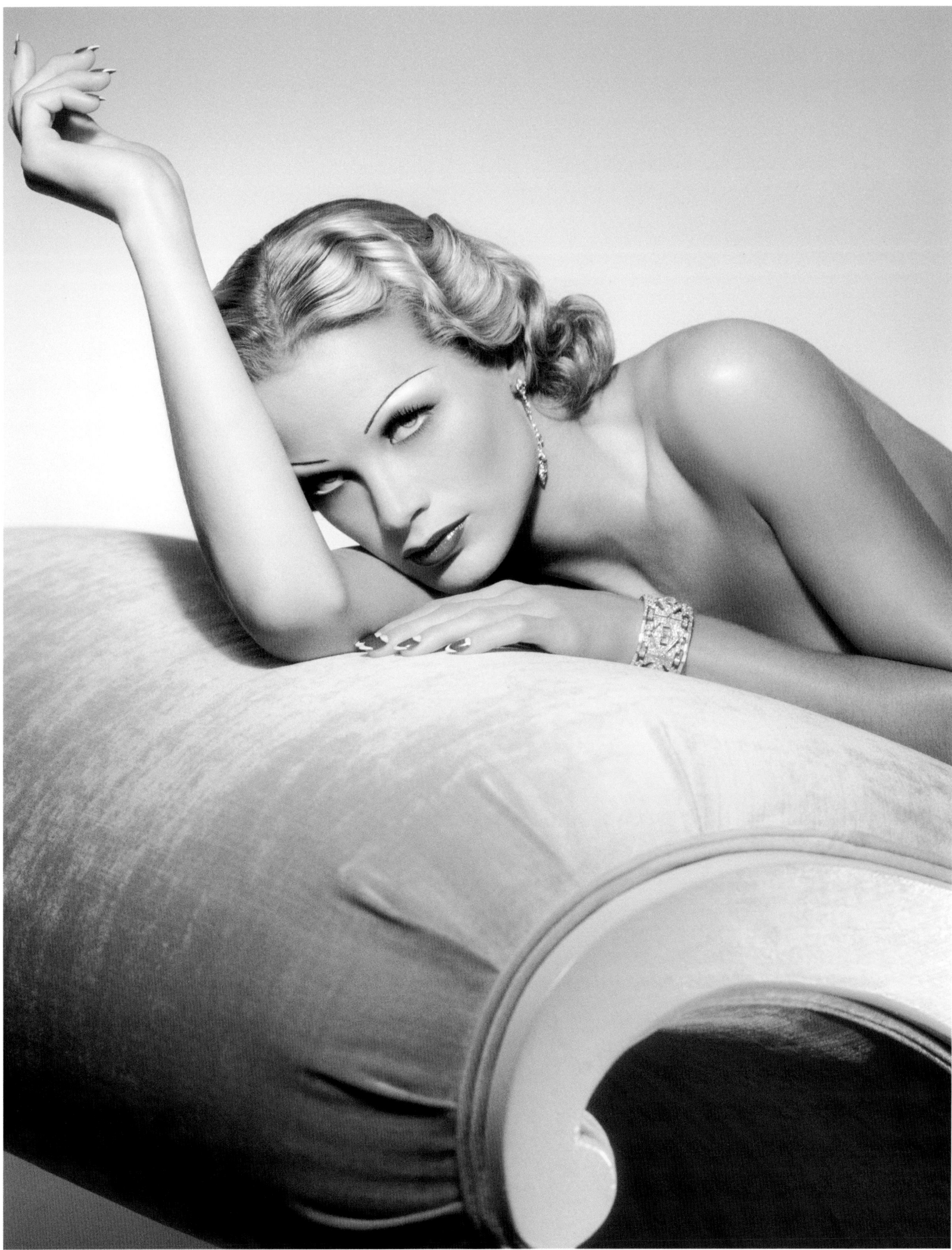

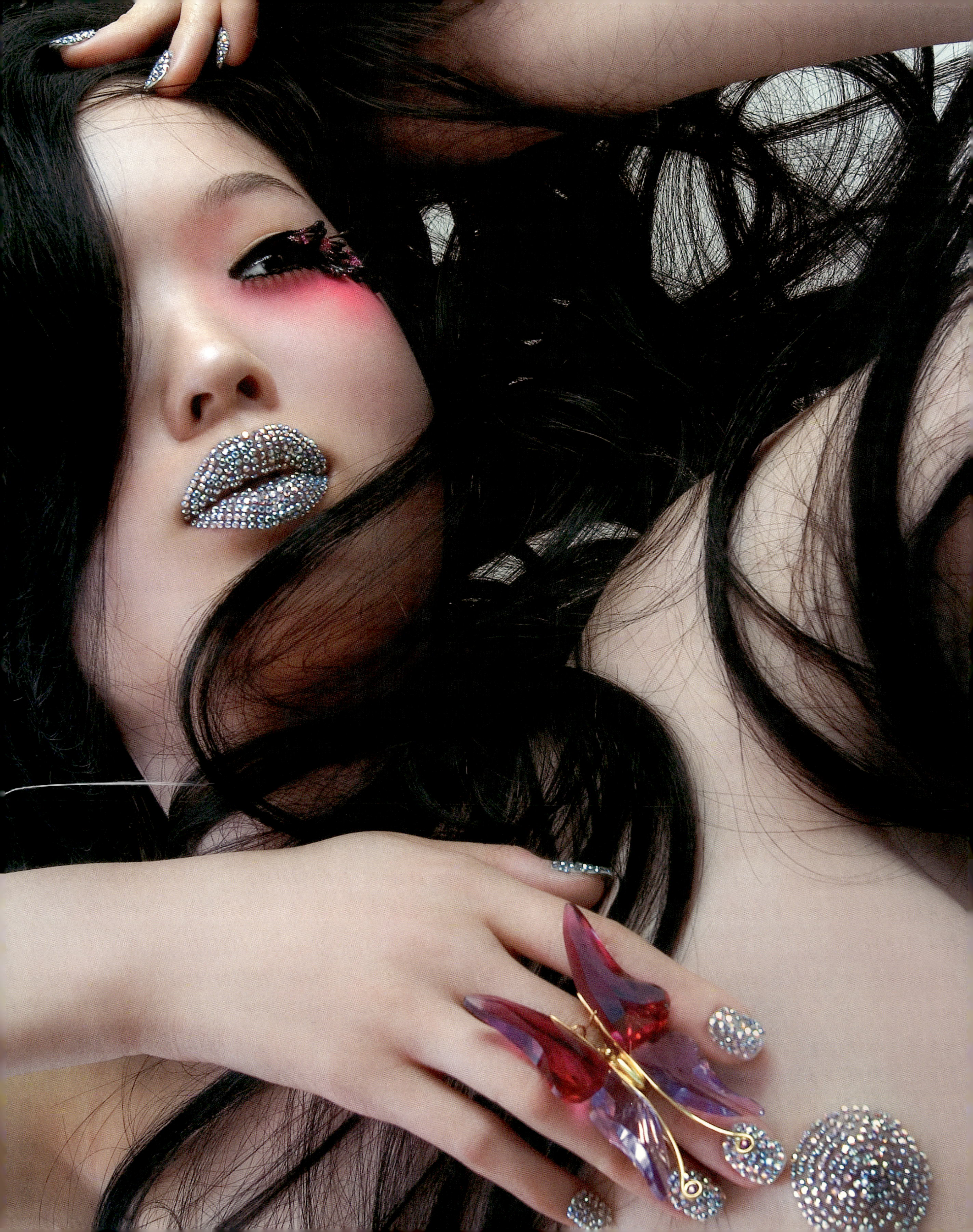

Sophia Lee Joanne Gair

Sophia Lee Joanne Gair

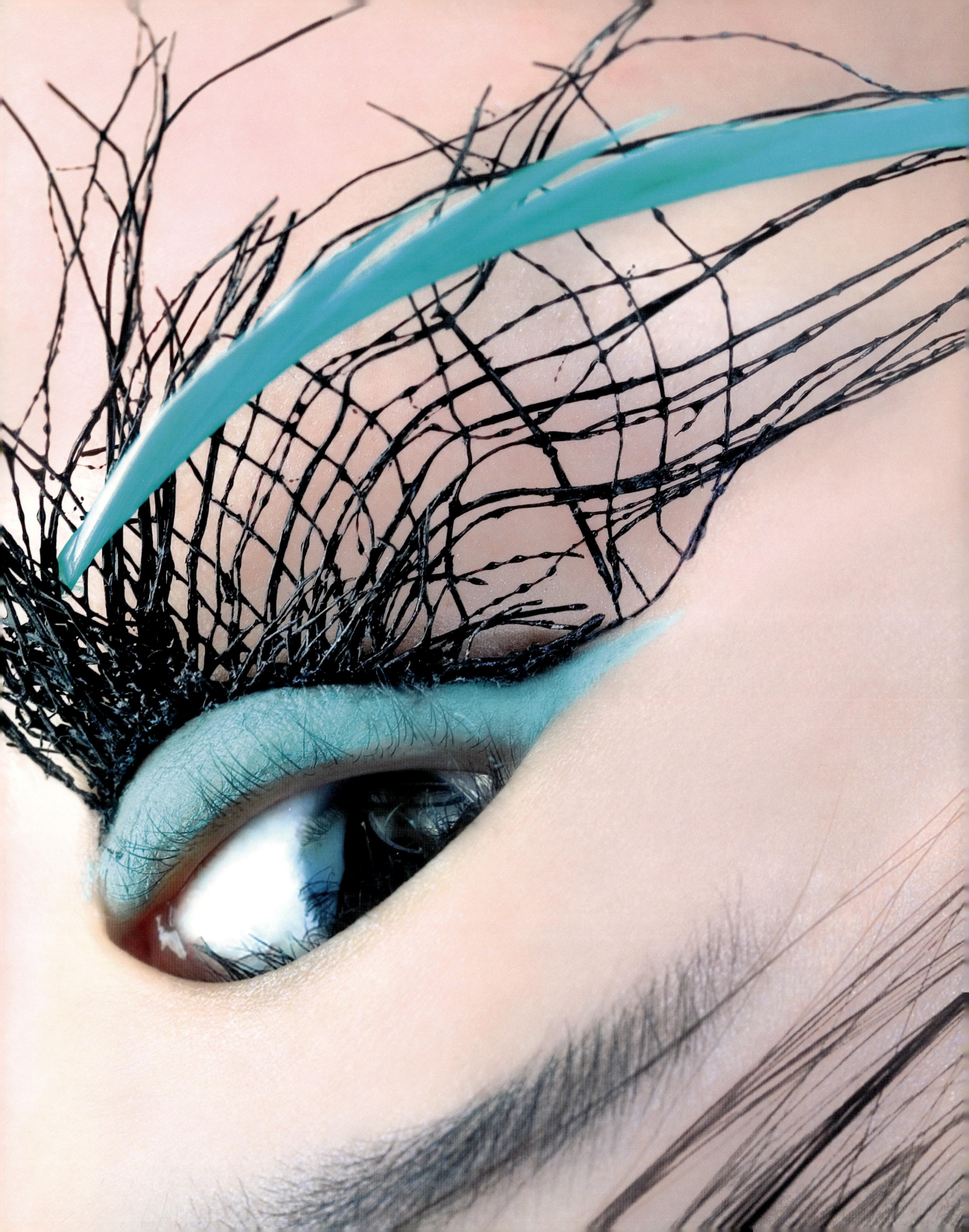

Eva Mueller

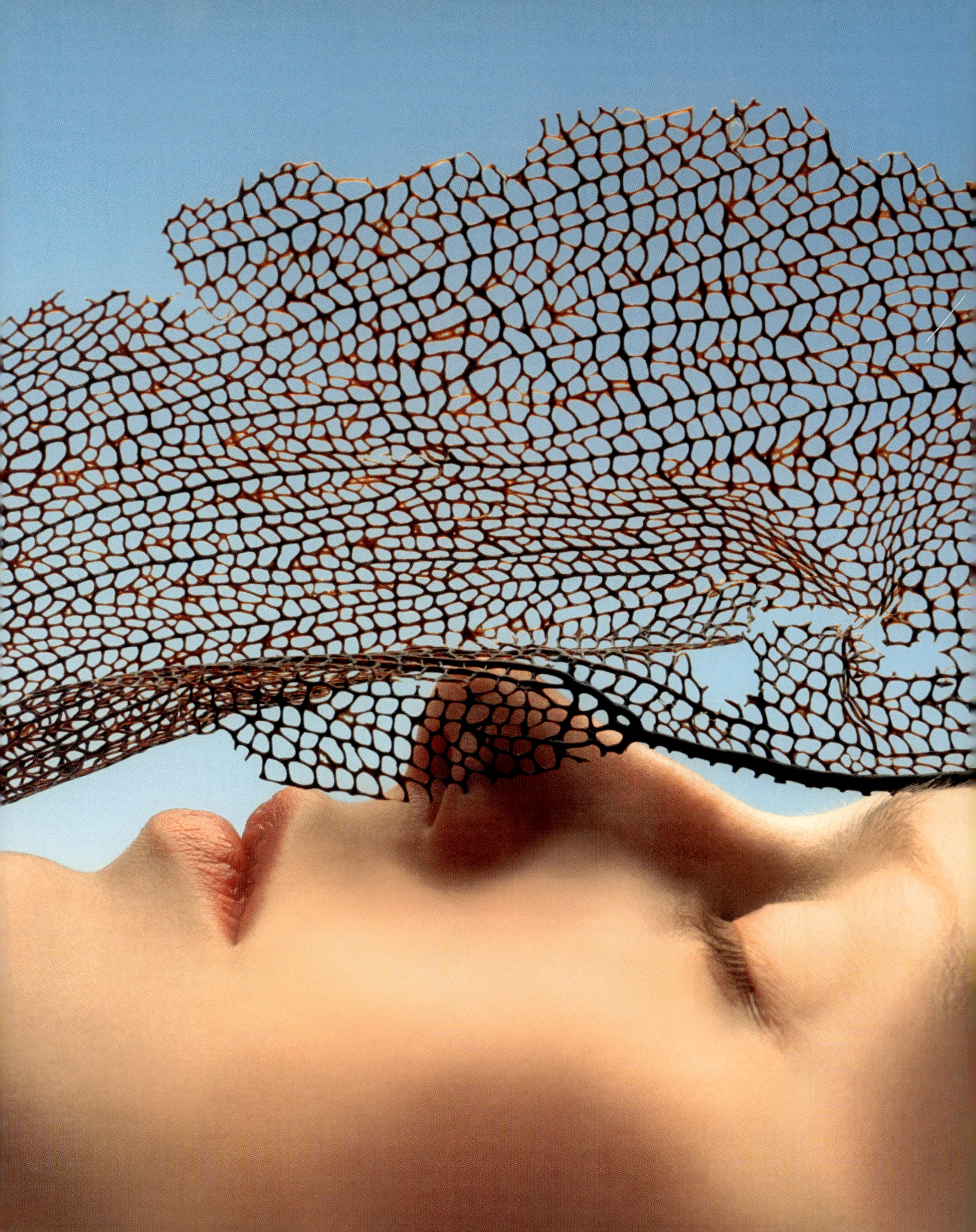

Mark Seliger

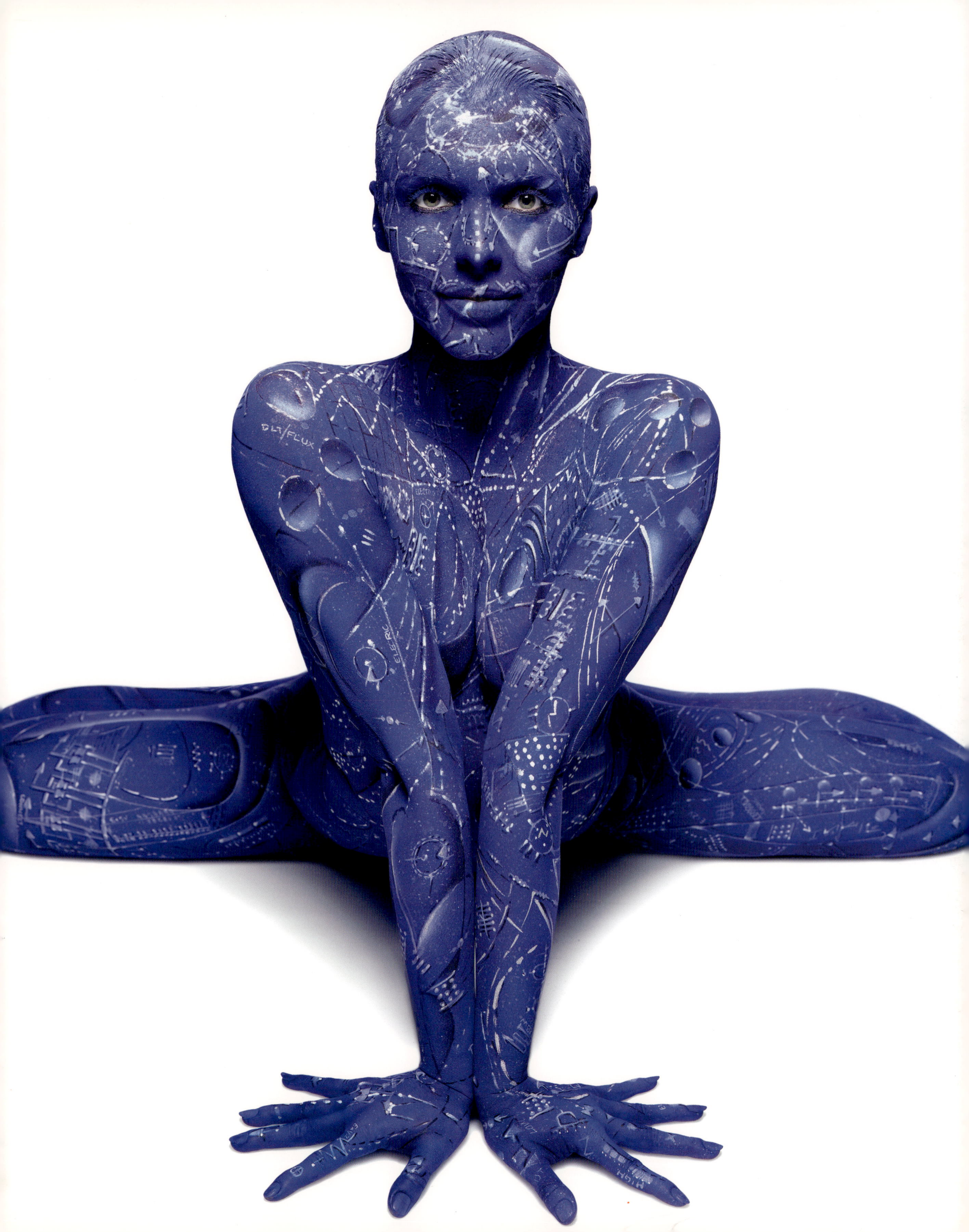

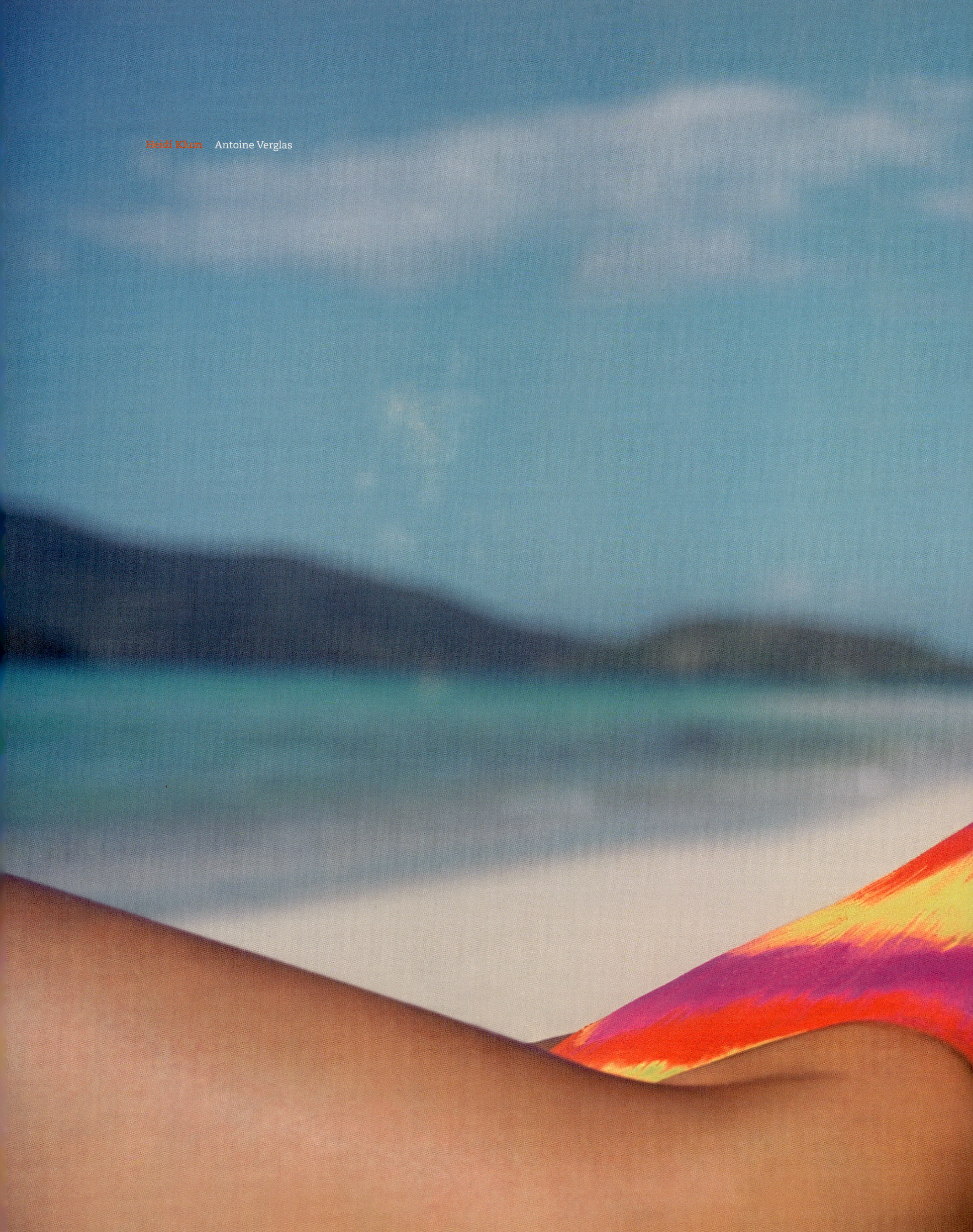
Heidi Klum Antoine Verglas

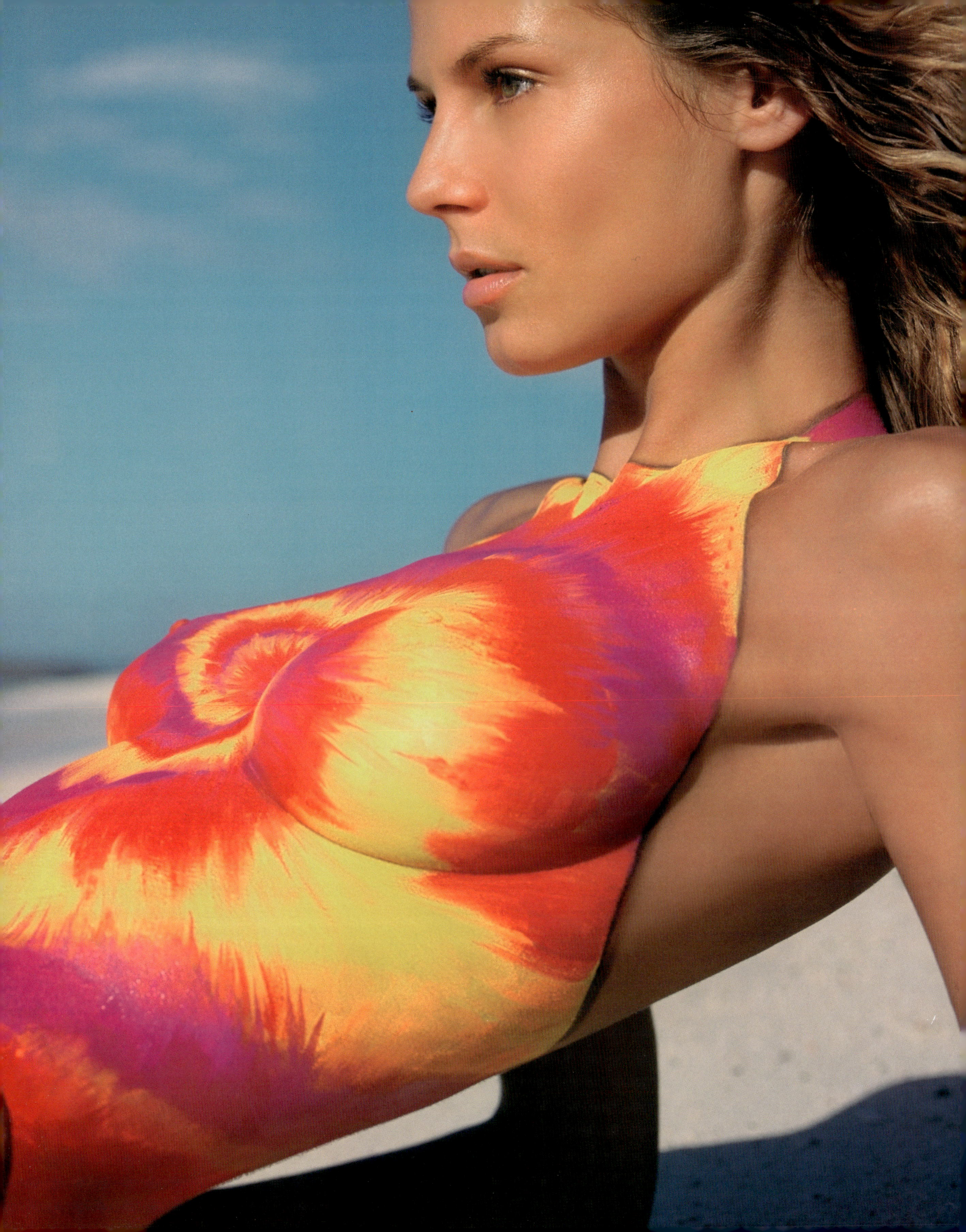

PLATES

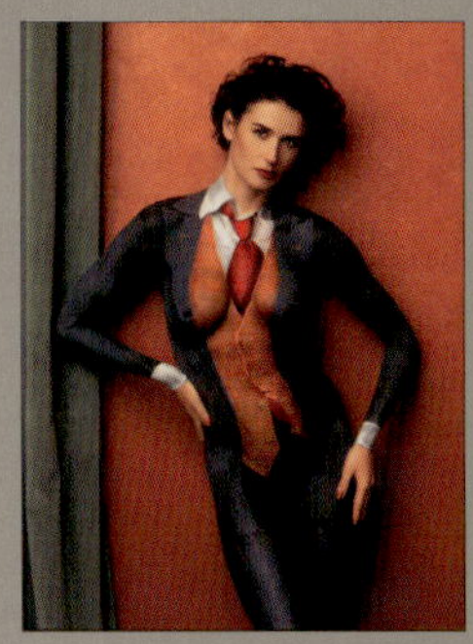

Demi Moore
Annie Leibovitz

Hollywood, 1992
This was a follow-up to Annie Leibovitz's famous 1991 *Vanity Fair* cover photo of a pregnant Demi Moore. We had all worked on that image a year earlier. During the week-long shoot in 1992, it was decided to try body painting for the August cover image. I was provided with a Richard Tyler three-piece, pinstriped suit. In those days I generally did not have an assistant to help me body paint. The day started at 6:30 a.m. at the Chateau Marmont in West Hollywood—it was a long day. Demi is probably the most disciplined person I've ever met—she even went home and slept in the suit, just in case we needed more coverage the next day.

Contact Press Images. First published as the cover of Vanity Fair, *August 1992.*

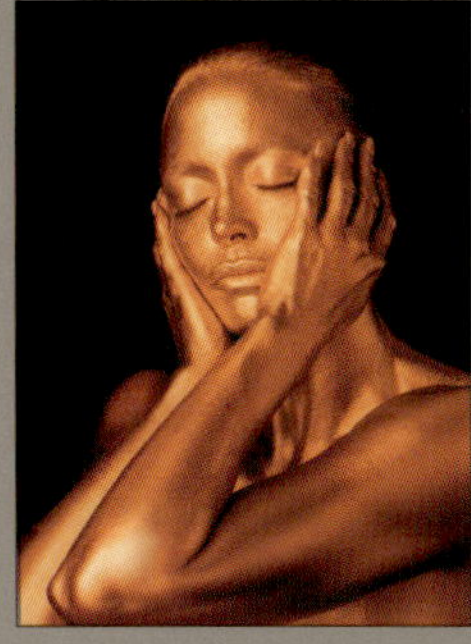

Goldie Hawn
Matthew Rolston

Hollywood, 1990
A "golden" Goldie Hawn was part of a photo spread that featured in the May 1990 issue of *Fame* magazine. Goldie was hand-painted from head to toe in a metallic oil-based, liquid gold makeup. She was an enthusiastic canvas and embraced the transformation.

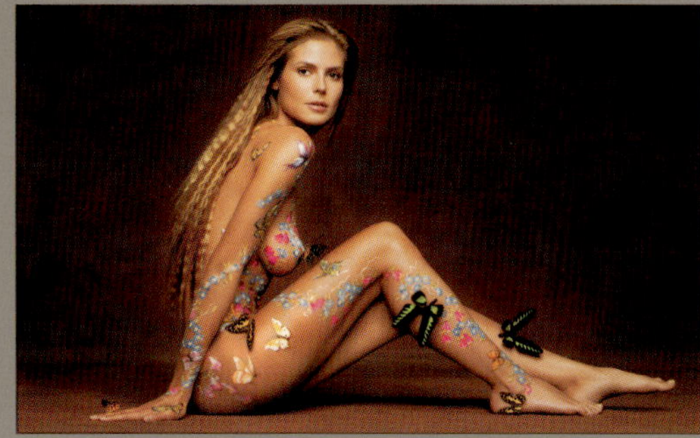

Heidi Klum
Christophe Jouany

Los Angeles, 2001
Shape magazine Art Director Jacqueline Moorby came up with the idea for an image representing "Mother Nature." We both thought Heidi Klum was the perfect model for the image. I painted flowered vines and exotic butterflies on Heidi and utilized farmed ones to create a three-dimensional effect.

My process is interactive, which makes for happy projects. Heidi herself even added a brushstroke or two.

Produced for Shape *magazine and used with permission. Art Direction: Jacqueline C. Moorby.*

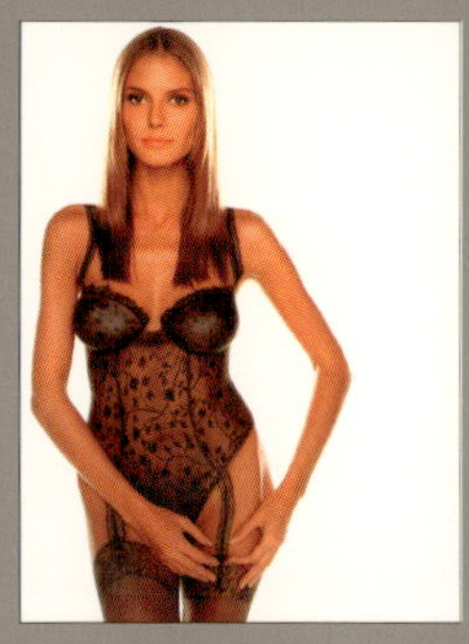

Heidi Klum
Antoine Verglas

New York, 1998
After working on several Victoria's Secret advertising campaigns with Heidi Klum and other models doing beauty makeup, I was inspired to attempt a body painting on one of my "off" days.

I am a fan of Victoria's Secret lingerie and their attention to detail. Heidi and I chose their best-selling lingerie outfit. I recreated it for these images using Dinair Airbrush Makeup and my favorite pen for detail—a black Sharpie. Heidi and Antoine Verglas kindly embraced this creative "day off" together with great enthusiasm.

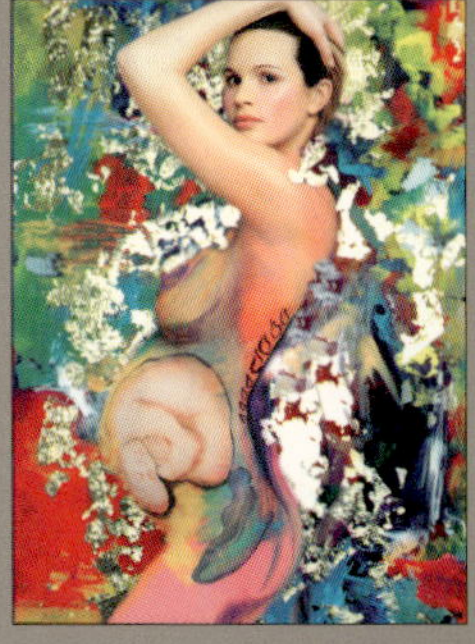

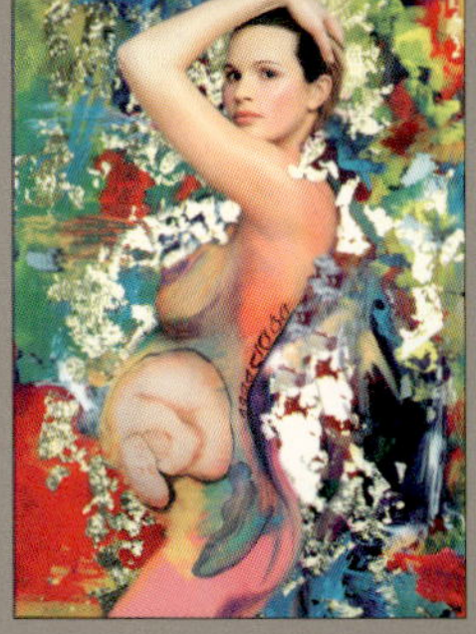

Elle Macpherson
Tony Duran

New York, 1997
Elle Macpherson was six months pregnant when I came up with a concept to celebrate the impending birth of her first son, Flynn. She loved the idea and together with Tony Duran we created an image titled "Celebration of Life." Elle was first body-painted and photographed. A sheet of glass that I had painted with gold leaf and vivid colors was then shot by Tony and married to the photo of Elle to create this image.

Thank you to Stuart Cameron, Artist Management Associates.

Ken Browar

Los Angeles, 1995
Ken Browar approached me to collaborate on a project with him. I had admired his beauty work in the past and was full of ideas to help him execute the many detailed images planned for our one-day shoot.

I brought an array of makeup supplies and paraphernalia for the four different images Ken photographed that day. This one had a model with big, luscious lips that I was able to make up with lipstick and glitter, making her mouth look like candy.

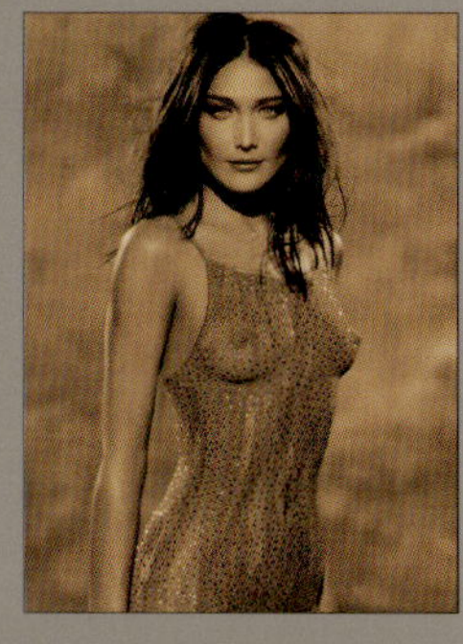

Carla Bruni
Holger Eckstein

Paris, 1999
This was a whirlwind international trip for me. I arrived in Paris the night before the shoot, having just completed a job in Los Angeles, and was thrilled to be working with both Holger Eckstein and Carla Bruni. Carla had always liked the idea of being body-painted and was looking forward to it. In this image, she is "wearing" an Italian Caractère wool-knit dress that I painted on her for Caractère's Fall/Winter collection campaign. I airbrushed as well as hand-painted her to get the desired effect. The tiny sequins were put on one-by-one with eyelash glue.

Used courtesy of www.holgereckstein.com.

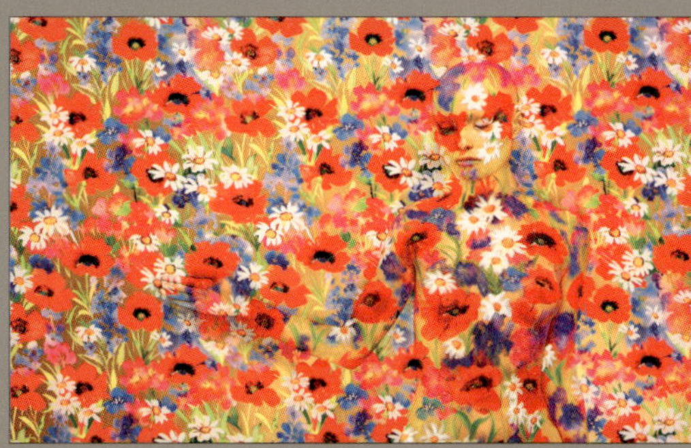

Sasha
Tracy Bayne

Los Angeles, 2000
Producer Gail Smerigan of the syndicated television program *Ripley's Believe It or Not!* contacted me in 2000 about a show featuring my body painting.

Their approach revolved around a photo shoot created especially for the episode. It featured my painting of Russian model Sasha and focused on the magical side of my work—how I can seemingly make people disappear with my brush. It turned out to be one of their highest-rated episodes.

Tracy Bayne for Opus Reps.

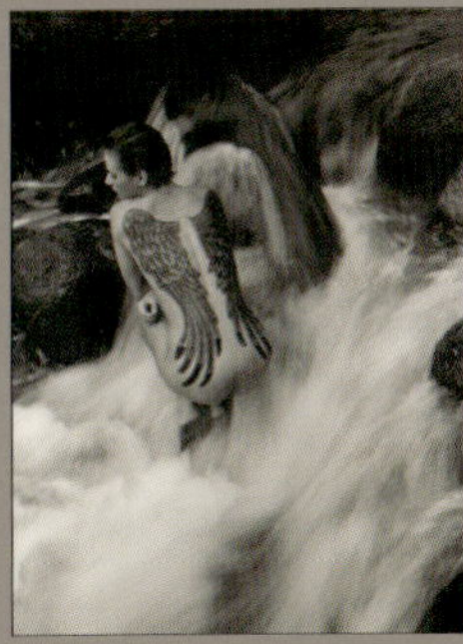

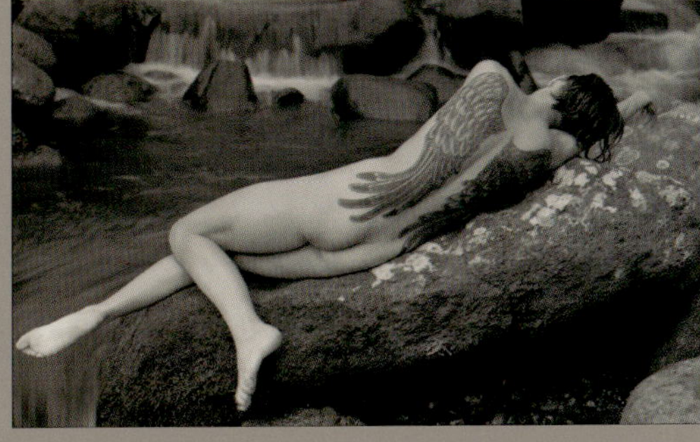

Demi Moore
Annie Leibovitz

Hawaii, 1992
In 1992, Annie Leibovitz was photographing a week-long pictorial with Demi Moore for the August 1992 issue of *Vanity Fair*. These images were created in Kauai, Hawaii the week before I painted the now-famous suit on Demi.

The location was a beautiful rain forest that Annie had chosen. I hand-drew the wings on Demi's back with multiple black Bic ballpoint pens to create the definition and detail seen in the photo.

Contact Press Images.

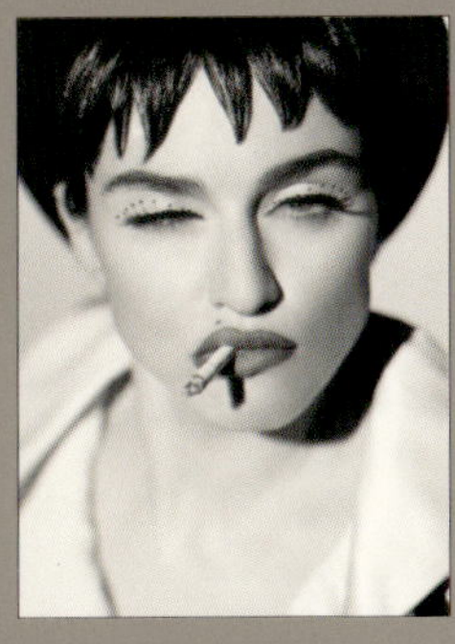

Madonna
Herb Ritts

San Pedro, 1990
I worked with Madonna over an exciting ten-year period. The late Herb Ritts photographed this iconic image, and it appeared in the June 1990 issue of *Interview* magazine and the Blonde Ambition Tour book. I love the way the focus is on the tip of the cigarette. I created the eyelashes by melting paraffin wax and mixing black eyeshadow. Madonna is amazing—she's very in control of what she creates and only has top people around her. When you work with Madonna, you know that what you produce will be innovative and stand the test of time; it was a privilege to work with her.

Gratefully reproduced with permission of the Herb Ritts Foundation.

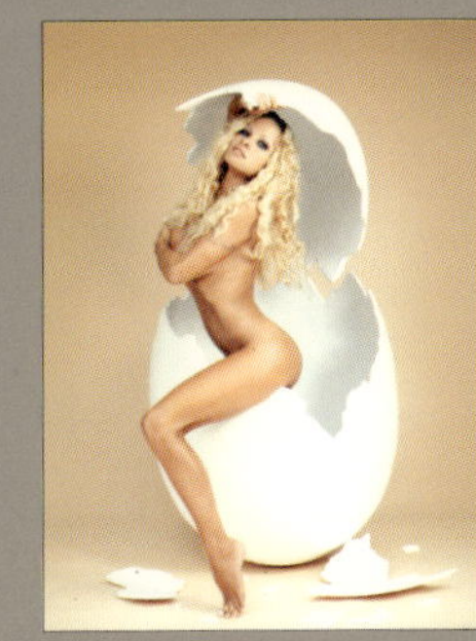

Pamela Anderson
David LaChapelle

Los Angeles, 1998
This image was part of a Pamela Anderson photo pictorial shot by David LaChapelle for the November 1998 issue of *Interview* magazine and was featured on the cover. David is such a talent at conceptualizing and executing his imagery. I think Pamela is one of his favorite subjects too, so you end up with fantastic images like this one—I think you can see the trust between subject and photographer here. Pamela has beautiful skin, so for me it was really just enhancing her natural beauty; I covered her in oils and shines to highlight and accentuate her curves and also did her face makeup.

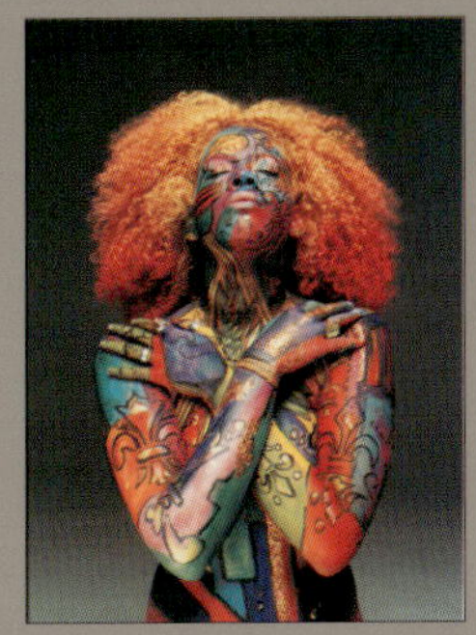

Kelis
Jonathan Mannion

New York, 1999
Virgin Records artist Kelis and I worked together for the first time on this image for her *Kaleidoscope* album cover. We had spoken on the phone previously and discussed what she was looking for: she wanted to appear as if viewed through a kaleidoscope or stained-glass window. I painted her by hand with water-based makeup, gold leaf, and diamond bindis. I think she really enjoyed the process and that it worked out beautifully, reflecting her dynamic personality.

Used with permission from Virgin Records America, Inc.

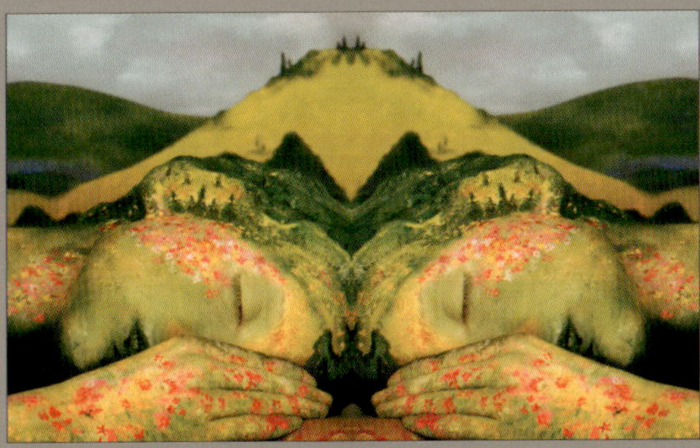

Lauren Gott
Matthew Rolston

Los Angeles, 1995
This shot was originally created as a single image for an Asprey jewelry print advertisement photographed by Matthew Rolston.

The original had model Lauren wearing the Asprey jewels. This is not the image that appeared in the campaign, but one from that photo session that was then digitally recreated to mirror itself, creating a "green hills" effect. I painted the model in water-based Aquacolor makeup and used clay for her hair.

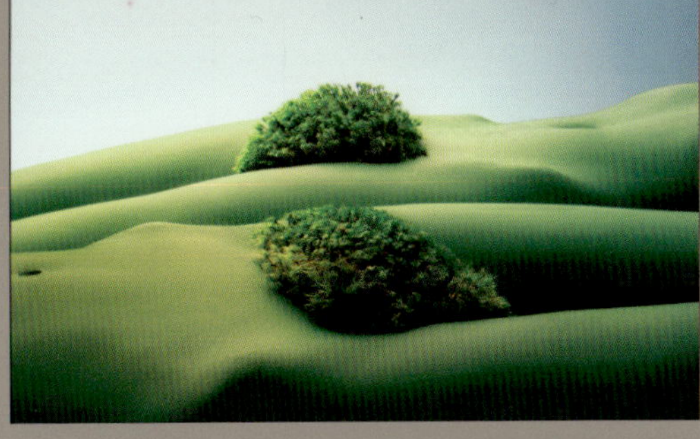

Eva Mueller

New York, 2000
Stylist Nikko Kefalas—then fashion editor of *Black Book* magazine and a dear friend—contacted me regarding a pictorial idea called "Skinscapes" that was being planned for their Summer 2000 issue. This beauty pictorial would use close-up, body-painted, and adorned shots of female bodies to give the illusion of landscapes. Nikko teamed me for the first time with photographer Eva Mueller—it was the start of a continuing collaboration and friendship with her.

This image features two women lying side-by-side, body-painted green, and covered in part with real moss to give the illusion of rolling hills. During the making of this pictorial, I agreed to become a beauty editor for *Black Book*—a role that lasted for a number of years.

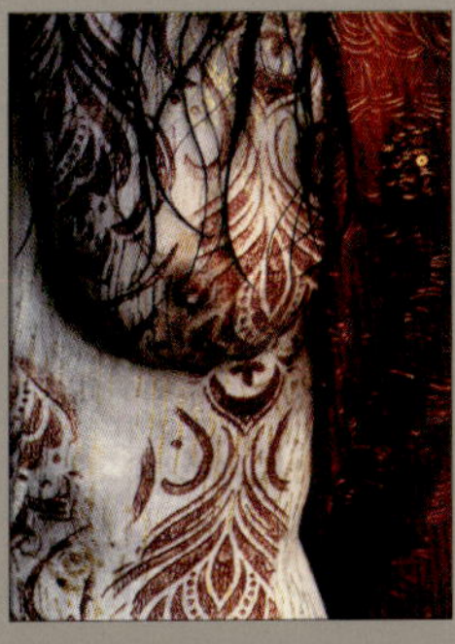

Yana
Alberto Tolot

Los Angeles, late 1980s
This was a collaborative personal project between Alberto Tolot, Peter Savic, and myself. It was photographed in Alberto's backyard on a hot summer's day. The model was Yana, a young, always enthusiastic subject. I layered what is essentially a sari wedding pattern on her long body by first whitewashing her with a water-based makeup. I then used a combination of freehand painting and stencils that I had designed with liquid gold and red makeup—it was really a layering process of different techniques.

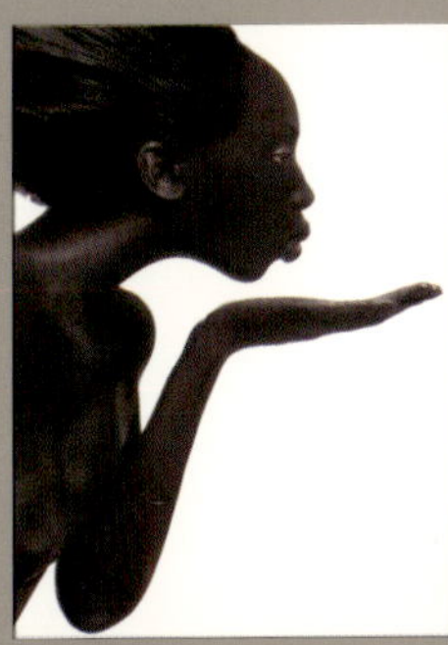

Suwana
Joanne Gair

Los Angeles, 2005
I love storytelling and movement. I really wanted to represent both elements with an action and reaction in this image and the following one.

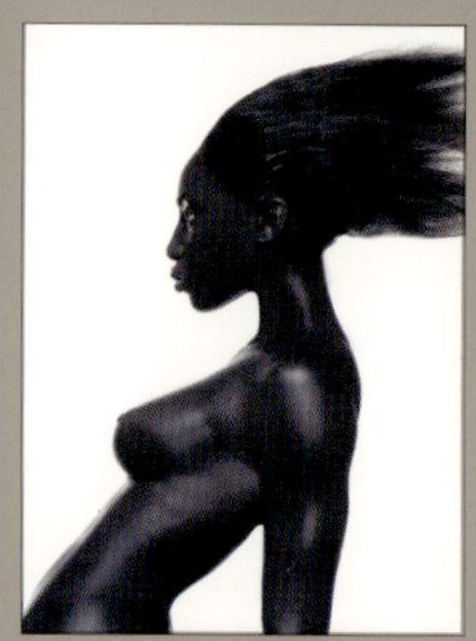

Suwana
Joanne Gair

Los Angeles, 2005
I shot this "reaction" and the previous "action" photographs at my home studio with model Suwana, who was just delightful to be around. My assistant Isaac Prado did the makeup, hair, and body painting, making her "dark black" with grease makeup.

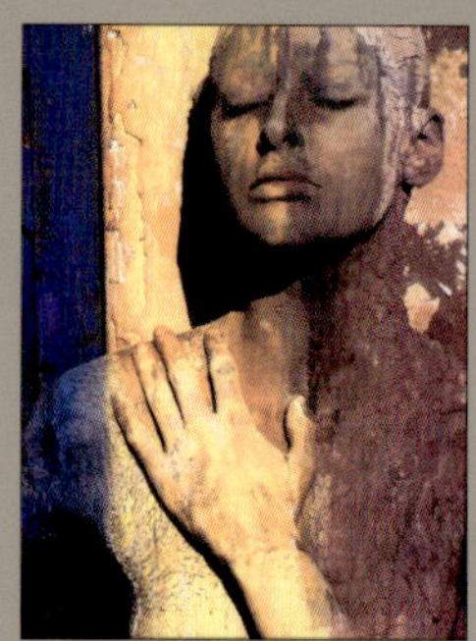

Broūn

California Desert, 1992
This image and the following were originally for an advertising job, which was shot as both a commercial and print campaign. The above photograph was shot on location in the California desert. A shack was constructed in what seemed like the middle of nowhere. I first covered the model's body in a clay base, then whitewashed over it with Aquacolor. Between traveling to the desert, painting, and the actual shoot time, it was one long day!

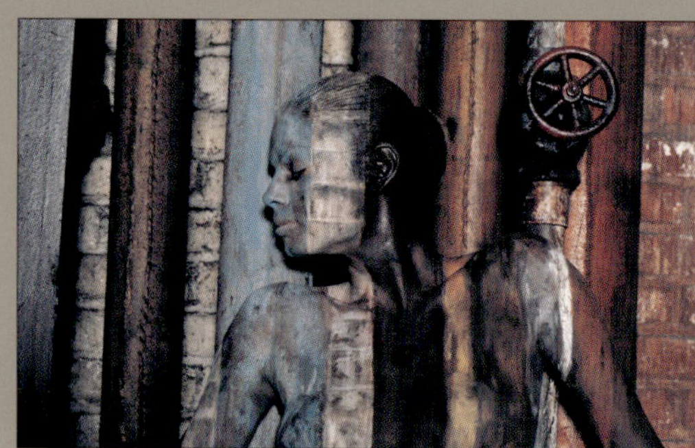

Broūn

Los Angeles, 1992
This second image was produced in a dark and derelict warehouse in downtown Los Angeles. I used water-based Aquacolor makeup to replicate the authenticity of the gritty, industrial set behind the model.

The photograph in the early pages of this book (page 8) captures a behind-the-scenes look at me painting the model on set.

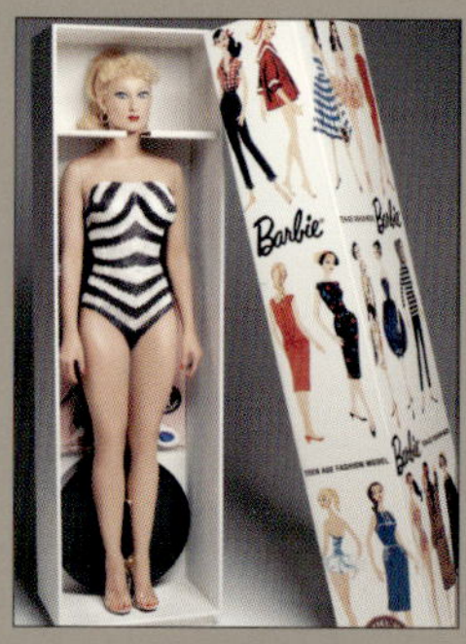

Demi Moore
Matthew Rolston

Los Angeles, 1995
Demi Moore loves dolls and is an avid collector—she came up with the concept of transforming herself into Mattel's Barbie while we were filming *Striptease*. With photographer Matthew Rolston, we decided to recreate two early versions of Barbie in one very long day of painting and shooting. Demi wanted to be painted as the original 1959 Barbie. With the help of my assistant Barry Bish, we prepared for two weeks. Matthew's company had the packaging box that the original doll came in replicated and custom-made to fit Demi. We tried to recreate every detail.

BARBIE ® is a trademark owned by and used with permission from Mattel, Inc. ® 2005 Mattel, Inc. All Rights Reserved.

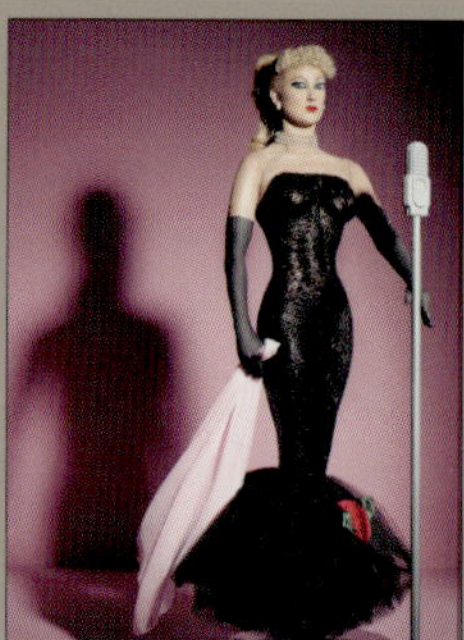

Demi Moore
Matthew Rolston

Los Angeles, 1995
This was the second image attempted in our twenty-three hour workday. We recreated Barbie "Solo in the Spotlight," which came out in 1960. I painted Demi black and then sprayed her with adhesive glue before applying glitter. The gloves were created with water-based makeup, and I used a pearlized makeup on her exposed skin to make her look more doll-like. I painted Demi's eyelids to create the illusion that the eyes were doll-like and oversized. When Demi shut her eyes, the doll's eyes came to life.

BARBIE ® is a trademark owned by and used with permission from Mattel, Inc. ® 2005 Mattel, Inc. All Rights Reserved.

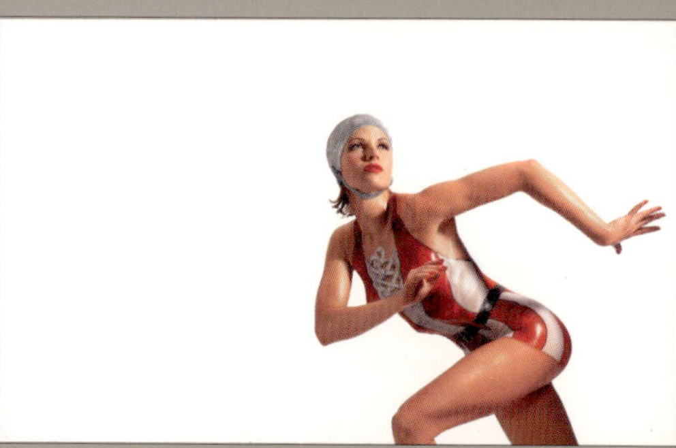

Tiffany Green
Dan Escobar

San Francisco, 1998
Dan Escobar had seen my body painting and wanted to work with me on an advertising campaign that he was photographing.

In 1998, body painting was less common in advertising, although now it's used frequently. Dan was a pleasure to work with, and I enjoyed the collaboration.

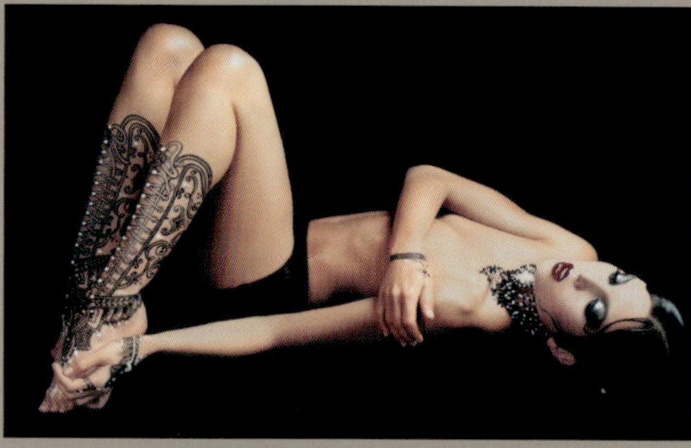

Libby McGinley
Tracy Bayne

Los Angeles, 2000
These boots are a similar design to one of my favorite pairs from Vienna. Nikko Kefalas sent me the sexy necklace as a styling idea, and the two worked really well together on Australian model Libby.

These photos were shot for *SOHO Style* magazine in Tracy Bayne's studio. I used a combination of Reel Creations ink and my trusty Sharpie pen, and embellished the design with glittering Indian bindis.

Tracy used Kino Flo lighting, so the light was amazingly soft on Libby's clean skin, which didn't even have foundation applied to it.

Tracy Bayne for Opus Reps.

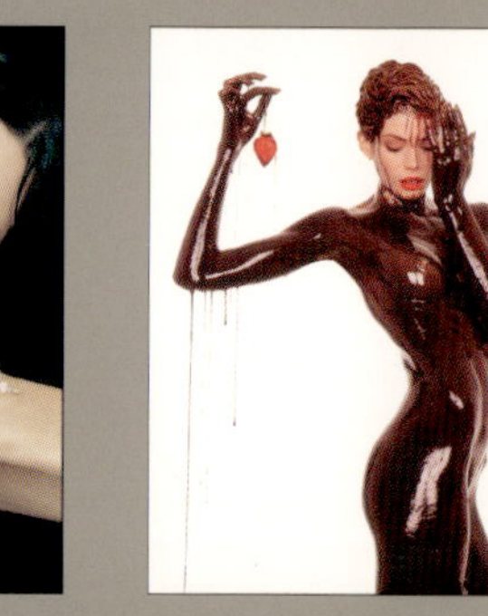

Howard Schatz

New York, 1999
Howard Schatz is well known for his ethereal underwater and botanical photography. This was a personal project that Howard, Beverly Ornstein, and I had conceptualized and decided to attempt. We used dark chocolate that had been melted in a large vat. My assistant and I continuously poured jugs of the warm, melted chocolate over the model, ducking in and out between shots. The chocolate found its own path of movement over her hair—which I had sculpted with clay—and down her body.

Nude Study #1273 by Howard Schatz from Nude Body Nude *(HarperCollins, 2000).*

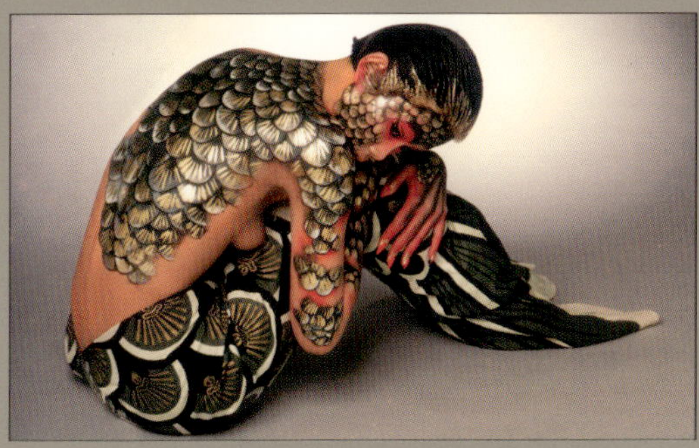

Geeling Ng
Bob Watson

Sydney, 1983
This image was created at the very beginning of my career. Model Geeling Ng and I were both New Zealanders living in the same building in Sydney. There was a beautiful Chinese weather balloon in Geeling's apartment, which I wrapped her in before painting the rest of her body to match. Bob Watson was her favorite photographer so between the three of us we captured something special. Geeling later garnered a lot of attention as David Bowie's "China Girl" in his music video.

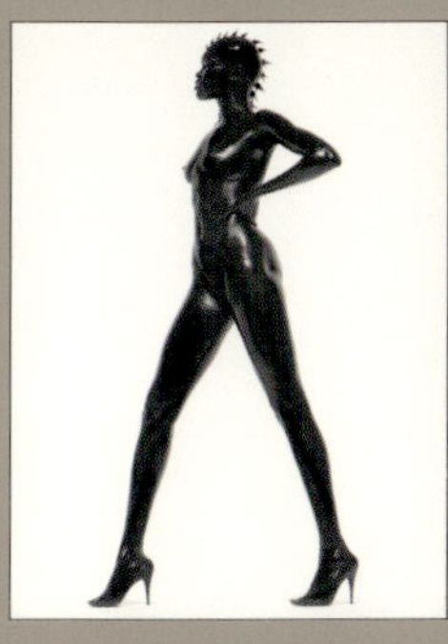

Alek Wek
Herb Ritts

Los Angeles, 1998
Herb Ritts photographed the 1999 Pirelli Calendar as a tribute to the twentieth century with each month's model representing a decade in time. This stunning photograph of Alek Wek was the December image and represented The Future. I handpicked the thorns that adorn her back from a bush in the Mexican jungle while on another shoot with Herb. The prosthetic latex feet were made by Mark Garbarino. Coupled with a little black oil grease and latex, Alek was transformed into our interpretation of the future.

Gratefully reproduced with permission of the Herb Ritts Foundation and IMG Models.

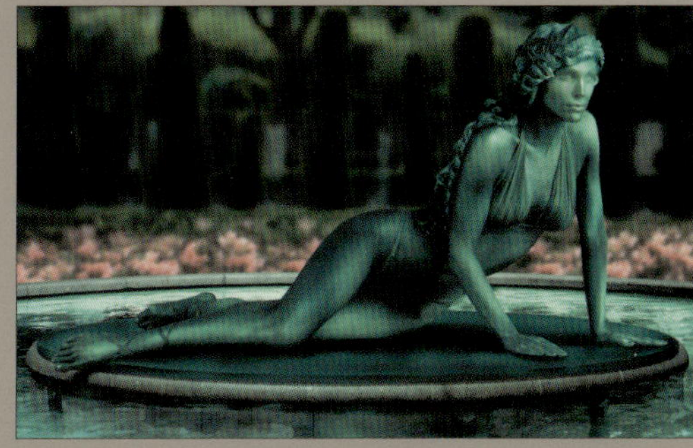

Molly Sims
James Porto

New York, 2000
This image was created for the 2001 *Sports Illustrated* Swimsuit Issue and was my second time working with the magazine. The theme that year for the models was "goddesses." It was a true collaborative project with SI Swimsuit Editor Diane Smith and photographer James Porto. In this image we turned model Molly Sims into Goddess Flora. She loved being "froggy green." I first body-painted her black and then put metallic green over it. Molly is completely airbrushed for this image with Reel Creations slate-green tattoo ink. James photographed her in his studio while the background was shot separately on location. He then put it all together digitally.

Courtesy of Time Inc./Sports Illustrated, Swimsuit Editor Diane Smith and Next Model Management.

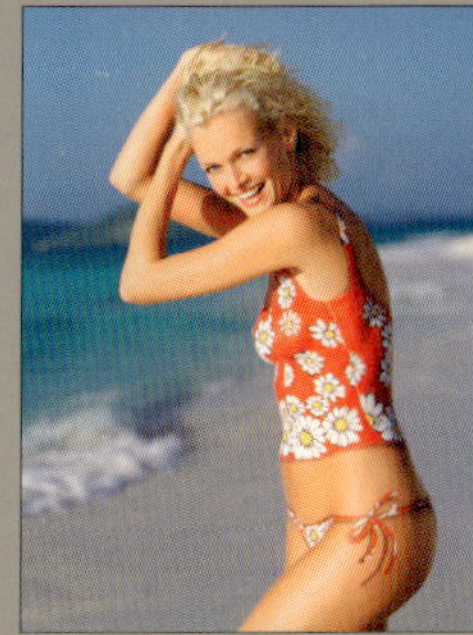

Sarah O'Hare
Antoine Verglas

Necker Island, 1998
Australian model Sarah O'Hare was delightful to work with. She was like a young Marilyn Monroe. This was part of a very large shoot on Necker Island, showcasing designer bathing suits for the following season's *Sports Illustrated* Swimsuit Issue (1999). Diane Smith and I chose each suit to match the girls' personalities and skin tones. I then recreated the suits in great detail. I love the finer details. For this shot, Sarah had to be ready at 6:00 a.m. for the beautiful morning light, so we started painting right after dinner and went straight through the night.

Courtesy of Time Inc./Sports Illustrated, Swimsuit Editor Diane Smith and Artist Management Associates.

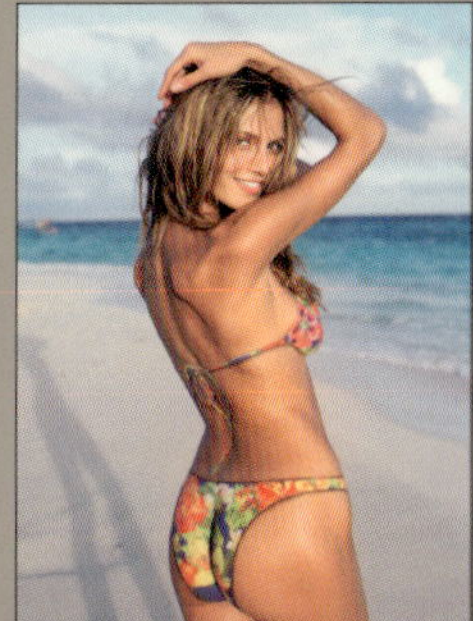

Heidi Klum
Antoine Verglas

Necker Island, 1998
This is another image that was created at Richard Branson's Necker Island retreat for the 1999 *Sports Illustrated* Swimsuit Issue. This particular suit was Heidi's personal favorite. My assistants Tipare Iti, Ramon Espinoza, and I used Dinair Airbrush Makeup and Kryolan Aquacolor to reproduce it.

Courtesy of Time Inc./Sports Illustrated, Swimsuit Editor Diane Smith.

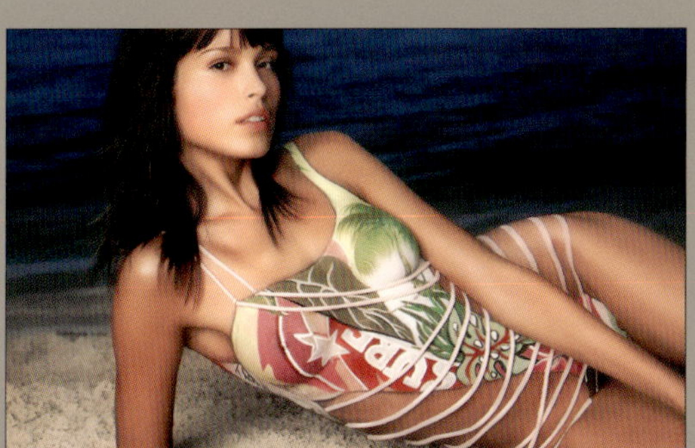

Petra Nemcova
Steven White

Florida, 2003
I tried very hard this year to create a more three-dimensional look for the bathing suits that appeared in the 2004 *Sports Illustrated* Swimsuit Issue. I had special rubber strings made to add to Petra Nemcova's suit. This was shot in the Florida Keys at dusk, and although you can't see it here, Petra was painted front and back.

Courtesy of Time Inc./Sports Illustrated, Swimsuit Editor Diane Smith and Next Model Management.

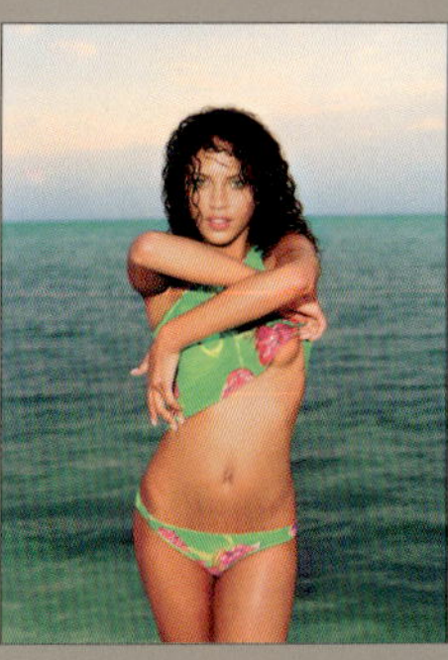

Noemie Lenoir
Steven White

Florida, 2003
I specifically wanted this body painting to be interesting and have attitude, so I worked to make it look like Noemie is taking the suit off. Giving a model something to do and the suit some movement avoids the body painting looking flat or one-dimensional.

Courtesy of Time Inc./Sports Illustrated, Swimsuit Editor Diane Smith and Ford Models.

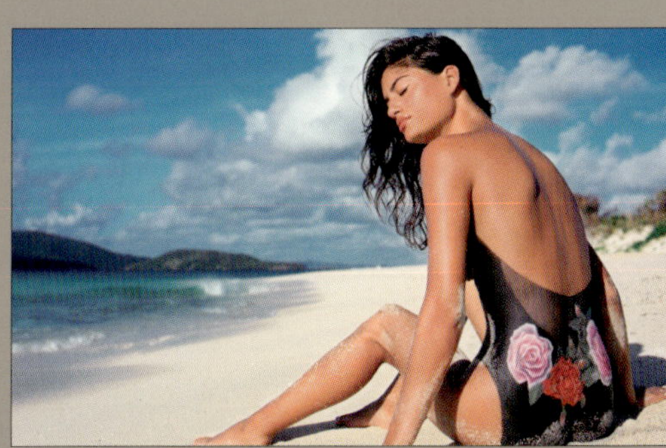

Yamila Diaz-Rahi
Antoine Verglas

Necker Island, 1998
This image was part of the series created in 1998 for *Sports Illustrated*. Unfortunately it did not make the 1999 issue of the magazine but it was later published in the 2001 body-painting calendar, which included all thirteen images from this period. Model Yamila Diaz-Rahi loved the body painting and the choice of costume with its Latin influence. This is also one of my favorites from the shoot.

Courtesy of Time Inc./Sports Illustrated, Swimsuit Editor Diane Smith and Next Model Management.

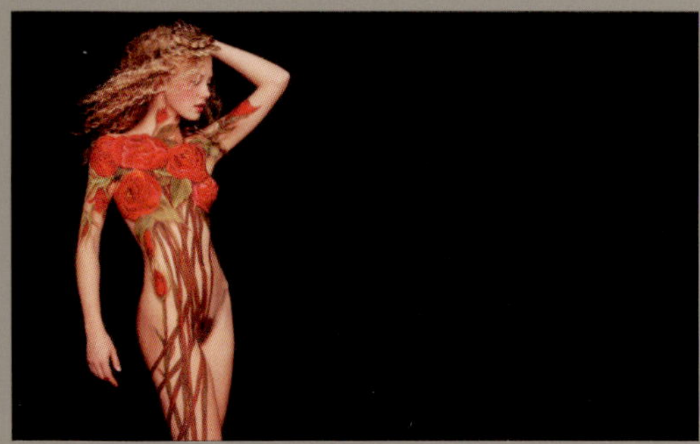

Howard Schatz

New York, 1999
Nikko Kefalas, a longtime stylist with Howard Schatz and Beverly Ornstein, introduced the pair to me in 1999. This was the first shoot to come out of that meeting and was a wonderful collaboration at Howard's Soho studio.

Nikko bought me a dozen red roses as inspiration for my painting on the model's beautiful skin. It was a long hand-painting process using only Aquacolor.

Nude Study #1178 by Howard Schatz from Nude Body Nude *(HarperCollins, 2000).*

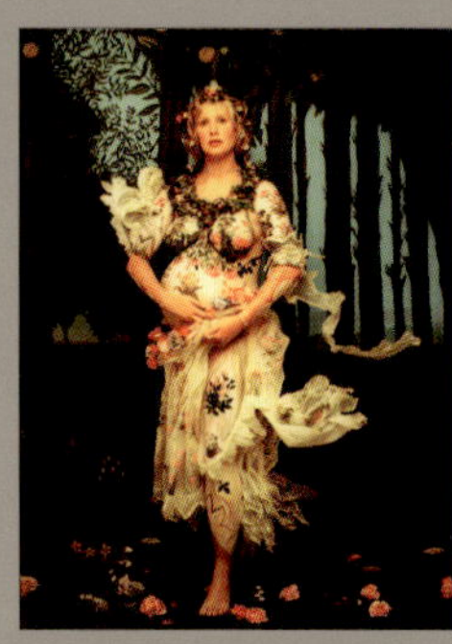

Demi Moore
Peggy Sirota

New York, 1994
While I was in Florence, Italy in late 1993, I had the time and privilege to view many of the original works of the great Renaissance painter, Botticelli. I was especially captivated by his attention to detail. Around the same time, Demi Moore—late in her pregnancy with Tallulah Belle Willis—phoned me interested in doing a body painting. Botticelli's *Primavera* stood out in my mind, and I proposed this to her as a concept. She loved it.

Demi's endurance was amazing—she was eight-and-a-half months pregnant at the time—and we worked almost twenty hours that day (between meeting, painting, and the photo session). I hand-painted her body and also pieces of chiffon fabric that were then attached to give her a three-dimensional look. Peggy Sirota photographed these beautiful images.

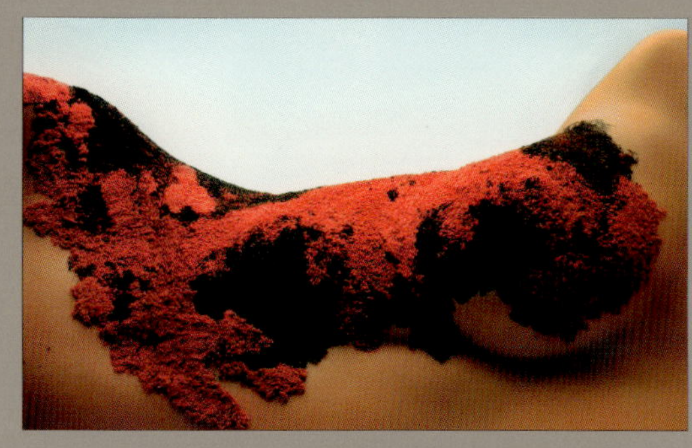

Eva Mueller

New York, 2000
I discovered "magic powder" at a voodoo shop, which is really just very fine-grain woodchips. I applied Vaseline to make it stick, and *voilà*. This was another image from the "Skinscapes" pictorial for *Black Book's* Summer 2000 issue.

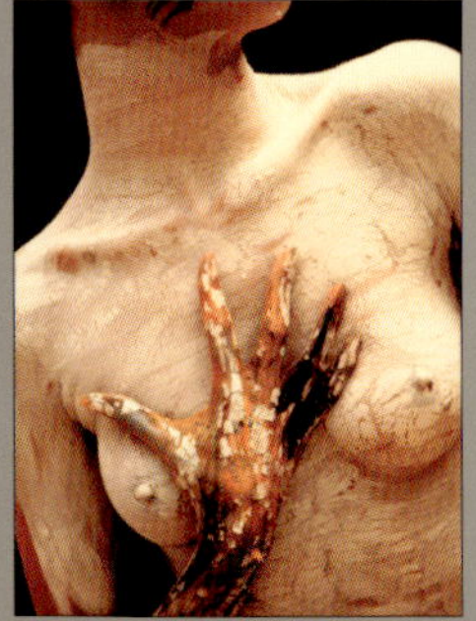

Kara Young
Alberto Tolot

Los Angeles, late 1980s
This is another very early experiment with clay. I was also exploring the use of pigment and gold leaf to make the arm look more organic. The materials were applied remarkably quickly for this shoot in the Hollywood Hills.

Thanks to Trump Model Management.

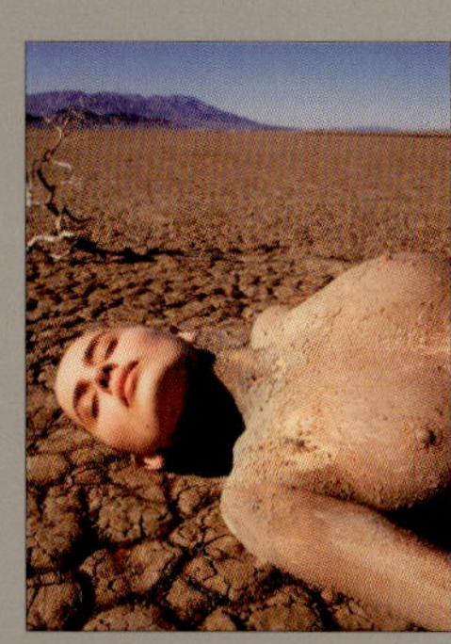

Mark Arbeit

California Desert, 1986
Mark Arbeit and I were on assignment for *Harpers & Queen* in 1986. We were heading to Joshua Tree, in the California desert, when we lost our way and ended up at a vast, dried-up lakebed. The existing dry mud at the location, with the help of a water spritzer, became the makeup for the Australian model, while the lakebed itself became the perfect backdrop.

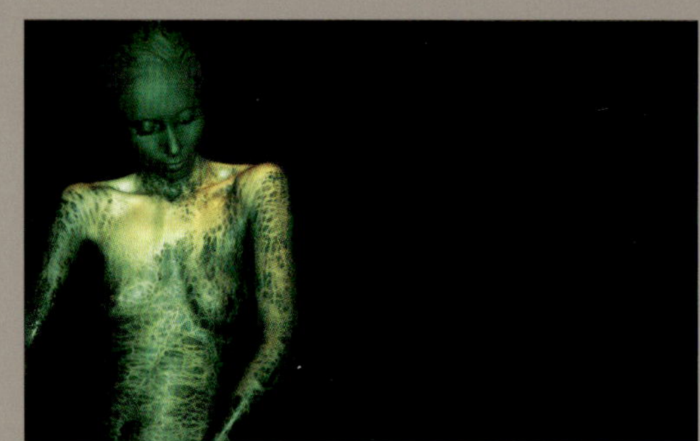

Tanya O
Joanne Gair

Los Angeles, 1998
Model Tanya O is seen here at the end of a very long day. After having black clay applied to her for a Jergens Lotion advertising campaign, she took a shower to clean up. As I was helping clean and remove the dry, cracking clay from her body, I noticed that the residue left on her skin was creating a lizard-type effect.

I grabbed my camera and started shooting her metamorphosis. With cross-processing, I was able to achieve the chameleon look. This is one of my earliest images as a photographer.

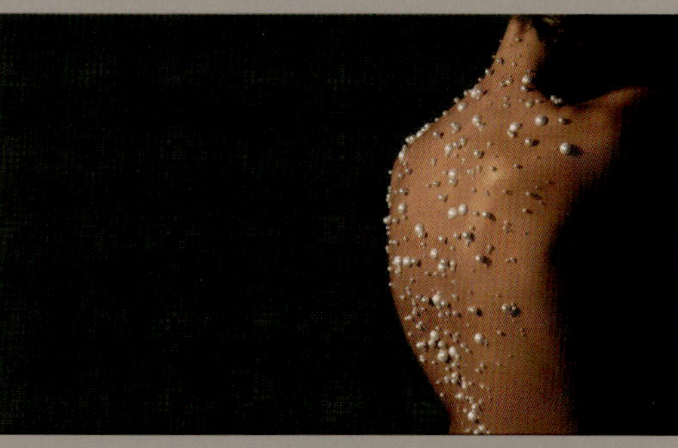

Joanne Gair

Auckland, 2004
While in New Zealand shooting my first book, *Paint A'Licious*, I took time out one weekend with my team. This was one of four images that were shot with the sea as a theme. Here the model is adorned with different-sized plastic white pearls.

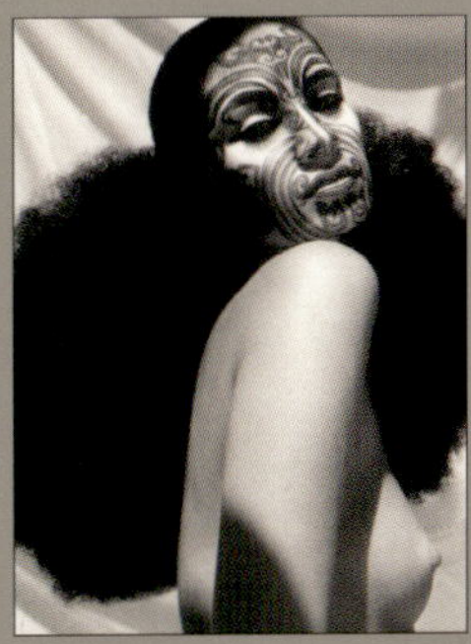

Yana
Alberto Tolot

Los Angeles, late 1980s
The pattern on Yana's face is an amalgamation of both male and female moko—customary facial tattoos worn by Maori, the indigenous New Zealanders. I was very homesick at the time. I had always been fascinated with facial adornment, and this was my own interpretation of the moko, combining patterns from each gender's tradition. It is all done with eye pencil, and once again, Peter Savic did the hair.

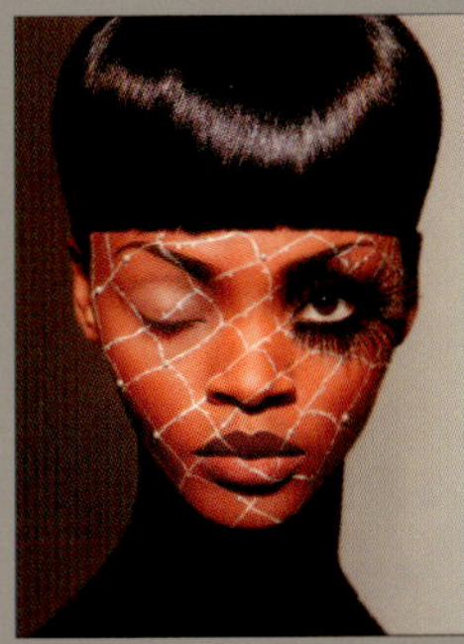

Lisa Butler
Matthew Rolston

Los Angeles, early 1990s
Rimmel Cosmetics ran an advertising campaign for their mascara called "Power Lash." This was one image in a series of four for which I dutifully recreated a very detailed storyboard, using multiple eyelashes for a spider effect. Water-based makeup was used for the spider web pattern across model Lisa's face. I created the water droplets by applying tiny plastic pearls. Matthew Rolston shot this image in two parts—with the eye open and then closed—to create the perfect wink.

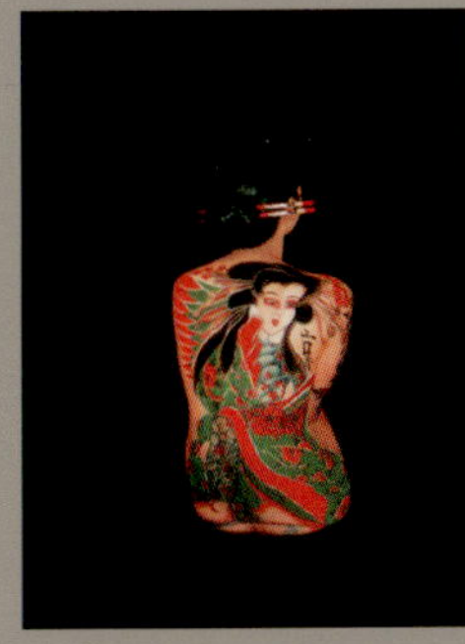

Deborah Lin
Tipare Iti

Los Angeles, early 1990s
While I was painting Deborah Lin for the Janet Jackson music video "If," my assistant Tipare picked up a 35mm camera and took this behind-the-scenes shot to document the painting. It turned out to be quite a beautiful image. In the video storyline, the girl drops her kimono to reveal her image "tattooed" on her own back.

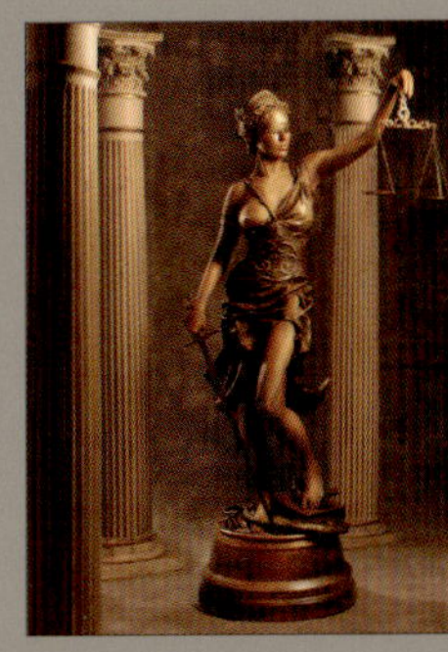

Michael Caulfield

Los Angeles, 2003
Nikko Kefalas and I were approached to participate in a calendar that was to be an artistic legal-oriented pictorial. Michael Caulfield photographed the thirteen images for the calendar. This partially body-painted image represented the "scales of justice." The costume for this shot was designed by Nikko and produced by Anthony Franco.

Michael Caulfield/WireImage.com.

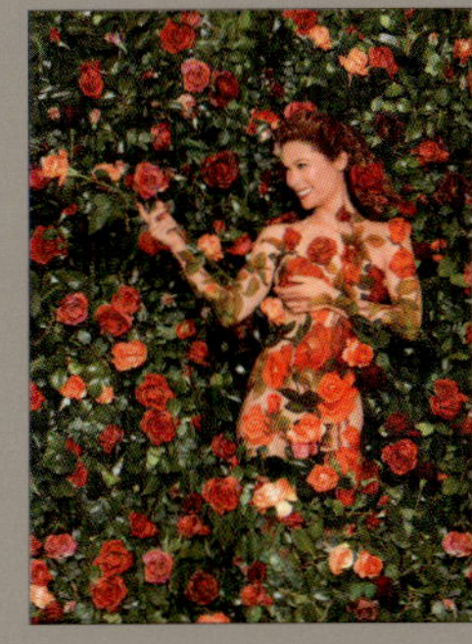

Emma Belcher
Joanne Gair

Auckland, 2004
Of all the rose stories and body paintings of roses that I have done throughout my career, this was by far the most involved. The roses that I painted on model Emma Belcher for my first book, *Paint A'Licious*, took the New Zealand crew and me approximately eighteen hours of intricate, detailed painting. It did not end there though—as I was also the photographer, I still had to shoot the image too! I am happy to say that everyone survived, and this image eventually made the cover of the US and UK editions of the book.

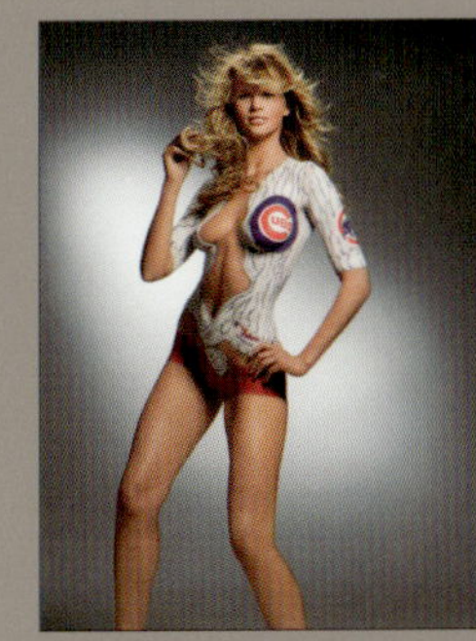

Anne V
Joanne Gair

New York, 2004
This image and the following one were part of an eight-page pictorial for the 2005 *Sports Illustrated* Swimsuit Issue that featured body-painted American sports team jerseys. In addition to body painting, I was also the photographer for this pictorial—my first time for *SI*. I photographed model Anne V wearing the jersey of MLB team the Chicago Cubs.

Courtesy of Time Inc./Sports Illustrated, Swimsuit Editor Diane Smith and One Model Management.

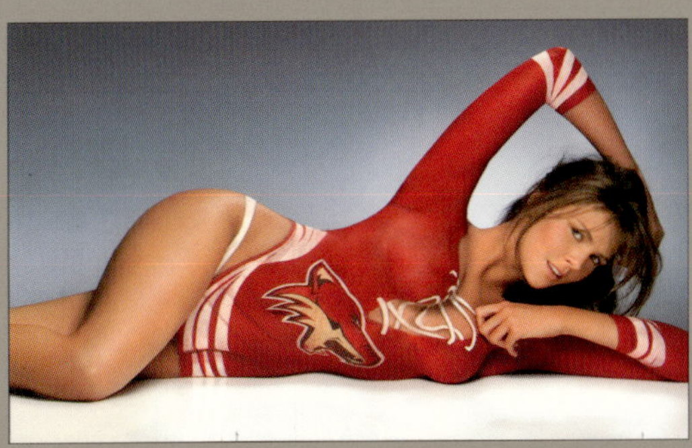

Daniella Sarahyba
Joanne Gair

New York, 2004
I photographed Brazilian model Daniella Sarahyba in the jersey of the NHL team, the Phoenix Coyotes for the 2005 *Sports Illustrated* Swimsuit Issue. As always, it was great to work with *SI* Swimsuit Editor Diane Smith again. I used both my airbrush and hand-painting techniques along with several makeup mediums to achieve the layered effect in this image.

My makeup assistants Reyna Pecot and Isaac Prado were invaluable to the success of this shoot.

Courtesy of Time Inc./Sports Illustrated, Swimsuit Editor Diane Smith and IMG Models.

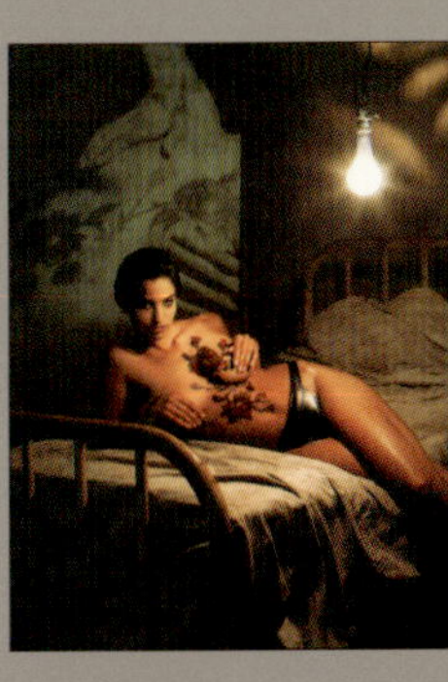

Phillip Dixon

Los Angeles, mid-1980s
I don't think I'll ever stop painting roses. This image was created very early in my career in the US. Phillip Dixon shot a detail of the body painting with black and white Polaroid film while the model was on set. He quickly developed it and projected it on the wall as a background before shooting the actual frame that you see here.

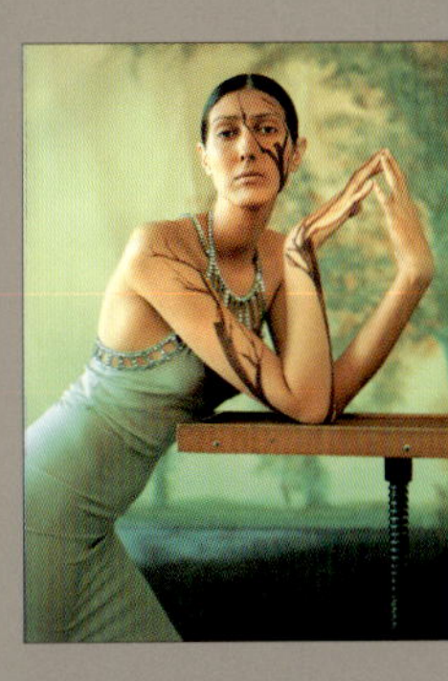

Ruven Afanador

New York, 1999
This was one of those fashion shoots where as the makeup artist, you just turn up with your box of tricks and they give you a theme or a word. This time Ruven Afanador said, "I'm thinking of a tree," and this is what he got. The image was part of a pictorial that appeared in the February 2000 issue of German *Vogue*.

Thanks to German Vogue, Jana Hallberg, Susanne Kolmel.

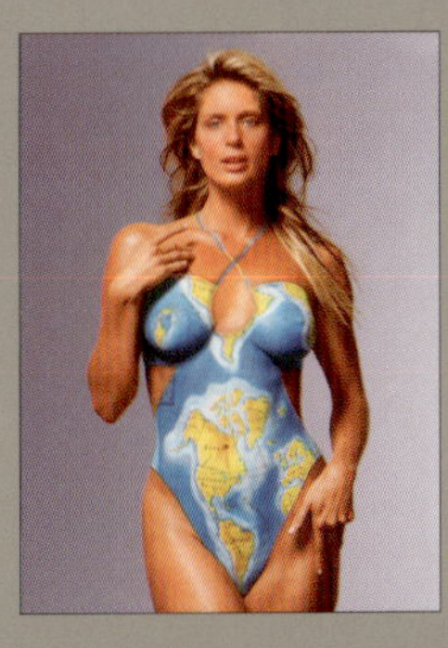

Rachel Hunter
Michael Zeppetello

New York, 2002
"Hottest Models, Coolest Places Around The World" was the theme for the 2003 *Sports Illustrated* Swimsuit Issue. Diane Smith wanted to capture this theme with a body-painted image and she came to me with the idea of painting a world map on Rachel Hunter's body. I had stencils made of the map and used Reel Creations inks for airbrushing. The ever trusty fine-tip Sharpie pen was also used for detail. Unfortunately, especially given the fact that Rachel and I are both Kiwis, New Zealand is tucked right around the back!

Courtesy of Time Inc./Sports Illustrated, Swimsuit Editor Diane Smith and Ford Models.

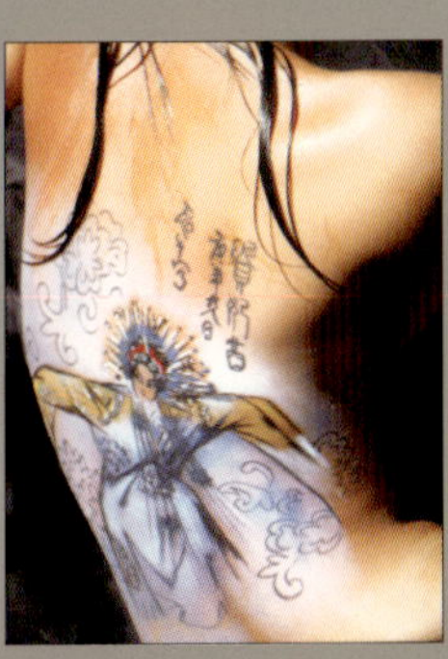

Yana
Alberto Tolot

Los Angeles, late 1980s
Here I have illustrated images and symbols assimilated from a Chinese opera onto model Yana's back. I used Chinese theatre makeup to paint, along with Aquacolor and Sharpie pens for detail.

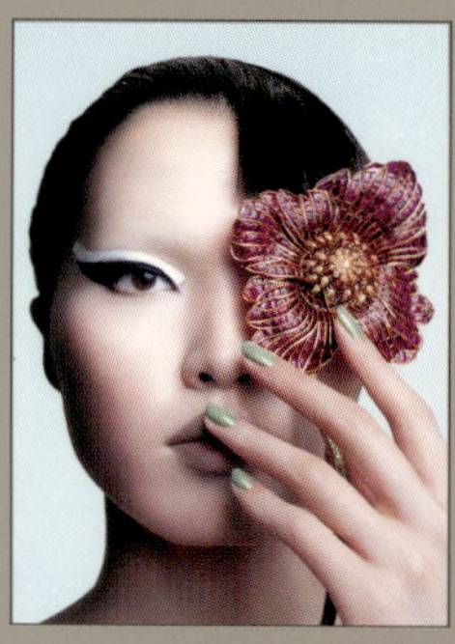

Torkil Gudnason

New York, 2001
Torkil Gudnason's mastery of beauty and skin perfection in the world of beauty photography is on prominent display here. This was an idea of German *Vogue's* Jana Hallberg for a jewelry editorial in their beauty section. They wanted me to create something graphic to help feature the ornate jewelry for the June 2001 issue.

Torkil Gudnason for German Vogue.

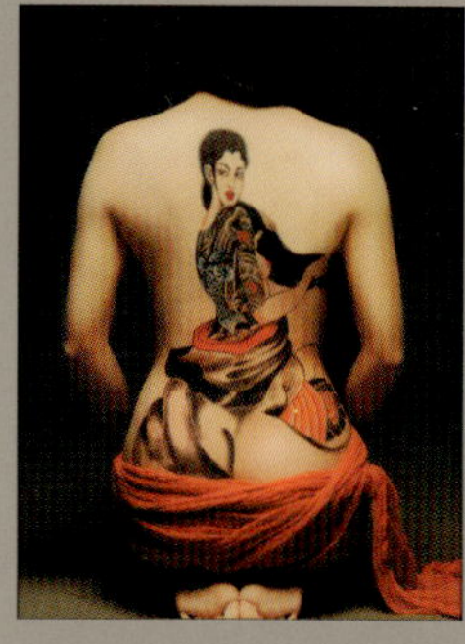

David Jacobson

Los Angeles, mid-1980s
This image is a personal favorite. I was intrigued by this young woman's beauty and long cascading hair when she caught my eye at a local gym. On an impulse I set up a painting and photographic session with David Jacobson, who also loves Asian skin tones—the smooth and perfect canvas. Through my painting, I projected a fantasy of her on her own back, and we told a story with multiple images.

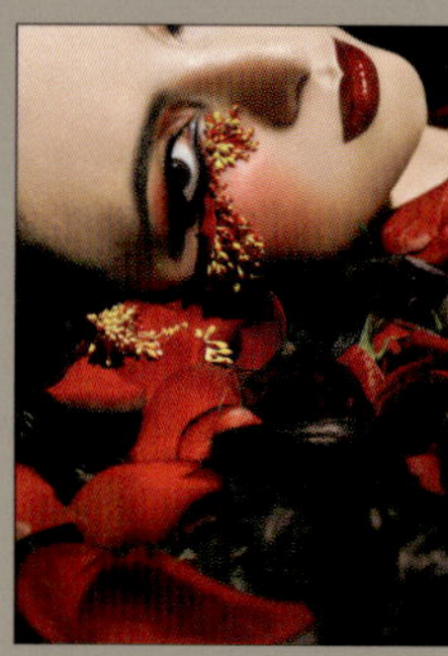

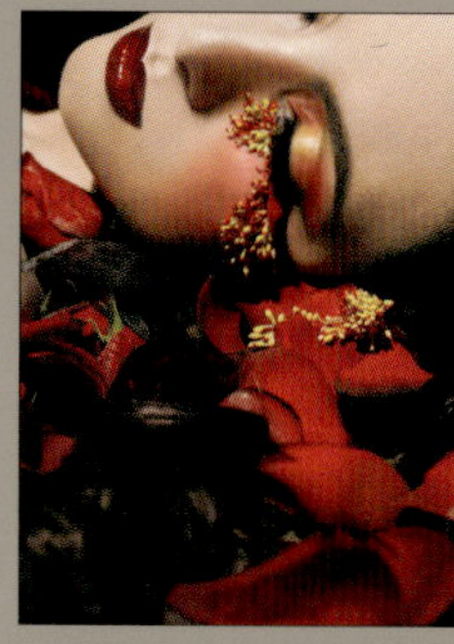

Nadia Riza
Joanne Gair

Los Angeles, 2003
People had been encouraging me to pick up a camera for some time, and this was one of my first attempts as both makeup artist and photographer.

The two images are part of a dream sequence themed "Rose Red." Again, my love of roses is very apparent.

Mark Abrahams

Los Angeles, late 1980s
These tattooed lips were the result of a creative moment. I used pen and ink to draw on the model's luscious lips. Mark Abrahams captured this image in black and white to make the illustration more graphic.

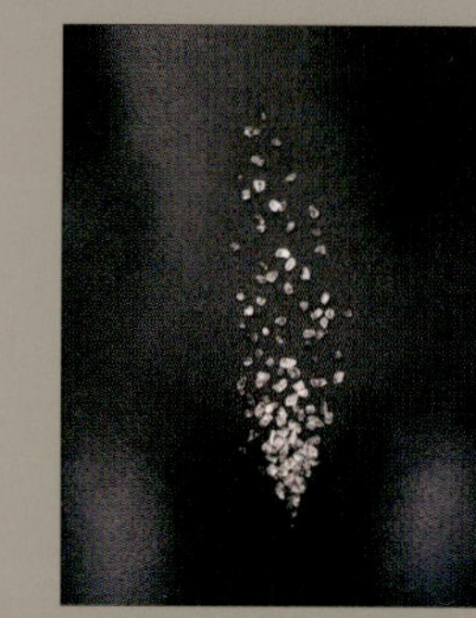

Eva Mueller

New York, 2000
I call this image "Salt Scrub." The model's skin was covered in black grease makeup and oil for shine while large chunks of rock sea-salt were sprinkled over her backside. She lay on her stomach while the salt pieces were placed along her lower back to give an organic feeling. Eva shot this image from above, looking straight down. It appeared in the "Skinscapes" pictorial for the Summer 2000 issue of *Black Book*.

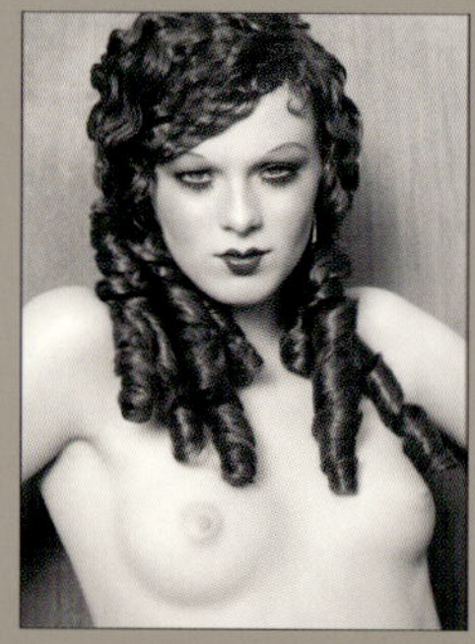

Karen Elson
Herb Ritts

Los Angeles, 1998
This is another image that appeared in the Herb Ritts-photographed 1999 Pirelli Calendar. Karen Elson represented the 1910s for the month of March. Hair stylist Peter Savic designed and executed all of the classic period hairstyles for the calendar. This was a wonderful, collaborative experience. For me, the images in this edition of the Pirelli Calendar are timeless.

Gratefully reproduced with permission of the Herb Ritts Foundation and DNA Model Management.

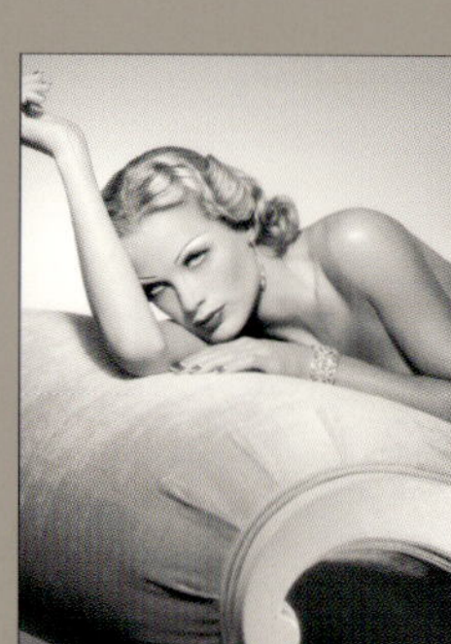

Carolyn Murphy
Herb Ritts

Los Angeles, 1998
Model Carolyn Murphy appears here portraying the 1930s for the month of May, again for the 1999 Pirelli Calendar. I did extensive research for this project as the time-span was the entire twentieth century and beyond. The art direction for the calendar was spot on thanks to L'Wren Scott's attention to detail.

Gratefully reproduced with permission of the Herb Ritts Foundation and IMG Models. Thanks to Estée Lauder for cosmetics, skincare, haircare, and fragrance.

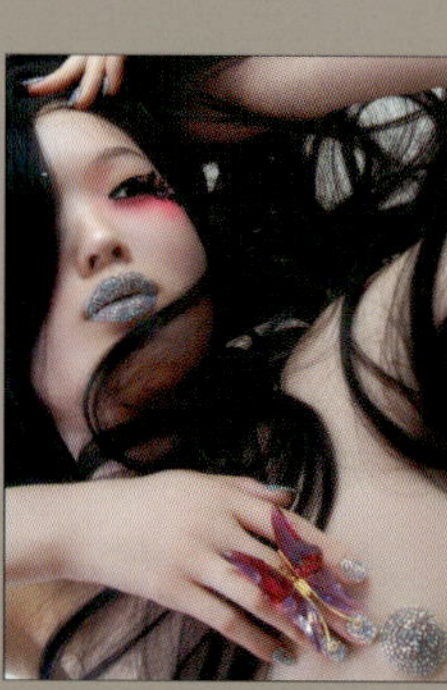

Sophia Lee
Joanne Gair

Los Angeles, 2003
This image and the following were done on a large, human-size light box in my home studio. As a photographer and makeup artist I particularly love close-up and beauty work. The jewels in this image are all Swarovski crystals, and I custom-made the eyelash. Sophia Lee was an absolute joy to work with.

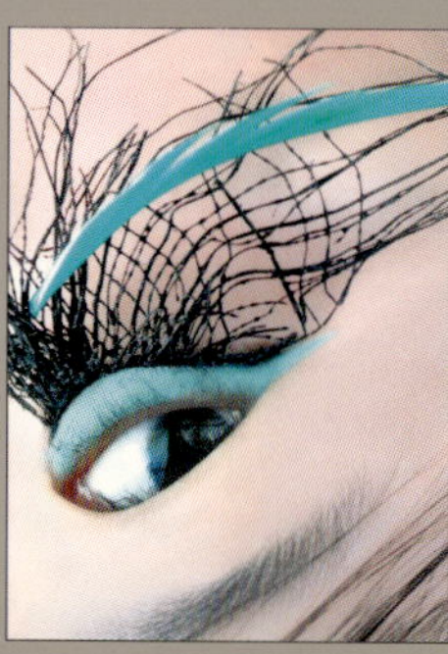

Sophia Lee
Joanne Gair

Los Angeles, 2003
That same day we shot the second image of Sophia. I made the black lash image by spray-painting a straw doll's hat and fraying the edges to give it a more organic appearance. The turquoise feather made the image look like the remnants of a bird's nest.

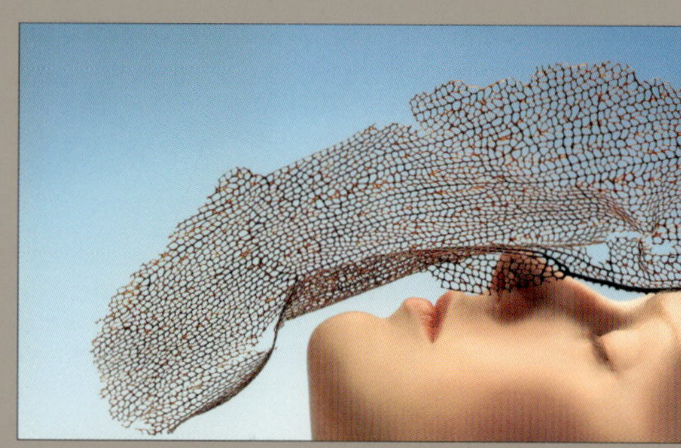

Eva Mueller

New York, 2000
I found the seaweed that was used in this image on a beach in central California while filming additional photography for Demi Moore's film *G.I. Jane*. There had been a major storm at the location the day before that had scattered deep-sea debris, including seaweed and kelp, over the beach. The unusual forms and shapes of the seaweed caught my eye, and I had to stop and collect some of it.

It would be several years, however, before I could use this netlike material for the right project. This image was part of the 2000 "Skinscapes" pictorial for *Black Book*.

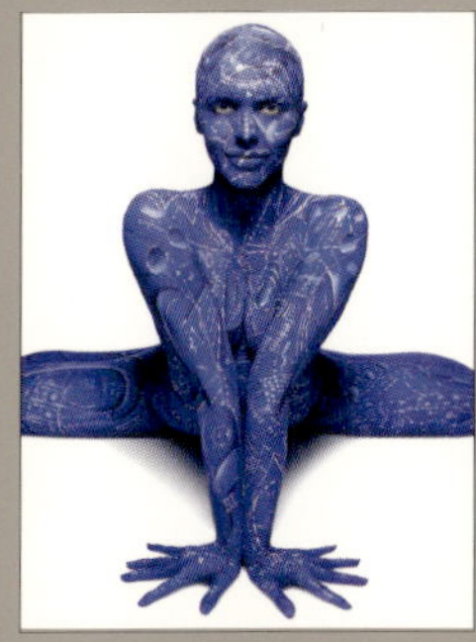

Mark Seliger

Los Angeles, 2000
Ericsson was running an advertising campaign to promote their cell phones linking to the web. Most of the campaign involved close-up shots on different painted faces to highlight sports, stocks, and entertainment. For this image, Mark Seliger shot the full body of the model after I had painted her as the client's interpretation of the World Wide Web. The model was completely comfortable with the process. She actually left the shoot still painted to have dinner at a trendy Los Angeles restaurant.

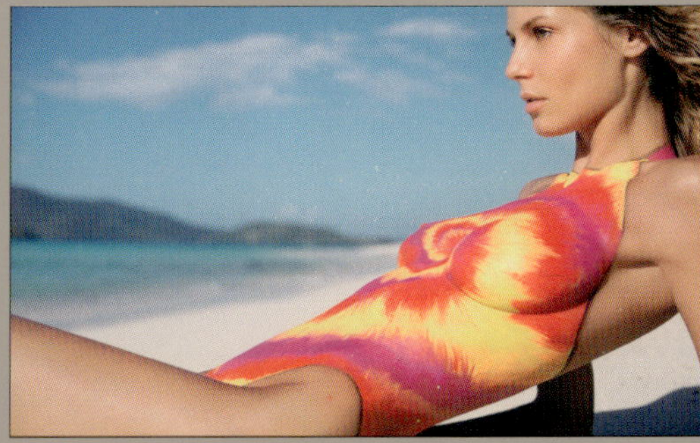

Heidi Klum
Antoine Verglas

Necker Island, 1998
When you are working on a large pictorial, there are sometimes variations of shots that are never used or published. This photograph of Heidi in profile in the tie-dyed swimsuit, from the 1998 Necker Island shoot, happens to be one such example.

This version never made the 1999 *Sports Illustrated* Swimsuit Issue, but is a beautiful representation of that body painting.

Courtesy of Time Inc./Sports Illustrated, *Swimsuit Editor Diane Smith.*

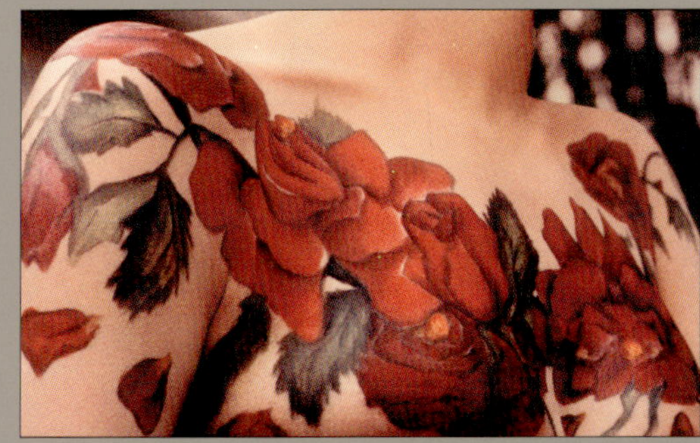

Davis Factor

Los Angeles, mid-1980s
This was produced with Davis Factor and Peter Savic. Flowers are my favorite thing to paint, I guess, having been influenced by my mother Fay who used to paint delicate flowers on china as a hobby. I think these are quite beautiful, especially the way they cascade down the model's shoulders. The roses are painted with lipstick and eye pencil, and the model's beautiful alabaster skin helped accentuate the colors.

It gives me great pleasure to dedicate this book to my parents, the Hon. George and Fay Gair. The work represented in the book spans the many years that I have been traveling and living abroad, entailing a sacrifice in precious time spent together. I thank my parents for encouraging me to explore the arts and to spread my wings and experience the world. Their devoted love and support have provided the greatest stability in my life. I thank them for the daily thought waves and messages they have sent, which have helped me immeasurably during the journey. Mum and Dad, I love you both.

ACKNOWLEDGEMENTS

I wish first to thank my family at home in New Zealand. In addition to my parents, my big brother Warwick and my sister Linda and their families have provided the greatest home base to return to. Being the baby in the family, I was deeply influenced by my brother and sister. Warwick was always building things for me when I was a little girl, while Linda was really the artist in the family, mastering photography, painting, sculpting, and music. Thank you both for your inspiration and for looking after your little sister so well.

Thank you Geoff Blackwell and Ruth-Anna Hobday for your continued collaboration, support, and friendship. PQ Blackwell and the great team you have assembled are a reflection of both of your creative leadership and vision. Rachel Antony, thank you for your hard work and dedication to this book—you have done a tremendous job.

To all the photographers who graciously agreed to have their work displayed in the book, I thank you. It has been a pleasure to work with all of you and to participate and collaborate on projects together. I will always treasure the experience.

Thank you to all the lovely models who appear on these pages. You were wonderful canvases to work with. Your beauty, personality, hard work, and patience have all really helped to bring the pictures to life.

During my creative time in the United States, three men have made a great difference in my life. They are Peter Savic, Spencer Franklin, and Nikko Kefalas, my creative and artistic partners in crime, whose work is reflected in many of the images in this book. They push me to discover new things, think differently, and laugh along the way. Most importantly, they are my trusted friends, whom I love dearly. I would particularly like to thank Spencer, my producer and associate editor for this book, for making the whole project possible.

I wish to thank two very special people from *Sports Illustrated*. They are Swimsuit Editor Diane Smith and Creative Director Steven Hoffman, who I first met in 1998 during my initial body-painting editorial for the magazine. We instantly hit it off when we began work on the Necker Island shoot that year, and I have now done six editorials for them. Both Diane and Steven have believed in me and championed my career, and in 2004 they awarded me my first *Sports Illustrated* swimsuit editorial shoot as a photographer. Thank you both for your trust and faith in me.

I first met former *Shape* magazine Art Director Jacqueline Moorby in 2001, when she came to my house in Los Angeles for a preliminary meeting to discuss her cover article idea for the *Shape* 10th Anniversary Issue. What came out of this meeting was a decision to approach Heidi Klum about modeling for the cover and the start of a professional and personal friendship. Jacqueline is my soul sister.

Years ago, Maxine Tall and Kim Zorros would book me for Herb Ritts' photo shoots. I always loved working with them and appreciated how they handled business and, in particular, how they dealt with me. They are now my agents while Kim is also my producer, and both are very dear to me. I thank them for their advice and for keeping me focused and ready to tackle the next assignment.

The Cloutier Agency was the first to represent me as an artist in the United States, helping me get a start and establish what has turned out to be a successful career. The agency was responsible for booking me on many of the jobs that resulted in the images that appear in this book. Thank you Chantal, Madeline, and Charnelle—I think of you all affectionately.

Terry Jacoby has been my business manager and good friend just about since the start of my career. I thank both Terry and Shirley Cooper for taking such great care of me. It is warmly appreciated.

Mark McKenna, it was always a great pleasure working on shoots with you and Herb Ritts all those years ago. Thank you for your support and assistance in obtaining permission from the Herb Ritts Foundation to reproduce some of the images that appear in this book.

I wish to thank all the makeup assistants and technicians listed below who have worked with me over the years, spending the long hours together that are necessary in this craft. Their commitment and dedication helped make the images as beautiful as they appear here.

Kylie Bell
Barry Bish
Carly Jane Chappell
Manjari Ehrlichman
Helen Eleftheriou
Ramon Espinoza
Linda Gair
Mark Garbarino
Lauren Harrington
Tipare Iti
Hannah Kearns
Reyna Pecot
Isaac Prado
Carol-Anne Ryce-Paul
Devoney Scarfe

It has been wonderful working with the exceptionally talented hair stylists below. They come to every shoot having done their prep and research, bringing with them great imagination and creative ideas.

Donna J. Anderson
Enzo Angileri
Shay Ashual
Gabriel Georgiou
Rick Gradone
Donald Hollingsworth
Richard Keogh
Enzo Laera
Patrick Melville
Pier Guiseppe Moroni
Ric Pipino
Bahram Rasizedeh
John Ruggiero
Peter Savic

The work of the following retouch artists can be seen in this book. I thank them all for the skill and dedication they bring to each job.

Berrin Moody
BowHaus
Digital Retouch
The Looking Room
Michael McCarty
Photo Impact
Tracy Bayne

Many of the following product companies and suppliers have been in my life for a very long time and they have all been great to work with over the years. The quality of their products, and their professionalism, help me do my job. Thank you.

AmazingCosmetics
Carter Sexton
Cinema Secrets
Classified Cosmetics
Dinair Airbrush Makeup Systems
Frends Beauty Supply
Gabel's Cosmetics
LORAC
M·A·C
Make Up For Ever
Naimie's Beauty Center
Reel Creations
Swarovski
Tinsley Transfers
Trendy Tribals

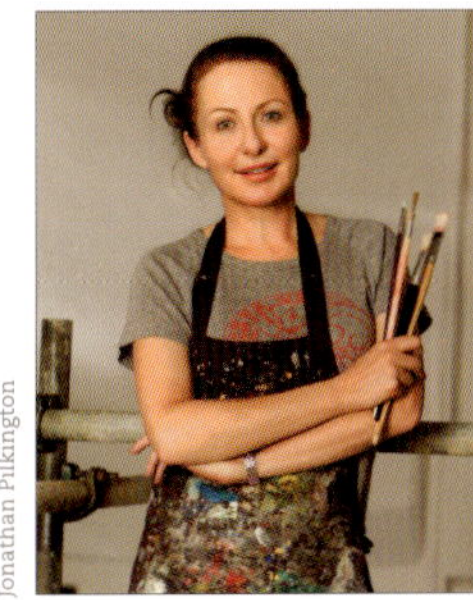
Jonathan Pilkington

For more information on Joanne Gair, please visit her website at www.joannegair.com

First published in the United States of America in 2006 by
Universe Publishing
A division of Rizzoli International Publications, Inc.
300 Park Avenue South
New York, NY 10010
www.rizzoliusa.com

Originally published in New Zealand as *Body of Work* in 2006 by
PQ Blackwell Limited
116 Symonds Street
Auckland
New Zealand
www.pqblackwell.com

The publisher is grateful to the photographers and models featured in this book for their consent to reproduce the photographs herein. Every effort has been made to trace the copyright holders and the publisher apologizes for any unintentional omission. We would be pleased to hear from any not acknowledged here and undertake to make all reasonable efforts to include the appropriate acknowledgement in any subsequent editions.

Design Carolyn Lewis
Associate Editor Spencer Franklin
Research Rachel Antony
Managing Editor Caroline Bowron

ISBN-10: 0-7893-1509-2
ISBN-13: 978-0-7893-1509-0

Library of Congress Control Number 2006903206

2006 2007 2008 2009 / 10 9 8 7 6 5 4 3 2 1

Printed in China by Everbest Printing International Limited